MARKETING IN THE 21ST CENTURY

MARKETING IN THE 21ST CENTURY

Company and Customer Relations

Volume 3

Linda M. Orr and
Jon M. Hawes
Volume Editors

Bruce D. Keillor, General Editor

Praeger Perspectives

Westport, Connecticut
London

Library of Congress Cataloging-in-Publication Data

Marketing in the 21st century / Bruce D. Keillor, general editor.
    p. cm.
  Includes bibliographical references and index.
  ISBN-13: 978–0–275–99275–0 (set : alk. paper)
  ISBN-13: 978–0–275–99276–7 (vol 1 : alk. paper)
  ISBN-13: 978–0–275–99277–4 (vol 2 : alk. paper)
  ISBN-13: 978–0–275–99278–1 (vol 3 : alk. paper)
  ISBN-13: 978–0–275–99279–8 (vol 4 : alk. paper)

  1. Marketing. I. Keillor, Bruce David.
  HF5415.M2194 2007
  658.8—dc22   2007016533

British Library Cataloguing in Publication Data is available.

Library of Congress Catalog Card Number: 2007016533
ISBN-13: 978–0–275–99275–0 (set)
ISBN-13: 978–0–275–99276–7 (vol. 1)
ISBN-13: 978–0–275–99277–4 (vol. 2)
ISBN-13: 978–0–275–99278–1 (vol. 3)
ISBN-13: 978–0–275–99279–8 (vol. 4)

First published in 2007

Praeger Publishers, 88 Post Road West, Westport, CT 06881
An imprint of Greenwood Publishing Group, Inc.
www.praeger.com

Printed in the United States of America

The paper used in this book complies with the
Permanent Paper Standard issued by the National
Information Standards Organization (Z39.48–1984).

10 9 8 7 6 5 4 3 2 1

CONTENTS

Set Introduction

It is my privilege to introduce this four-volume set, *Marketing in the 21st Century*. Given the myriad changes that have taken place in the area of marketing over the past several years, and the increasingly dynamic nature of marketing as a business discipline, the publication of these volumes is particularly relevant and timely. Each volume deals with an aspect of marketing that is both a fundamental component of marketing in this new century as well as one that requires new perspectives as the marketplace continues to evolve.

The set addresses four of the most compelling areas of marketing, each of which is changing the foundation of how academics and businesspeople approach the marketing tasks necessary for understanding and succeeding in the changing business environment. These areas are global marketing, direct marketing, firm-customer interactions, and marketing communications. By using recognized experts as authors—both academic and business practitioners—the volumes have been specifically compiled to include not just basic academic research, but to speak to business people in terms of how they can translate the information contained in each chapter into long-term success for their firm or organization.

Volume 1, *New World Marketing,* edited by Timothy J. Wilkinson and Andrew R. Thomas, deals with the salient aspects of the global marketplace. More specifically, it focuses on the realities of the 21st-century global market and then moves into how to identify emerging markets of opportunity, operate in these markets successfully from the perspective of the customer, and develop global strategies that are grounded in the concept of constant improvement through the use of value-added strategies. Authors of numerous books and articles related to international marketing, with extensive experience in executive education in international/global marketing, the editors are uniquely qualified to create a cutting-edge volume in their area of expertise.

In Volume 2, *Interactive and Multi-Channel Marketing,* edited by William J. Hauser and Dale M. Lewison, the focus shifts toward the various mechanisms through which firms and organizations can establish a means for direct interaction with their customers, whether individual consumers or other businesses. Using a two-step approach, Volume 2 discusses in great depth issues related to understanding the various direct-marketing options and then moves on to the application of these options to maximize results. As Director and Associate Director, respectively, of the Taylor Institute for Direct Marketing at The University of Akron, the leading institute worldwide for direct marketing, the editors have the ability to draw on the knowledge of the "best and brightest" in this rapidly emerging and influential area of marketing.

Volume 3, *Company and Customer Relations,* edited by Linda M. Orr and Jon M. Hawes, tackles the challenges of not only establishing and maintaining a functioning relationship between company and customer, but also how to sell successfully in the 21st century. Along the way, they deal with thorny issues such as when to disengage customers and where technology fits into what are, typically, personal interactions. Dr. Hawes is a well-recognized expert in building and maintaining customer trust, while Dr. Orr has a wide range of business and academic experience in organizational learning. This combination of perspectives has resulted in a volume that deals head-on with issues of immediate concern for any business organization.

Finally, Volume 4, *Integrated Marketing Communication,* edited by Deborah L. Owens and Douglas R. Hausknecht, addresses the various means of creating a basis for communication between company and customer that goes well beyond the traditional approaches of advertising, public relations, and sales promotion. The volume begins by considering how the new age customer "thinks" in the context of consumer behavior and then segues into methods to construct an interactive communication platform. Both editors are widely recognized in business and academic circles as experts in the field of marketing communication. They are also known for their ability to view traditional marketing communication tools "outside of the box." The result is a volume that puts a truly fresh perspective on communicating with customers.

Each of the volumes in the set presents the most advanced thinking in their respective areas. Collectively, the set is the definitive collection of the necessary new paradigms for marketing success in the 21st century. It has been my pleasure to work with the volume editors, as well as with many of the chapter authors, in bringing this collection to you. I am convinced that, regardless of your area of interest in the field of marketing, you will find *Marketing in the 21st Century* an invaluable and timeless resource.

Bruce D. Keillor, General Editor

Part I

21ST CENTURY RELATIONSHIP MARKETING

CHAPTER 1

WHAT DOES "RELATIONSHIP MARKETING" REALLY MEAN?

Linda M. Orr

> Society is always taken by surprise at any new example of common sense.
> —Ralph Waldo Emerson

> There is one key ingredient that separates the great salespeople from the good ones: The ability to build relationships.
> —Jason Karem, Sales Manager at ADP

We know that it costs, on average, anywhere from six to ten times more to get a new customer than to keep an old customer. Yet, most *Fortune* 500 companies lose 50 percent of their customers in five years. Furthermore, the average company communicates only four times per year with current customers and six times per year with prospects. That translates into the fact that customer loyalty is worth more than ten times a single purchase. Some statistics even show that a 5-percent increase in customer retention can increase profits 25–125 percent!

When we first started to write this book on selling in the context of the 21st century and what is different now, we wanted to highlight what is different about selling and sales management today. The steps of the selling process are time-honored steps that must occur with every sale, but in terms of what is different today, that took some thought. So selling is selling, right? Not much has changed, correct? Absolutely not! We could put together another book that teaches the basics of selling: how to handle objections, SPIN (situation, problem, implication, and need-payoff) selling, and other questioning techniques, or great ways to close. Do not get me wrong. These are very important topics that we spend a great amount of time teaching at the Fisher Institute for Professional Selling at The

University of Akron. Learning how to master these techniques is a critical element for any great salesperson. But, selling in the 21st century is light-years from what it was in the 20th century. Let us face it, in the 21st century, selling is not about manipulation and it is not about each individual sale. Competition is too fierce, markets are saturated, and customers are too smart.

Great sales pitches, well-crafted marketing strategies, and creative advertising can be very persuasive, and they can even get people to buy your product. But, to keep customers in the long run, you must treat them right and build relationships with them. Even if you have a very expensive product that people buy only once in their lifetimes, you will be rewarded through positive word-of-mouth advertising if you treat your customers the right way. You have to make every moment about more than just that individual sale, but about the long term.

Most people think this is common sense, and it really is, but the problem is that managers get caught between two places: they are either so desperate for business that they become manipulative and pushy, or they are doing so well that they become complacent. Both are dangerous states of mind. When you fail, you tend to blame external factors. It must be the competition, the economy, or the weather; people rarely look inward for faults. Then, the simple solution seems to be to pour more and more into selling and advertising. The reverse is true for managers who are succeeding. Then, you want to think about how good you are. We externalize failure and internalize success. These two dangerous places cause us to rarely see the true problem and/or the cause for success. No matter which situation you are in, the same argument exists. To make money you have to have sales that outweigh your expenditures. To have success in the long term, you have to continue to either bring in new customers or keep your old customers, or preferably both.

To bring in new customers and to keep old ones, you have to realize that the externalizing of failures and internalizing of successes holds true for the customers as well. Remember the old adage "Nobody likes to be sold; but everyone likes to buy." That means that if a customer has a problem or feels manipulated, it becomes your fault. If a customer makes a great choice or hunts down the perfect "bargain," he or she will give himself or herself the credit. Where does that leave you? It means you have to leave your ego at the door and realize it is not really all that simple. You have to focus on keeping customers happy, and the only way to do that is by building and maintaining a relationship with each one. You have to get past the 1950s pushy marketing in which the answer to is "persuade" new customers. You have to realize that you must go beyond the basic psychological processes and work to maintain a relationship. When relationships are formed, single failures and even successes can be over looked. Customers really want convenience, too, and they know just as well as you should that it is expensive to find new providers. In today's service-oriented economy, relationship building and excellent service are more than competitive weapons. They are survival skills.

WHAT IS RELATIONSHIP MARKETING?

Relationship marketing is a total strategy that involves all the marketing mix variables to create and keep loyal customers. Remember back to Marketing 101 and keep in mind the 4 P's of the marketing mix, which are the "elements" of a marketing strategy that a firm has at its disposal to utilize to reach the target customer (see Figure 1.1). Product, place, price, and promotion: these are all key factors even today in the 21st century. Basically, as will be mentioned many times in this book, it is all about strategy. You have to have a clear strategy first and make this well-defined in your mission statement. You will find many of the authors starting their chapters with a discussion of mission. That is because it always must come back to strategy. Without a clear, well-defined strategic direction that is translated to everyone (all stakeholders) and filtered down throughout every part of the organization, you have nothing. You will be operating blindly and be forced into a reactive mode instead of a proactive mode that can take you where you truly want to go.

Within your strategy you must figure out what your unique selling and value proposition is. What do you have to offer the consumer? How are you different?

Figure 1.1
The Marketing Mix

How will you stand out in the marketplace? Why is the consumer buying your product? To determine this, you will need to go back and revisit every element of the marketing mix and decide which direction to take, keeping in mind that whatever path you choose, you must be consistent and have all your elements integrated together to send one, clear, dependable message. The importance of this consistency of strategy cannot be understated.

However, if you revisit Figure 1.1, it becomes apparent how one-sided traditional marketing approaches were. Even given the fact that Figure 1.1 is simplified and does not include the environment and the competition, everything about the heart, the very key to the equation, is missing. Now, think back to your strategy or marketing mix variables and your value proposition. A critical component of your value proposition must include how you plan to satisfy your customers, which will then create beneficial and long-lasting relationships. These relationships must become the heart of any business's strategy that is operating in the 21st century. We spend too much time and effort formulating our strategies and learning about our customers to not follow through and assess satisfaction and then work to maintain relationships. In the 21st century, strategies have to be a two-way street and have to include the long term. A focus on one-time transactions cannot succeed anymore. As mentioned, relationship marketing is a total strategy focused on creating and maintaining long-term, mutually beneficial relationships.

THE ORIGINS OF RELATIONSHIP MARKETING

Much of what we know about relationship marketing came from earlier research in sociology, psychology, and anthropology about dating, relationships, and marriage. After all, we are working to create bonds that will last forever; the only difference is that we want to create these bonds with multiple consumers. Relationship selling is like a marriage. To make it work, you must work at it. It is not easy and, at times, the costs to you will outweigh the profits that you are receiving in return. Much as in marriage, awareness, credibility, trust, and chemistry govern the relationship. The importance of each must be emphasized continuously. You must be prepared to deliver on every promise. If you do not deliver, you must be prepared for a fight or struggle. If you have enough negativity, be prepared for divorce.

The stages of the formation of a business relationship follow that of the dating/marital relationship. It is important to think about how much time and effort must go into each stage, which, just as in dating relationships, will determine the value of the relationship and the potential for that relationship to continue. Initially, young single people must search for mates. In selling, this stage is called prospecting. Prospecting is hard work and nobody likes it. You have to get shot down numerous times to hear just one yes. People do not want to give out their phone numbers. You have no trust, no awareness, and no credibility at this stage. It is really hard work.

Then you get a phone number; in social relationships, you begin the process of dating. In selling, you begin to establish rapport. No matter which situation you are referring to, the same thing is happening: you are searching for some mutual attraction and chemistry. Does this person have something to offer that I want? Then, as the sales process continues, astute salespeople will probe for needs. In social relationships, this is when the courtship begins. In a selling situation, sales-people who have listened to needs can then appropriately respond to those needs. They can present a product or service that most likely fulfills all of the customer's needs and provides a satisfying solution. In social situations, this is when a couple begins to fall in love, if and only if appropriate needs are met.

Next, if all has gone well, is either the closing of the sale or wedding bells. As we know from both sales knowledge and relationship knowledge, this step in no way ensures commitment. Buying a product (or entering a marriage) requires some degree of a leap of faith. Just as you truly never know a person until you actually live with him or her and begin to build a life with him or her, you do not know if you will be satisfied with a product until you actually use it. Will the quality hold up? If not, will the company be there to fix it? Will it honor all warranties? This part of the process, the after the sale/commitment, is when trust is truly built. So many marketers (and daters, for that matter) assume that trust has been created because the sale was made, when in actuality, the most critical component of the relationship—trust—does not form until the after-the-fact use of the product and the follow-up. Customer satisfaction can come from a one-time successful sale. Customer loyalty, which is the Holy Grail to all marketers, can come only from repeated transactions and the formation of a relationship.

So, are your customers satisfied or loyal? A satisfied customer is a buyer who has a good purchasing experience with a particular supplier, but plans to buy from whichever vendor offers the best opportunity in the future. Meanwhile, a loyal customer is a buyer who has selected a particular supplier over time and intends to buy from that same supplier in the future. Customer loyalty is the ultimate goal of relationship marketing. It takes a solid, consistent, well-thought strategy directed at satisfying customer needs to achieve this over a long period of time.

HOW RELATIONSHIP SELLING IS DIFFERENT

Traditional 20th century transaction selling was synonymous with terms like the "Hard Sell," "My Way or the Highway Selling," or "Manipulative Selling." Many mind-sets existed about selling in the 20th century. Selling was thought to be a contest. Selling was persuasive. Customers must be talked into buying certain products; they must be sold. Great salespeople are great manipulators. Buyers and sellers alike might be lying. There was even a key acronym in older selling textbooks, as late as the late 1990s: ABC. ABC stood for Always Be Closing because, of course, the close is everything. Who cares about the future? You got your sale, right?

The 20th century sales process many times included a canned presentation, which was very much one-sided. In this presentation, the salesperson did all the talking and barely let the customer get a word in. If the customer cannot talk, he or she cannot say no, right? The salesperson was focused on persuading and overcoming objections. It always goes back to convincing the customer that he or she is wrong and you are right. Salespeople were seen as an annoyance at a minimum and even as someone to fear at the maximum level. They could not be trusted. Salespeople out on the road were considered very lonely people, and they probably were.

Contrast all of this to relationship selling. Even the terminology is different. We use words like "Collaborative Selling," "Partnering," "Nonmanipulative Selling," "Consultative Selling," "Problem-Solving Selling," and the "Soft Sell." All in all, 21st century relationship selling has a completely different mind-set. Selling is thought of as a service in which salespeople help customers find solutions to problems. Customers love to buy because, once again, they have needs and want to find solutions to satisfy those needs. In relationship selling, buyers want to trust the salesperson. They know that this trust will be mutually beneficial because there will be reduced search costs on both sides of the equation. In relationship selling, customer service comes first. Great sellers truly care. And most importantly, it is not a one-time event, it works—again and again and again.

The 21st century relationship selling process is completely different from the 20th century process. The sales process is a two-sided, flexible interaction. In fact, many great salespeople realize that it is better to let the customers do most of the talking. The salesperson takes on the role of a person probing for needs by asking questions. It is talking *with* the customer and not talking *to* the customer. All 21st century salespeople seek to be helpers who can resolve concerns. They are not feared. Salespeople are thought of as partners and sometimes even as friends. These are the keys to relationship selling in the 21st century. It is a very different process, strategy, and mind-set.

RELATIONSHIP MARKETING AND CUSTOMER SERVICE = SATISFACTION AND LOYALTY

As the research shows, building relationships is almost always more successful and profitable than creating one-time transactions. Over the long run, nothing is more cost-effective than establishing a base of satisfied customers. In some industries, over 80 percent of all future sales come from the existing customer base. This is done through the provision of exceptional service, especially after the sale has been made. Customers make initial purchases because of the *promise* of great service. Repeat sales are made because of the *provision* of great service. Firms that can achieve a very lofty goal and be rated *high* by customers in their *provision* of customer service grow twice as fast as companies rated poorly, and they charge an average of 9 percent more. Imagine that: treat customers well, let the word get out there, and you can charge more. That increase in profits is in addition to the added revenues and decreased expenditures created by having loyal customers.

Thus, even though we have discussed service, satisfaction, and loyalty, it is equally important to understand customer dissatisfaction. Unfortunately, only 1 customer in 27 will volunteer his or her feelings to the seller when dissatisfied; others just buy elsewhere next time. Thus, it is critical to provide proper service and follow-up to continually gauge and track customer experiences. When customers are dissatisfied, managers often wonder whether or not they should placate complaining customers. There is an often-asked question: What can a firm afford to spend to convert a complaining customer into a satisfied customer? Remember the figure just mentioned: most sales (perhaps 80 percent) come from prior customers. In the business-to-business sector, the average cost of securing an order from a *new* prospect is $1,673. Meanwhile, the average cost of securing an order from an *existing* industrial account is only $717. Thus, the difference is $956. Additionally, existing firms are more likely than new firms to place large orders and orders with higher margins. Thus, relationship marketing equals satisfaction, loyalty, and increased profits.

21ST CENTURY RELATIONSHIP MARKETING

The facts are really quite simple. No matter how you look at it, even if it seems like complete common sense or a big, burdensome hassle, relationship marketing is critical to the success of any firm operating in the 21st century. Thus, when developing this book, we decided to focus on relationship marketing instead of just selling. Part 1 of the book examines key strategies that sales managers must utilize to develop and organize their sales functions for success. Subsequently, Part 2 of the book covers opportunities and challenges faced by salespeople who are attempting to build relationships in the 21st century. These components are shown in Figure 1.2 and summarized in the following chapters of the book.

THE UTMOST IMPORTANCE OF TRUST

As described, the first research into relationship marketing evolved from the marriage literature. Thus, courtship and dating are always good examples to use when describing the characteristics of relationships and why they are so

Figure 1.2
Company and Customer Relations: Key Strategies for Successful Selling in the 21st Century

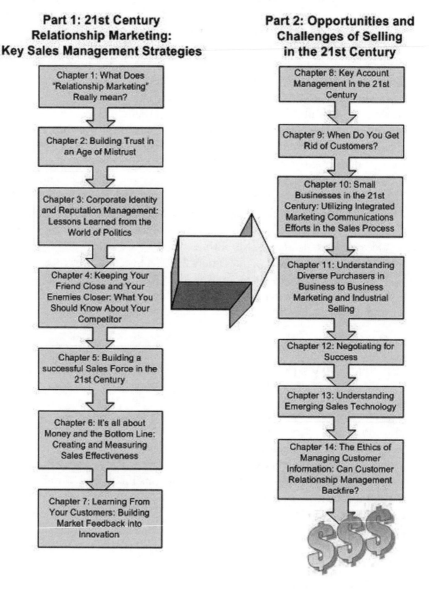

Part 1: 21st Century Relationship Marketing: Key Sales Management Strategies

Chapter 1: What Does "Relationship Marketing" Really mean?

Chapter 2: Building Trust in an Age of Mistrust

Chapter 3: Corporate Identity and Reputation Management: Lessons Learned from the World of Politics

Chapter 4: Keeping Your Friend Close and Your Enemies Closer: What You Should Know About Your Competitor

Chapter 5: Building a successful Sales Force in the 21st Century

Chapter 6: It's all about Money and the Bottom Line: Creating and Measuring Sales Effectiveness

Chapter 7: Learning From Your Customers: Building Market Feedback into Innovation

Part 2: Opportunities and Challenges of Selling in the 21st Century

Chapter 8: Key Account Management in the 21st Century

Chapter 9: When Do You Get Rid of Customers?

Chapter 10: Small Businesses in the 21st Century: Utilizing Integrated Marketing Communications Efforts in the Sales Process

Chapter 11: Understanding Diverse Purchasers in Business to Business Marketing and Industrial Selling

Chapter 12: Negotiating for Success

Chapter 13: Understanding Emerging Sales Technology

Chapter 14: The Ethics of Managing Customer Information: Can Customer Relationship Management Backfire?

important. As just briefly described, we enter into relationships, personal or business, to minimize effort and risk. Just as it becomes tiresome and burdensome to continually find new people to date, it is extremely expensive for new businesses to constantly gain new customers. Plus, as a consumer enters into a relationship with a business, the business gains because it better understands the customer's needs and it knows how to better serve that customer. Likewise, the customer gains because he or she does not have to continually seek alternative suppliers. Just think about when you move to a new city. It is stressful just to figure out which local grocery stores you like best and where you will find the right doctor. Thus, hopefully, the act of forming a relationship creates a win-win situation. This is, of course, until one or both parties of the relationship begin to feel that the relationship is no longer fulfilling their needs and they could then probably be better served elsewhere.

On that note, would you have an interpersonal relationship with someone you do not trust? Why or why not? Usually the answer depends on what you have to gain and what you have to lose. What are the risks and what are the rewards? Of course, as with all relationships in life and in business, there are risks and rewards. Maybe you have a relationship with someone you do not like because he or she is family. Thus, the risk of maintaining civil harmony within your family becomes a greater reward than the risk of whatever the annoyance is of the family member. In business, the greatest risk is financial, but there are also many other types of risk, such as time and ego risks. But, from the customer's perspective, with greater and greater saturation of markets, why would you ever do business with someone you did not trust? And more importantly, once trust is broken, would you ever continue to conduct business with someone? What if you just heard from a *trusted* friend or colleague that an establishment or salesperson is untrustworthy? The answers to these questions are fairly obvious to most of us. Unless that business has something that we really want or need, that we cannot get anywhere else, the lesson is very simple—no trust, no sale. Thus, Chapter 2 breaks down one of the most important steps in the relationship-building process. As the author describes, the purpose is not to help untrustworthy salespeople do a better job of tricking customers. Instead, Chapter 2 provides businesses and salespeople with a road map to utilize to reap the rewards of having high integrity in the sales process.

REPUTATION IS EVERYTHING: GUARD IT WITH YOUR LIFE

Chapter 2 also describes a principle of consistency. Honest people should work for honest companies and vice versa (honest companies should hire honest people). Chapter 2 describes trust mainly from the perspective of the salesperson and how salespeople can be perceived to be more honest. However, in the 21st century, it is just as important to trust the company as it is to trust the salesperson.

Once again, would you do business with someone you do not trust? NO! Thus, the basic elements of public relations, reputation management, and corporate identity are critical in the 21st century.

Chapter 3 expands on what is described in Chapter 2 about trust and then explains how businesses should manage and guard their reputations to be seen as trustworthy. At some points, Chapter 3 may almost seem out of place in a book focusing on sales and relationship marketing. But, in the 21st century if you do not have a good, healthy corporate image, do not worry about anything in the rest of the book. Also, in the days of heavy media presence and extremely educated consumers, it is essential to know how to rebuild a damaged reputation. Without a trustworthy sales force (Chapter 2) and a solid corporate image (Chapter 3), you have nothing.

KNOWING AND UNDERSTANDING THE COMPETITOR

In light of the extreme importance of strategy, it would be utterly foolish to examine any strategy, even a sales strategy, without careful consideration of the competition. Nobody operates in a vacuum. We are constantly dealing with competition from every angle. And even with the most trustworthy sales force and the best corporate image, competition can come in and disrupt the equation and cause the best-planned strategies to fail. While a full examination of competitive analysis is outside the scope of this book, Chapter 4 examines this topic from a sales management and a salesperson viewpoint. The author of Chapter 4 makes a brilliant and often forgotten point. When you are a salesperson, who is your competition? Is it the competing businesses? Is it their products and/or services? As an individual out in the field, it is much more basic than that. Your primary competition from this level is the other salespeople. As is mentioned so many times in this book, the 21st century is one of hypercompetition (extreme competition), created from fragmented and saturated markets, more knowledgeable consumers, greater technology, and more globalization, just to name a few. So, when you are out in the trenches, what distinguishes you from the competition, what sets you apart? Well, the easiest answer is you!

It is up to each and every individual salesperson to build an ongoing, solid, lasting relationship with each customer. When that loyalty is built, then you have a differential advantage. It is also up to each salesperson to learn and understand how the other salespeople in the industry behave and build relationships. No matter how great the technology and innovation of the 21st century is, we are all still just people selling products and services to other people. And given the increased changes, this concept becomes even more important than ever. We are right back to the basic principle of relationship marketing, which is once again why it was so incredibly important to focus this "selling" and "sales management" book on relationships.

So many books about competitive analysis go into great detail about why competitive analysis is important. The author of Chapter 4 does stress why competitive analysis is so important, but does so from a relationship marketing perspective. Then, the author shows how salespeople and sales managers can actually go out and get competitive intelligence and also distinguishes which types of information are more important and why. This hands-on, practical advice can provide enormous benefits to anyone interested in learning about their competition—as all businesspeople should be.

KEYS TO SUCCESS FROM THE INSIDE OUT: BUILDING A SUCCESSFUL SALES FORCE IN THE 21ST CENTURY

According to the president of a shoe company, two shoe salespeople were sent to a poverty-stricken country. The first wrote the president and said, "Returning home immediately. No one wears shoes here." The second, more optimistic salesperson approached the situation in a very different way. She described the situation to management as "Unlimited possibilities. Millions of people here are still without shoes."

This cute story illustrates that one of the most important jobs sales managers perform is the personnel function. The work of sales managers in personnel activities starts with finding and hiring individuals for sales slots in the organization—people who are both interested in sales jobs and qualified to fill them. An organization cannot survive without a good, competent, energetic, and creative sales force.

From the chapters so far, we have learned each and every time how important it is to go back to square one. As a business owner, the utmost important thing is to always have a clear strategy. This must come first. Thus, just as in all other areas of managing a 21st century sales force, your guiding principles and choices of action must be rooted in a carefully planned and deeply rooted strategic mission and vision statement. From these statements, more specific, tangible objectives can be established. These goals and procedures must not only have strategy as their guiding principles, but must also emerge from a set of ethical standards. Does this line of thought seem repetitive at this point? Good! A well-developed strategic direction that is founded on a solid ethical foundation is the single most important step.

As the author of Chapter 5 discusses, once these tasks are accomplished, then sales managers can begin the tasks of hiring, training, motivating, and keeping employees who take special care of the customer. Profitability stems from customer satisfaction, and customer satisfaction and loyalty are deeply rooted in employee satisfaction and loyalty. As many other businesses have learned this lesson the hard way, so did T.G.I. Friday's. After years of very dismal store results, T.G.I. Friday's started focusing on internal operations such as the cleanliness of the store and the happiness and the attitude of the servers. When it did this, sales doubled in six months.[1]

As described in the introduction to this chapter, few business owners want to look inward to find the fault for problems. It is also easier to blame something external. We have almost an instinctual response left over from the 20th century to try to dig out of sales slumps by increasing advertising spending. Pumping thousands of dollars into promotion is not going to solve problems that form the very backbone of relationship marketing. With whom do customers actually have a relationship? It is the business, but more specifically, they remember the waitress who actually waited on them or, in the case of sales, the salesperson who took care of them. Therefore, the issues of Chapter 5 are not human resource (HR) problems, and they cannot be left to HR departments to solve. These issues must become central to any marketing and sales campaign and must be integrated within the total efforts. Finding and keeping the best sales talent is a key competitive weapon of the 21st century.

SALES EFFECTIVENESS, MONEY, AND THE BOTTOM LINE

What is the end result of all this fluffy relationship stuff? Hopefully it is money, of course! A reoccurring theme of the 21st century is hypercompetition. Competition comes from more than just potential competition for your customers; it also includes competition for your employees. As we learned in Chapter 5, relationship marketing is just as much about the relationships with your employees as it is about the relationships with your customers. Customer satisfaction and loyalty comes from employee satisfaction and loyalty. So how do you get satisfied, loyal employees? Studies have shown that more than 80 percent of all behavior is determined by the reward system.[2] As a consequence, 80 percent of behavior is within your control as a manager. You must pay employees correctly, and you must use a proper balance of the other types of motivational tools.

Then, it is just as critical that you enact the proper mix of measurement tools, for both the sales force and the organization. You cannot know what to fix if you do not know what is broken. As Chapter 6 describes, many performance indicators must be collected. Simply looking at financial indicators is not sufficient. After all, money is a lagging indicator, meaning once you are looking at an income statement, the mistake (or accomplishment) has already happened in the past. Customers must be enticed to buy first, must be satisfied, must have time to tell their friends and/or co-workers, and must have time to possibly rebuy or look elsewhere before the outcomes of their behaviors will show up on an income statement. Thus, it is critical to take a multifaceted approach to evaluating effectiveness. Chapter 6 will discuss many tools to ensure that your salespeople are operating at their peak performance to ensure continued, lasting customer relationships.

LEARNING FROM YOUR CUSTOMERS TO INCREASE INNOVATION

Once we have taken care of some basic strategic decisions, built a great company from the inside out through the development of a great sales force, and paid very careful attention to the competition, we have to remember the most important component of the relationship. With whom are we trying to build a relationship? It is the customer, of course! Customer relationship management (CRM) has become a very popular term of this century. CRM is a term that is commonly used to refer to software packages that have become commonplace in the 21st century for managing and handling consumer data. However, CRM goes beyond software applications. The term encompasses a total strategic approach to managing customer relationships. Specifically, CRM is the processes that identify customers, create knowledge about those customers, build customer relationships, and shape customers' perceptions of a firm and its products and/or services.

Chapter 7 briefly discusses the CRM processes and their importance to an overall relationship marketing strategy. One of the most important parts of this process is the knowledge-building component. What do your customers want and how do you modify your product based on that? How do you get them to talk to you so that you can find out what they want? How do you interpret what they say? Chapter 7 answers some of these important questions in practical, straightforward terms. It also demonstrates how market knowledge can be applied in order to adapt or improve products to create new products and services. Understanding innovation and adaptability, and more importantly how to be innovative, is a necessity in an age of such turbulence.

KEY ACCOUNT MANAGEMENT IN THE 21ST CENTURY

As we learn in Chapter 7, CRM of the 21st century involves a very strategic handling and managing of accounts. Since partnerships are hopefully long term, you need and will have tons of data about customers. These data need to be stored and utilized to make key decisions. Then, salespeople need to utilize this information to determine which accounts to serve and what levels of service to provide each account. Some accounts just want a phone call every now and then. Some need personal visits every week. Consequently 21st century key account management requires careful consideration of these questions. Key account management is simply about learning who the most profitable customers are. As we will see in Chapter 7, the 80/20 rule, that 80 percent of your sales come from 20 percent of your customers, holds true. Thus, sales managers and salespeople need to make key decisions to determine who those 20 percent are. But, it goes much further than that. What do you do with the other 80 percent? They need careful consideration and classification as well. What if you could take some of that 80 percent and "move them up," or get them to purchase more?

Chapter 8 also covers the other side of the key account management equation. How do you organize your sales force around these accounts as well as all other accounts? Territory management of the 21st century has become harder and harder than ever before. On the one hand, as a sales manager, you want to utilize whatever system is most efficient and effective and allows the customers to have the best possible service available. On the other hand, you want to be fair to your salespeople. Sometimes sales representatives perform poorly not because of their own skills and abilities, but instead because they are simply in a bad territory. It can and does happen frequently. If your compensation system and motivation system is based upon this, you have problems. Therefore, just as relationship marketing has caused us to take a more careful and strategic approach to account management, sales managers must also take a more careful and strategic approach to sales force and territory management.

Sales managers want to get the most bang for their buck no matter how they make decisions. They want value. Value refers to the perception that the rewards exceed the costs associated with continuing the business relationship—on all sides of the equation. For the seller, investments in building the business relationship may be considerable, but a highly committed buyer may be the seller's most important asset. The seller can leverage skills and resources, build strong competitive positions, and enjoy the benefits of a long-term relationship without continuing to experience customer search costs. Buyers also enjoy the benefit of long-term business relationships. They can avoid costs associated with extensive product search procedures, receive favored treatment from suppliers, and can often achieve a reduction in total costs, even if the price is the same as (or even higher) than that charged by others.

The value and the efficiency that both the buyer and the seller want make the tedious process of customer relationship management, key account management, and territory management worth it in the long run. However, these are processes that require a great deal of skill and effort. All 21st century sales managers and salespeople must understand these principles, which is why a chapter is devoted to this subject.

GETTING RID OF THOSE THAT ARE NOT PROFITABLE

In the 21st century, many companies are operating on even tighter margins, and managers are forced to be more accountable. Thus, just as the tried and true approaches of the past are still necessary, 21st century sales managers must learn when to get rid of customers just as they must know when to get rid of certain employees. Keep in mind the definition of relationship marketing, which was mentioned earlier in this chapter. Relationship marketing is a total strategy focused on creating and maintaining long-term, *mutually* beneficial relationships.

As we see in the key account management chapter (Chapter 8), through our efforts, we will find that some accounts are not as profitable as others.

The author of Chapter 9 states some stunning statistics. To repeat, a recent analysis of customers in a major bank in Australia revealed that 12 percent of its customers contributed to the majority of the profits, 60 percent were at a break-even level, and the remaining 28 percent cost the bank money (see Chapter 9 for more information). The author continues to cite studies from the largest banks in the United States, which found that only 6 percent of the customers were the most profitable. On average, they produced $1,600 in revenue and cost $350 to serve. Compared to this, 14 percent of customers contributed to loss and produced only $230 in revenue while costing $700 to serve. The percentage of profitable customers varied from a mere 7 percent of the customers for a software company to 16 percent for a media company.

We all know it is true to some degree, but the actual statistics presented can be somewhat daunting. These numbers may make sales managers want to go back and reread Chapter 8 over again to make sure they have been segmenting their accounts correctly. Chapter 9 takes these concepts and goes into even greater detail expressing that key account management also needs to incorporate other variables into the equation, which adds the costs associated with serving each customer. If you are making a lot from a customer, but calling on him or her every day and refunding his or her purchasing constantly, that customer still may not be profitable. Now comes the tricky part: What do you do with unprofitable customers? Chapter 9 discusses the many strategies and alternatives to take care of these accounts. In the 21st century, managers must consider these crucial elements along with their customer relationship management and key account management decisions. Margins are simply too tight in this century.

UTILIZING INTEGRATED MARKETING COMMUNICATIONS IN SMALL BUSINESSES

Because the 21st century is all about customer relationship management, it is necessary to discuss some of the special types of businesses and customers and their respective needs. Small businesses have always existed. In fact, the origins of all businesses were in small businesses. However, the 21st century has brought with it changes that have and will continue to change the role small businesses play in our economy. In some ways, it is easier than ever to thrive and succeed with a small business. In others, it is harder and harder to succeed when faced with competition from major corporations and their mega-brands. So, what are the alternatives for selling in small businesses in the 21st century?

As with so many other things that we have seen, it all comes back to strategy. Many feel that the 21st century will see a continued dominance of "pull" strategies instead of "push" strategies. That means, instead of companies pushing the product to the consumer with mass advertising and a heavy sales force presence, consumers will pull the product through the channel. They will do so because they are so educated these days. With blogs, and all other forms of technology and word-of-mouth advertising, customers can find out information about products and services as soon as, if not before, they hit the market. Thus, strategies for the 21st century have and will continue to change.

Luckily, the 21st century has brought amazing advancements in technology, which can help the small business owner succeed. These are all basically "tools" that a sales manager can add to his or her "tool box" and utilize to communicate with the customer. The author of Chapter 10 discusses direct marketing, database marketing, e-mail marketing, using Web sites, and utilizing search engine technology. To the small business owner with a considerably smaller sales force, of which many of the salespeople are performing multiple functions, these technological tools make the small business owner an equal competitor in this century. It all comes back to strategy because even with the use of these tools, they all must be integrated back into the company's strategy to send one consistent and unified message to the customer about the company's products and services. If the messages say the same thing, it really does not matter what the "channel" or "medium" is. As long as the customer receives correct, timely, and relevant information, the technological breakthroughs of this century help the small business owner succeed right along side of the large companies.

UNDERSTANDING DIVERSE ORGANIZATIONAL BUYERS

Once again, with customer relationship management and key account management being two crucial elements of a relationship marketing strategy, it is vitally important to understand a firm's largest accounts. Usually, just due to sheer purchasing power, the largest accounts are the industrial and other business-to-business accounts. These customers have many distinct differences from ultimate consumers in the marketplace. Many of these differences are the same as they have always been throughout the 20th century. However, some of these aspects are so important that they deserve repeating. On the other hand, just like everything else, the dramatic changes of the 21st century have brought dramatic changes in organizational selling characteristics and processes.

The author of Chapter 11 discusses some of these changes and identifies strategies to take advantage of these opportunities and challenges. Some of the biggest changes that have occurred in the 21st century, with regard to business-to-business purchasing, deal with the purchasing and buying center functions of the organization. Many of these changes were brought about by the same forces that are requiring changes in all organizations—increased accountability and lower operating margins. There is not as much room for trial and error in this century. Salespeople calling on business-to-business and industrial accounts need to recognize these changes and deal with them effectively. Although the changes mentioned in Chapter 11 are unique to business-to-business and industrial selling, the solutions are the same. To succeed in this century we need to have a greater emphasis on relationship marketing and all of its elements that are discussed throughout this book.

NEGOTIATING FOR SUCCESS

As with all relationships, communication is critical. As we have discussed in this chapter, 21st century selling is not about a pushy, manipulative salesperson who monopolizes all of the talking time and, then, the customer eventually breaks down and buys. In order to have a successful negotiation, communication must be a two-way street. As this chapter discusses, the best negotiations are ones that involve a win-win situation for both parties. Therefore, instead of having a chapter in this book that covers how to sell, in a canned speech context, this book includes a chapter on negotiation (Chapter 12), which explains how salespeople can create win-win situations and solve their customer problems by offering solutions. This is the heart of 21st century sales tactics.

UNDERSTANDING EMERGING SALES TECHNOLOGY

Any book that covers the changes that have occurred in selling in the 21st century has to cover the changes that have occurred with technology. The changes in technology are one of the biggest, if not the biggest, changes of this century. They have impacted all types of sales forces in all industries. Sit down with a group of salespeople anyday, anytime, and you will hear the same complaints and comments. I have heard praises for personal communication devices in the same sentences that I have heard these devices called foul names. Why is this? Simply put, technology has brought us closer to the customer and made the world much smaller. Sometimes we want to be closer to our customers, and even in a world of relationship marketing, sometimes we want our space.

Chapter 13 discusses the specific technological advancements of the future and provides illustrations as to how salespeople utilize these forms of technology in their jobs. More importantly, Chapter 13 covers the pros and cons of technology implementation. Does implementing sales force automation (SFA) help or hinder productivity? This is one of those million-dollar questions that is yet to be fully realized; however, the authors of Chapter 13 provide some research into this question. Moreover, the authors make suggestions as to how SFA implementation can be handled more effectively and efficiently so that sales managers and salespeople can make the most of this technology. It all comes back to one thing: we want to implement and utilize technology that helps build customer relationships and not utilize technology that would detract from these relationships. We want technology that improves productivity and performance to positively help our bottom line and the bottom line of our customers.

THE ETHICS OF MANAGING CUSTOMER INFORMATION

All of our customer relationship management efforts and all of our increasing technology have brought with it one tremendous opportunity and challenge too great to be mentioned in the previous chapter: What do we do with all this information? What are the ethical issues involved? What about consumer privacy, does it matter? Chapter 14 covers these and many other issues associated with the 21st century. First and foremost, salespeople have to reach the customer. All the information that exists has, quite frankly, produced "information overload." Therefore, from a sales perspective, it has become harder and harder to reach customers. So, the first question managers must answer is how to reach customers through the clutter of information. Then, if you do reach the customers, you then have a whole new set of issues of managing their information. Chapter 14 covers the ethical issues involved with this information management to both protect you as a business owner and legally ensure that you are doing everything properly. Moreover, it can be a benefit to your company if you manage this information correctly. Just as companies that mishandle consumer data can end up in a public relations nightmare, companies that learn to properly use and respect consumer information gain an added advantage of enhancing their reputation.

CONCLUSION

The only way to survive in the 21st century is by building relationships. Relationship marketing seems like a term caught between a cliché and common sense. However, no matter how cliché and like common sense that it may seem, it is a complex set of processes that must be utilized to cope with the rapid changes of this century. The following chapters will cover some of these processes in greater detail and help sales managers and salespeople understand how to better take advantage of these processes and strategies. With the implementation of the processes covered in this book, companies can forge stronger bonds with their customers to build relationships and create better success and, hopefully, ultimately, greater profitability.

NOTES

1. Michael LeBoeuf, *How to Win Customers and Keep Them for Life* (New York: Penguin Putnam Inc., 2000).
2. Ibid.

CHAPTER 2

BUILDING TRUST IN AN AGE OF MISTRUST

Jon M. Hawes

The golden rule of sales is the golden rule.

—Dan James[1]

Working as a professional salesperson is a terrific career. A lot of satisfaction comes from making your living by helping customers solve important business problems. Of course, this job is much easier after the salesperson has spent a few years developing a number of trusting relationships with high-volume customers. It may take a while (always longer than the salesperson would hope!), but trustworthy salespeople who sell good products, work hard, have integrity, and therefore do what they say they will do eventually become trusted partners for many of their customers. Given a long enough period of time for the client's evaluation, a trustworthy salesperson will become trusted by a particular customer. This is because over the long term, most people accurately assess the behavior of others.

In an earlier article several years ago, the author wrote:

> Trust is the binding force in most productive buyer/seller relationships. No amount of detail in a formal written contract, no abundance of legal staff to fight for recompense, no form of recourse can provide the buyer with such a high expectation of a satisfying exchange relationship as a simple, basic trust of the salesperson and the company that he or she represents.[2]

And now, decades later, not only does this still apply, but it is even truer today in the 21st century. Indeed, earning the buyer's trust by the salesperson is the foundation for all that has been written about relationship selling. Earning trust is a prerequisite for business success within most sectors of the business-to-business or the business-to-consumer marketplace.

The recent series of widely publicized business scandals at firms such as Enron Corporation, WorldCom, Tyco International, Adelphia Communications Corporation, Fannie Mae (the Federal National Mortgage Association), HealthSouth Corporation, and Global Crossing, however, have made earning the prospect's trust even more difficult. The process of earning the prospect's trust was tough enough and took far too long before these well-known scandals hit the front page. It would be great if customers paid more attention to what Jack and Suzy Welch recently reported. Of the many millions of people working in business, only about 1,000 individuals have been convicted of corporate crime during the past four years. As they reminded us, "Enron-like behavior is rare. Most businesses play by the rules, and the rules work."[3]

It is, of course, true that only a very small percentage of business executives engage in criminal behavior. Most business executives possess ethical standards similar to those of others within the community. Nevertheless, the public's perception of integrity from business executives has fallen dramatically over the past few years. This chapter will provide some practical advice to sales and marketing executives about how to build trust with clients and speed the rightful attribution of trust under such challenging times. First, let us define trust and the benefits that accrue to a trusted salesperson.

WHAT IS TRUST?

Earned trust is a thing of beauty for the sales professional. A classic definition of interpersonal trust was provided by Julian B. Rotter who defined it as "a generalized expectancy held by an individual that the word, promise, oral or written statement of another individual or group can be relied on."[4] When the salesperson has earned the prospect's trust, it means that the prospect is willing to engage in a risky activity (such as a purchase) feeling that the salesperson will (a) handle the transaction in a way that appropriately serves the needs of the prospect, (b) provide all of what had been promised, and (c) not take advantage of the prospect if that should become possible as a consequence of the purchase agreement being completed.

In essence, the prospect expects the salesperson to be honest as well as competent and furthermore expects at least some degree of benevolence on the part of the seller. The prospect believes that the purchase decision will result in a satisfactory exchange for both parties. This is a powerful concept. The salesperson profits by being able to make the sale, and the prospect also benefits by experiencing a lower level of perceived risk than would otherwise have been the case. Trust enables a relationship to be maintained and strengthened over time.

Trust is a notion that evolves ever so slowly over time, or at least it seems that way for sellers. The salesperson qualities that lead to the development of trust by prospects include all five of the following: being *likable, competent, dependable,*

Figure 2.1
Necessary Salesperson Characteristics for the Development of Trust

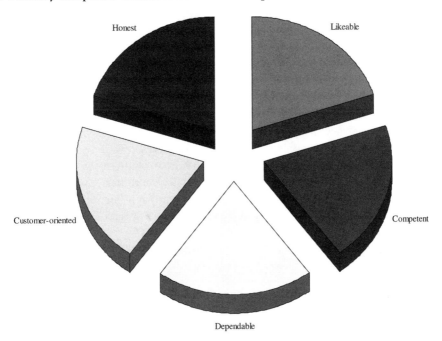

customer-oriented, and honest (see Figure 2.1).[5] These basic components must exist for trust to be developed. First, we just like people and tend to trust those who seem friendly, likable, and also resemble ourselves. We trust those people who appear to be competent and know how to do their jobs. Is there anything more frustrating than being a customer dealing with someone who obviously has no clue or has to continually ask his or her manager questions? We trust people who know what they are talking about and understand their company and their products. Thus, proper training (covered in Chapter 5) is crucial.

Also, dependability is key because trusting relationships evolve over time. If someone is trustworthy and delivers on his or her promises nine out of ten times, we will remember that tenth time when he or she failed. Additionally, no one likes to be sold to, but everyone likes to buy. Customers must feel that the salesperson has their best interests at heart. One of the biggest damaging factors in the salesperson-customer relationship is the fact that we do not trust salespeople by nature. Why? Because we know that their basic livelihoods and commissions depend on them making the sale. Thus, salespeople must go out of their way to demonstrate that the customer is king and it is not all about revenue. And finally, as will be described later, just be honest. This basic principle does not require any explaining, but is critical to the relationship and is often missing.

All of these qualities cannot be assessed at the beginning of a salesperson-customer interaction. It is highly unlikely that a prospect would attribute the quality of trustworthiness to a salesperson during the first sales call. Unlike love, there is no such thing as "trust at first sight." In fact, given the fact that the prospect knows that a salesperson would receive a personal financial benefit from making a sale, it is more likely that the prospect would initially mistrust the salesperson or, at best, be neutral regarding trust for a salesperson until there is clear reason to change that view based on a series of positive interactions over time. If the buyer has had some bad experiences with other salespeople in the past, it is even more likely that a situation of negative trust will exist at the beginning of a business relationship with another specific salesperson.

How long does it take for a prospect to rightfully attribute trust to a truly trustworthy salesperson? While it varies depending upon the context, one study found that on average, it took 5.6 sales calls for this to occur.[6] It is interesting that a well-respected professional selling textbook published slightly later reported that the average number of sales calls required to close a sale was 5—just slightly less than the average number necessary to earn the prospect's trust.[7] Apparently, prospects are willing to place an initial order prior to the full attribution of trust in the salesperson, but need to personally verify that the salesperson's promises have been fulfilled through a satisfactory first purchase in order for trust to be more fully attributed. Evidently, to repeat a wise saying, "seeing is believing." This can occur only after the first purchase (often a trial order) and receipt of the goods or services in a manner which positively reinforces the promises made by the salesperson.

THE BENEFITS OF BEING TRUSTED

How would you feel as a business owner if you found out that the millions of dollars that you spent on advertising were a complete waste? They might have been if trust was not there. John E. Swan and I. Fredrick Trawick conducted an important study in which salespeople shared their feelings about the outcomes of gaining trust from customers.[8] Eight benefits were identified and the first of these is that the trusted salesperson's primary role changes from selling to servicing the account once trust has been earned. The role of persuasion becomes much less important and instead the salesperson's role shifts to much more emphasis on simply providing excellent service to the customer. The second outcome from earning the buyer's trust is a change (improvement) in customer receptivity to the salesperson's purchasing suggestions. Buyers become more open to salesperson suggestions, including information about other products that may also receive consideration for other projects in the near future. In addition, it becomes easier to make appointments with the buyer, and the relationship generally becomes more relaxed, open, and friendly.

The third benefit of earning buyer trust is that clients begin to serve as receptive gatekeepers for these salespeople who then more easily gain access to other people at a variety of levels (often higher) within the buyer organization. This can facilitate the sale of other products to other units within the corporation. Not only do revenues increase, but profits increase at an even better rate once trust has been established. This is due to a reduction in selling costs coupled with the fact that price discounting is generally less necessary. A fourth benefit is that the salesperson gets more time for sales presentations, including more time per call. He or she also has a better chance of getting in to see the prospect without an appointment and a better quality of time during the sales calls. These time-related benefits help the salesperson achieve even more selling success with the client.

The fifth useful outcome of earning buyer trust is that industrial salespeople have greater ease in scheduling appointments with less waiting time. This provides more opportunity as well as increased productivity. The sixth identified benefit is that customers often inform the salesperson about future buying needs, enabling the salesperson to be involved earlier in the buying process. This provides an opportunity for the salesperson to suggest product specifications that may provide him or her with advantages over other competitors for this new business. The seventh benefit identified is that customers simply became more relaxed. This also serves to the advantage of the well-known and trusted sales representative. Finally and perhaps of greatest importance, there is a change in the buying patterns with more being purchased. As salesperson quotas continue to increase, this concentration of purchases with his or her firm is a most welcome outcome from this now highly productive business relationship.

EARNING THE PROSPECT'S TRUST

With such extraordinary benefits for the salesperson, it is no wonder that trust is such a sought-after attribute. For example, consider the persuasive challenge confronting a new, but trustworthy salesperson selling a new product for a new company in a new market. In the long run, of course, the best way to win a potential buyer's trust, and to keep it, is to simply deserve it by being completely trustworthy throughout this lengthy period of time. Not only is being trustworthy the best way to earn the buyer's trust, it is also important for the salesperson's own sense of well-being and overall job performance because it impacts his or her self-confidence, self-esteem, and freedom from guilt. A trustworthy salesperson will become trusted once the potential buyer has taken enough time to get to know him or her and understands his or her way of doing business. The salesperson needs to create an environment in which the potential buyer is willing to devote the time needed to get to know the seller and the sooner the better.

Most salespeople are, however, very impatient. Not very many ambitious salespeople are simply willing to wait around for whatever period of time is necessary (an average of 5.6 calls per prospect) for trust to evolve naturally. New salespeople are among the least patient because so few potential buyers already know them well enough to already trust them. These rookie salespeople are in a hurry to earn trust sooner because they need to generate revenue and demonstrate achievements to their bosses. Veteran sales executives also want to speed the attribution of trust. Professionals with more than 20 years of sales success and an abundance of solid long-term relationships with major accounts are continually meeting new people, whose trust must be earned, at new or even existing accounts. And as far as the veteran sales rep is concerned, this valuable trust cannot be earned too soon.

The point is that there are a lot of highly trustworthy individuals who would like to know how to convince people of their trustworthiness in shorter periods of time. They are searching for more productive and efficient methods to achieve this highly desirable goal. Here are some great ways to achieve this worthy goal.

TOP TEN WAYS TO EARN THE PROSPECT'S TRUST SOONER

In the spirit of David Letterman's "Top Ten List," what follows is a description of the top ten ways that trustworthy salespeople can speed their rightful attribution of trust from prospects. The goal of this section is to provide very specific and practical advice for salespeople. Remember, tonight's category is "ways to earn the prospect's trust sooner."

Number 10: Develop a Record of Fulfilling Promises

Trust evolves over time as the prospect comes to rely upon the salesperson's word. One way to speed this process is to make more promises early in the relationship and to be sure to keep those promises. By taking a *proactive* stance, a deserving salesperson can decrease the length of time it takes to earn a buyer's trust. The key here is to begin early in the series of interactions by making a number of promises *that are kept*. By doing so, the salesperson proves that his or her words and deeds are linked. Remember that old experiment with Pavlov's dogs? That researcher rang a bell immediately before feeding the dogs. Eventually, the dogs learned that the ringing of the bell meant food could be expected to follow. Over time, the dogs learned to make this association, and they began to salivate in anticipation of the food whenever the bell was rung. While potential buyers are not dogs (!), prospects do learn in the same manner, and this learning does occur over time. When a salesperson makes enough promises that are kept, the potential buyer eventually learns to expect that the salesperson can be trusted to fulfill his or her promises.

For example, the salesperson can begin by making an appointment for the first sales call, rather than cold calling. Rather than suggesting a meeting during the "first of the week," consider asking for an appointment at 2:15 P.M. on Monday. Then, the salesperson needs to walk into the reception area at precisely 2:10 P.M. on Monday. At this point, the learning process of making and keeping promises that links salesperson words and deeds has begun.

During the first sales call, the salesperson is likely to be asked about some aspect of the product that may need to be researched. He or she should promise to provide that information by telephone at a certain scheduled time, say 9:45 A.M. on Wednesday. When the seller makes the call at precisely 9:45 A.M. on Wednesday with the information sought, another promise has been made and kept. While each of these has a small impact, the cumulative effect will become very significant. To the extent that the salesperson can consistently demonstrate truthfulness over time, in a variety of settings, and with an array of people within the buying organization, these efforts will contribute toward the buyer's development of trust for the seller.

Number 9: Be Extraordinarily Honest

Honesty is, of course, a prerequisite for being considered trustworthy. To speed the attribution of trust, however, the salesperson can exhibit *extraordinary* honesty to the prospect. For example, a potential buyer may ask a number of competing salespeople to recommend an order quantity for a given project. If other sellers recommend a quantity that could exceed the buyer's initial needs and the buyer has an excellent understanding of the true quantity needed, the salesperson who suggests a more modest and accurate initial order quantity is likely to be perceived as "extraordinarily truthful," or distinctively honest in comparison to the competition who guessed on the high side relative to the amount the prospect would need.

Another way to exhibit extraordinary honesty is to explain the product's pros as well as its cons. Such a two-sided argument helps demonstrate trustworthiness and may also be quite persuasive, especially when the buyer is well informed and sophisticated. Other means of demonstrating truthfulness include the use of facts and figures rather that generalities when describing a product. For example, the seller should describe the product by saying "it weighs 74 pounds," rather than "it's really heavy." Other ways to exhibit extraordinary truthfulness include backing up claims with proof such as testimonials and other third-party verifications, using written rather than verbal contracts, and providing a written guarantee.

Being extraordinarily truthful relates to a concept known in the social science literature as "the cost for lying."[9] Both the salesperson and the potential buyers know that if a salesperson gets caught telling a lie, she is likely to lose the order.

In addition, perhaps she will lose the account and possibly even her job. The higher the salesperson's cost for lying and the more widely recognized this is by the prospect, the more likely that her message will be perceived as truthful due to the prospect's assumption that she would not take such a risk of lying when the potential penalty is so high. The salesperson can highlight this cost for lying in discussions with the potential buyer thereby increasing the prospect's perception that the salesperson is extraordinarily truthful because to do otherwise would be foolish given the high cost for lying.

Number 8: Be Friendly, But Not Too Friendly Too Soon

Salespeople should be friendly to prospects and work toward the achievement of the affective dimension, but they should not try too hard, nor too soon. It is critical that the friendliness be viewed as appropriate for the circumstances under which the salesperson and the prospect find themselves. As reported earlier, likability contributes to the attribution of trustworthiness. When a salesperson behaves in a way that is viewed as appropriately friendly by the prospect, this can contribute to the attribution of likability.

A key issue in successfully implementing this tactic is to avoid making the prospect feel uncomfortable. The friendliness needs to be suitable to the occasion and the context and done in a way consistent with how the prospect is responding to it. Being too friendly too soon or in a way that violates the social norms of the prospect will be counterproductive. For example, hugging would be viewed as an unacceptable practice on an initial North American sales call. In addition, suggesting that the initial meeting be held over drinks at a bar would probably be perceived as outside of the socially acceptable norms within the North American context. Meeting for lunch at a nice restaurant near the prospect's place of business for the initial meeting might or might not be viewed as socially acceptable within North America, depending upon the industry. It is so important for the salesperson to develop an understanding of how prospects want to conduct business and then to behave in that manner while being just friendly enough to encourage the view that he is a likable and therefore trustworthy salesperson.

Beyond the contextual issues, the manner in which the seller shows friendliness to the prospect is also important. To contribute to the successful attribution of trust, the seller's friendliness must be perceived as genuine and natural. Any feelings by the prospect that the seller's expressive smile, firm handshake, or pleasant conversations are contrived aspects of a learned persuasive appeal will be highly counterproductive. A senior sales executive once described this issue to the author as follows: if a particular salesperson is a jerk, when she tries to act friendly with the prospect, this will probably be perceived by the prospect for what it is, a disingenuous persuasive tactic that fails. Many would argue that the demonstration of friendliness is not a trainable tactic for most members of the sales force. Instead, sales managers need to recruit and select salespeople who are genuinely nice people by nature. Jerks need not apply!

Number 7: Get It Done and Get It Right

It is very important, especially early in the relationship, to get things accomplished and the salesperson's work should be accurate. Competence is a critical factor in earning the prospect's trust, and the salesperson needs to demonstrate proficiency within the context of the sales relationship. This can be done in a variety of ways. Obviously, avoiding mistakes during the early phases of the relationship is important. Build some flexibility into the deal so as to minimize the probability of mistakes. If typical shipping time is one week, quote a shipping time of "within the next ten days." This increases the chances of getting it right.

Another tactic that can contribute to the perception of competence is to let the prospect know about the salesperson's customer-service awards, education, experience, or other indications of expertise. This is a good tactic, but only if it can be executed effectively. Bragging is unquestionably a bad idea. Enabling the prospect to feel like the salesperson is engaging in impression management is also a bad idea. There are times, however, when tangible accomplishments can be worked into the conversation. For example, when setting an appointment, perhaps the prospect suggests meeting at a time when the salesperson is out of town receiving an award for excellence in customer service. It would be totally appropriate to apologize about being unable to meet at that time and to explain the nature of that prior commitment.

Furthermore, during early discussions the conversation often involves a search for common ground. A typical topic of conversation may involve something about the prospect's college experiences. If the prospect attended a prestigious university and the salesperson is also a graduate of that institution, discussing that common experience may work well to gain rapport as well as demonstrate the salesperson's capabilities.

For senior salespeople, an easy way to demonstrate competence is to refer to the length of time spent in serving customers who have had similar needs. Customers are likely to believe that extensive experience working with clients facing similar problems contributes to a salesperson's competence within this context. During the sales interaction, there are many appropriate and useful ways to make reference to a lengthy career in the field of sales.

Number 6: Show Concern for the Prospect

Prospects need to know that the salesperson truly cares about the prospect's needs. Since most salespeople get rewarded for making sales, prospects may feel that their purchases are nothing more than a way for the salesperson to make money. To earn the attribution of being trustworthy, a salesperson needs to be viewed as customer oriented, not self-centered.

Of course, the worst thing a salesperson could do when writing up an order would be to take out a calculator and compute her commission in full view of the prospect! Tom Hopkins, a highly successful and very experienced sales trainer, goes so far as to suggest that "commission" is an ugly word that salespeople should avoid. If the customer asks about the salesperson's compensation system or asks if he will receive a commission for making the sale, Tom suggests that the salesperson reframe the concept as the salesperson's "fee for services provided."[10]

A very good way for the seller to demonstrate true concern for the prospect is to talk about other highly satisfied customers and how she helped the client solve an important problem. By focusing on how the customer was well served, the attribution of customer orientation can be enhanced.

Another useful tactic to demonstrate customer orientation is for the salesperson to simply and honestly say with genuine sincerity that his goal in working with this prospect is to create another satisfied client. This can be supported by the fact that a large proportion of the salesperson's new business comes from referrals who are provided by highly satisfied customers. Being a very good active listener also helps demonstrate concern for the other party. When a salesperson really does have a customer orientation, the persuasive challenge is greatly diminished and a frank discussion of how the seller does business is a productive way of demonstrating this quality.

Number 5: Demonstrate Trust of the Prospect

If a salesperson wants the prospect to trust her, she needs to trust the prospect and let the prospect know this. Trust is a quality that tends to be reciprocated. When a salesperson shows that the other party is trusted, the other party tends to respond in kind with trust for the salesperson.

Consider, for example, the matter of credit extension to customers. The salesperson can explain her company's policy and then make a comment such as "and we know that we can trust you to make your payments on time." This highlights the fact that trust is a two-way street and the prospect often comes to the conclusion that if she can trust me, I should be able to trust her.

Another way that a seller can exhibit this trust of the prospect is when delivering proposals, sales literature, or other written documents from your company. Upon turning such material over to the prospect, the seller can comment on how he has kept the information relating to the prospect's needs analysis confidential and that he knows he can expect the same of the prospect regarding the seller's documents.

Number 4: Speak Slowly and Make Eye Contact

Have you heard the expression "a fast-talking salesperson"? When customers complain about bad selling experiences and/or about salespeople who have been dishonest, the phrase "fast-talking" often gets included as a descriptive, general criticism of these disliked sales behaviors. Perhaps customers feel that if a salesperson talks very fast, she can more easily slip a falsehood into the conversation. Or, perhaps customers believe that they will not be able to verbally defend themselves by getting a word in edgewise with a fast-talking salesperson. At any rate, the salesperson who is trying to earn the attribution of trust from a prospect would be well advised to slow the pace when speaking to a prospect. This, of course, is also impacted by local expectations relative to pace of speaking. People often talk at a faster pace in Brooklyn, New York, for example, than is common in Mobile, Alabama.

While speaking more slowly, the salesperson should also be sure to make adequate eye contact with the prospect. It is widely believed that a lack of eye contact is a potential indication of dishonesty. So the advice here is very specific and very direct. Look your prospect right in the eyes and slowly speak the truth. Speak clearly, articulate, be consistent, and where possible present third-party evidence or other forms of proof.

This does not sound difficult, but many of us speak more quickly when we are nervous, and we also tend to avoid eye contact when we lack confidence. Unfortunately, both of these conditions are often present when we begin an interaction with a new prospect. Consequently, under the very circumstance when we need it the most, we often fail to speak slowly and make eye contact. If we do, there is a better chance of earning trust. When we do not, prospects are likely to incorrectly feel that we are trying to hide something. Salespeople need to make a more conscious and focused effort to speak slowly and make eye contact with prospects.

Number 3: Work for a Trustworthy Company

A trustworthy salesperson will earn the rightful attribution of trust from the prospect sooner if she works for a company that has a golden reputation for integrity. The path that companies must take to achieve this is described in Chapter 3. However, for companies that do have a golden reputation, salespeople are well advised to share evidence of their employer's stellar corporate reputation with prospects. There is an association in the prospect's mind about the salesperson and her employer. Both go into the equation that eventually determines the prospect's view of trustworthiness. For example, at the Goodyear Tire and Rubber Company's corporate office in Akron, Ohio, there are signs throughout the building with the slogan "Protect our good name." When the good name of Goodyear is maintained, it is easier for its salespeople to earn a prospect's trust.

The consistency principle has a significant influence on how buyers think about this issue. In the prospect's mind, the consistency principle suggests that a trustworthy firm would hire a trustworthy salesperson and an untrustworthy firm would hire an untrustworthy salesperson. Obviously, this is not always true. There are many instances of individuals who are not trustworthy, but are nevertheless currently employed at firms with generally good reputations. On the other hand, there are some trustworthy people who currently work for firms that are not at present viewed as model corporate citizens.

For a prospect who is trying to quickly size up a potential buying opportunity, however, in the absence of other more convincing information, there is great advantage for the salesperson representing a more trustworthy firm. In fact, within the short run, the persuasive challenge for a trustworthy salesperson representing a tarnished company may be inordinate. For this reason, when a company that previously had a very favorable reputation gets itself into trouble for a widely publicized ethical violation, product failure, executive misconduct, or other problems, some of the firm's best salespeople are likely to leave the firm for more attractive opportunities with other more highly respected firms.

This concept also offers very practical career advice to a young person considering a career in sales: choose an employer carefully. For the rest of that person's sales career, she will be known as the person who worked for Company X. If that firm has a bad reputation, the seller's association with it will continue to influence her career success for a very long period of time. On the other hand, if the firm is widely respected for a reputation of integrity and professionalism, she will always be known as the person who was hired by Company Y, which has very high standards of conduct. Even after a salesperson leaves the firm, she will continue to benefit from that association.

Number 2: Never Wear a Plaid Sports Coat

Remember the television show *WKRP in Cincinnati*? There was a character on that show who sold advertising. His name was Herb Tarlek, and he always wore a plaid sports coat. Herb's father was also a salesperson, and he appeared in a few episodes. Of course, he also wore similarly hideous plaid sports coats. Even though the show has been off the air since 1982, people still identify the character of Herb Tarlek with stereotypical, unprofessional, bribe-offering, desperate salespeople. In fact, Herb has even made it into Wikipedia, the free Web-based encyclopedia, which reports Herb's atrocious sales behavior for the entire world to see.[11]

So, what does this mean? If you work in sales, never wear a plaid sports coat! If you do, others may make a linkage between your clothing selection and that of the highly untrustworthy Tarleks. That association is very bad news for any salesperson attempting to gain the prospect's trust. Beyond the Herb Tarlek association, plaid sports coats are typically not very attractive, they are certainly currently out of style, and even if they were fashionable, they would never be acceptable in formal business settings because sports coats are intended for more informal occasions.

What should you wear? That is a much more difficult question, especially given the wide range of what is considered acceptable attire across so many different industries and around the world. Many years ago, some companies had formal or informal dress codes that made it easy to know what to wear. At IBM in the 1970s, for example, all male salespeople (then called "Marketing Representatives") wore dark business suits with white shirts, black leather dress shoes, and very conservative ties. It was simple, but so very boring!

In the 21st century, it is much harder to know what the employer as well as the prospect expects in terms of attire. A guideline that is useful is to dress slightly above what you expect the prospect to wear during your sales call. Another guideline especially useful for salespeople with an interest in management is to emulate the manner of dress among the company's most successful top executives. When in doubt, identify up, not down. While these guidelines are not inconsistent, they provide excellent advice for ambitious salespeople who seek an advantage.

And do not forget the right color. Some colorologists get carried away with this notion, but there is value in knowing that dark blue is a good choice when trying to earn the prospect's trust. It is a conservative color associated with serious occasions. Some also associate blue with truthfulness, as in the phrase "she is a 'true-blue' friend." Blue is also a dominant color in our American flag, and that linkage to patriotism may also serve the salesperson in a positive way.

Number 1: Be Trustworthy!

A salesperson cannot become trusted unless he is, in fact, trustworthy. While it is the perception rather than the reality of trustworthiness that influences a prospect, any salesperson violating social norms relative to this attribute will surely lose the opportunity to earn trust over the long run. Even more critical, once trust has been lost due to dishonesty, incompetence, unreliability, or any of the many other ways that trust can be lost, it is very, very, very difficult to rebound and build any form of momentum toward the redevelopment of trust. A doubling of efforts after such a mistake is not likely to be enough to recoup the loss of trust from the demonstration of an untrustworthy behavior.

The prior advice has been directed at *speeding the rightful attribution* of trust to trustworthy salespeople. Being trustworthy is a necessary prerequisite for earning the buyer's trust. The specific ways suggested in Number 10 through Number 2 are intended to simply cut down on the length of time it takes for a truly trustworthy salesperson to earn this attribution from prospects. Even trustworthy salespeople start the buyer-seller relationship with a lot of doubt on the part of the prospect who widely recognizes the self-interest of the salesperson to obtain sales revenue in order to succeed financially. With such an initial trust deficit, very few untrustworthy salespeople have enough impression management skill, acting ability, and Machiavellianism to earn trust from buyers.

Sales managers should seek to build a trustworthy sales force through recruitment by hiring high-potential salespeople who, by their general nature, have integrity, high moral standards, and a genuine concern for others. They should consider the advice of Warren Buffett. When asked how he made hiring decisions, Mr. Buffett thoughtfully answered, "I look for three things. The first is personal integrity, the second is intelligence, and the third is a high energy level." After a slight pause, he added, "But if you don't have the first, the second two don't matter."[12] This is solid advice for sales managers when recruiting salespeople in any industry at any time, but it is especially valid now when building trust is essential as an element in the practice of relationship selling. The process to hire the right salespeople is described in more detail in Chapter 5.

In addition to careful hiring practices, thorough training and considerable experience are necessary to develop competence, another key component of trustworthiness. Then, relative to the attribution of trust, the persuasive challenge for the salesperson is simply to encourage prospects to learn the truth about the salesperson's intentions and tendencies. No acting worthy of an Academy Award on the part of the seller is necessary. The two parties just need to get to know each other. While the salesperson may find it challenging to persuade the prospect to devote enough attention to the matter for this rightful attribution of trust to evolve over time, the seller simply needs to be herself.

An important issue relative to "being trustworthy" involves the ethical standards of the two parties involved in the buyer-seller dyad. While it goes without saying that salespeople need to practice high ethical standards, this is easier to say than to do. Furthermore, it is the ethical standards of the prospect that will determine how the seller's behavior is viewed. This can create some mismatching problems when the two parties belong to different demographic groups. For example, men have lower ethical standards than women; young and less experienced people have lower ethical standards than older, more experienced people; and competitive people have lower ethical standards than cooperative people.[13] Unfortunately, salespeople often belong to the demographic group that tends to have the lower ethical standard. Consequently, salespeople must kick it up a notch in terms of how they deal with prospects, especially when the prospect has different demographics. When it is a close call, the error should always be on the side of practicing higher ethical standards, not questionable ones.

A similar argument can be made relative to perceptions of fairness. What seems fair to a party in a dispute is a function of self-interest. When a problem arises in the buyer-seller relationship, as the salesperson begins to conceptualize a fair resolution that can be proposed to the buyer, she should take into consideration what "fair" means from the buyer's perspective, not her own. This might involve asking the buyer to suggest how to resolve the issue or providing a more generous offer than what the seller might consider fair in terms of restitution.

CONCLUSION

Given the current adoption of a relationship selling philosophy by many corporations, salespeople must develop buyer trust in order to succeed. Now more than ever before, being trusted is important for the salesperson as she works with prospects to develop partnering types of business relationships.

Unfortunately, several corporate scandals have recently received very widespread attention. This extensive array of bad publicity has made people more skeptical about the integrity of all business executives, including salespeople. Consequently, just when large numbers of salespeople have finally bought into the notion of relationship selling, it has become more difficult to earn the buyer trust that is necessary in order for the partnering business philosophy to take root.

This chapter has examined the nature of customer trust relative to salespeople, highlighted the many benefits that a trusted salesperson experiences when dealing with clients, and suggested the top ten ways for trustworthy salespeople to speed the rightful attribution of prospect trust. These suggestions follow: develop a record of fulfilling promises; be extraordinarily honest; be friendly, but not too friendly too soon; get it done and get it right; show concern for the prospect; demonstrate trust of the prospect; speak slowly and make eye contact; work for a trustworthy company; never wear a plaid sports coat; and be trustworthy!

Of course, the most reliable way to be perceived as a trustworthy salesperson is the last one: "be trustworthy!" The goal of this chapter is *not* to help untrustworthy salespeople do a better job of tricking customers into making bad deals. Instead, what the chapter has attempted to do is to provide a road map so that salespeople with high integrity can sooner reap the rewards of doing the right thing when serving the needs of customers. In the long run, it has been said that nothing succeeds like success. So, too, it is with regard to earning prospect trust. Treat customers as you would like to be treated. Have high ethical standards. Do what you say you will do. It is really very simple, is it not?

NOTES

1. See http://www.zaadz.com/quotes/Dan_James, last accessed on July 25, 2006.

2. Jon M. Hawes, Kenneth E. Mast, and John E. Swan, "Trust Earning Perceptions of Sellers and Buyers," *Journal of Personal Selling and Sales Management* 9 (Spring 1989): 1.

3. Jack Welch and Suzy Welch, "The Real Verdict on Business," *Business Week* (June 12, 2006): 100.

4. Julian B. Rotter, "Interpersonal Trust, Trustworthiness, and Gullibility," *American Psychologist* 35 (January 1980): 1.

5. Jon M. Hawes, Kenneth E. Mast, and John E. Swan, "Trust Earning Perceptions of Sellers and Buyers," *Journal of Personal Selling and Sales Management* 9 (Spring 1989): 5.

6. John E. Swan, I. Fredrick Trawick, and David W. Silva, "How Industrial Salespeople Gain Customer Trust," *Industrial Marketing Management* 14 (August 1985): 205.

7. Rolph Anderson, *Professional Personal Selling* (Englewood Cliffs, NJ: Prentice Hall, 1991), 33.

8. John E. Swan and I. Fredrick Trawick, Jr., "Building Customer Trust in the Industrial Salesperson: Process and Outcomes," *Advances in Business Marketing* 2 (1987): 81–113.

9. Svenn Lindskold, "Trust Development, the GRIT Proposal, and the Effects of Conciliatory Acts on Conflict and Cooperation," *Psychological Bulletin* 85 (July 1978): 773–774.

10. Tom Hopkins, *Sales Closing for Dummies* (Foster City, CA: IDG Books Worldwide, 1998), 126.

11. See http://en.wikipedia.org/wiki/Herb_Tarlek (accessed on June 23, 2006).

12. Adrian Gostick and Dana Telford, *The Integrity Advantage: How Taking the High Road Creates Competitive Advantage in Business* (Layton, UT: Gibbs Smith Publisher, 2003), 3–4.

13. Roy J. Lewicki, David M. Saunders, and Bruce Barry, *Negotiation,* 5th ed. (Boston: McGraw-Hill Irwin, 2006), 262–263.

CHAPTER 3

CORPORATE IDENTITY AND REPUTATION MANAGEMENT: LESSONS LEARNED FROM THE WORLD OF POLITICS

Angela McMillen

Reputation is only a candle, of wavering and uncertain flame, and easily blown out,
But it is the light by which the world looks for and finds merit.
—James Russell Lowell

My auto mechanic, Mike, is the perfect illustration of a man who understands the value of a good reputation. He is a second-generation Greek man who owns a small service station in Copley, Ohio. His business, which bears his family name, was started by his father about 50 years ago. Mike does not have a fancy operation, but he does not need to have one. He is not known for those kinds of things. What he is known for is his low cost, good quality work, and his honesty. When my air conditioner broke in my Chevy, I brought it over to him. He called me a few hours later and said, "Honey, the problem is one of two things. It's either covered under warranty or it's a part I can't get to unless I tear off your dashboard, which will take a lot of time. Run it over to your dealership and they'll do the computer diagnostic for you."

I took it over to the dealership and, of course, it was the part under the dashboard that was not covered by warranty. To fix it would be $420. I called Mike and told him what the problem was. He looked up the part—it was $50. "Oh, honey," he exclaimed, "Go get that car and bring it to me! With labor, you're only looking at about $160." I did, he fixed it, and he even loaned me his very own white Mercedes sedan for a few hours. Top off Mike's reputation for low cost, good quality work, and honesty with kindness as well as generosity and throw in an incredible Greek feast customer appreciation Christmas party at the service station every year and what do you get? A stellar reputation to be sure! In fact, Mike's reputation is like a built-in warranty. It is like a warranty, because customers know that due to his reputation their risk is lowered. In other words, because people trust him, they worry less about being scammed, losing money, or even the stress, hassle, and lost time that comes with missing work. His reputation also sends a message to his customers that their expectations will be met and sometimes even exceeded. Mike does a great business and is successful enough to drive around in a big Mercedes.

Mike has what the Chinese call "face," of which there are two types. *Lien* is his community's perception of his integrity and moral character without which he could not operate his business. *Mien-tsu* refers to the kind of prestige that is gained by getting on in life through success and ostentation.[1]

This chapter is about building a corporate image, identity, and reputation from a political marketing perspective. Political candidates have many of the same marketing needs and problems that companies have. In fact, it is very beneficial to look at corporate identity and reputation management from the viewpoint of a politician, because not only do political candidates have the same challenges that goods marketers face, but, furthermore, the challenges that politicians face are even more exaggerated. Let us face it, everyone has faults. And when you are selling a person as a candidate, these faults become magnified. The more popular the candidate is, the more the media will search for and find faults to have a field day within the media. Thus, you can take what I have learned from marketing political candidates and apply these same basic principles to your business, whether you are selling a good or a service or are a large or a small company. If you can learn how to overcome some of the insane things that candidates have done, like getting intoxicated in public or having extramarital affairs, then you can easily learn how to make your company look better in the public's eyes.

The approach taken by political consultants in the marketing of a candidate is very straightforward. There is a "recipe" for creating a candidate. This recipe can help companies approach reputation building in a systematic manner and, therefore, create a better business.

Reputation has a power like magic: With one stroke of its wand, it can double your strength. It can also send people scurrying away from you.[2]

Cultivating a solid reputation is worth every ounce of energy. When people think highly of your company, more opportunities come your way and you do not even need to spend energy creating them. A poor reputation can have the opposite effect—people do not trust the company, its market offerings, or what it says about itself. Here are some of the ways in which a good reputation can help your business:

1. It adds extra psychological value (for example, trust) to your products and services (for example, when it is difficult to differentiate the service between two companies, the company with the better reputation will get the deal).

2. It helps reduce the risk customers feel when buying products or services.

3. It helps customers choose between products (for example, televisions) and services (for example, auto repairs and legal services).

4. It increases employee job satisfaction (good companies seem to generate a halo effect on employee job satisfaction ratings).

5. It provides access to better quality employees when recruiting (most people would rather work for a highly respected company).

6. It increases both advertising and sales force effectiveness.

7. It acts as a powerful signal to your competitors.

8. It provides access to the best professional service providers (for example, the best advertising agencies want to work for the best clients—so they can benefit from the clients' good reputations).

9. It provides a second chance in the event of a crisis (for example, after the two Tylenol product-tampering crises, Johnson & Johnson's marketing share bounced back, in large part because of the good reputation of the company).

10. It acts as a performance bond when dealing with other businesses such as suppliers and service providers (for example, consultants).

The process of building a reputation is as central to the marketing of a political candidate as it is to a corporation or product. However, with a new candidate, this process occurs over a period of months, not years. The concept of taking an ordinary product (candidate) and turning him or her into a superbrand follows a marketing model, which is called the Market-Oriented Candidate Model. This model argues that to win an election, a candidate needs to identify and understand public priorities, concerns, and demands before designing a campaign that reflects them. It does not attempt to change what people think, but to deliver what they think they need and want. This model can be applied in the business world as well.

This marketing concept is not new to politics, and it should not be viewed as a major flaw in the political process. Sure, there have been new methodologies including opinion polling (that is, market research), computer analysis of voting patterns (that is, sales analysis), and professional campaign consultants (that is, marketing firms). Before this, candidates got elected by making speeches, attending tea parties, and kissing babies. The new technologies have not introduced new marketing methods to politics; it has just increased their sophistication.

The 2000 campaign of George W. Bush can be used to illustrate the four steps involved in the Market-Oriented Candidate Model. Bush's campaign got off to a good start because he had credibility in each of the political domains. He was an above-average candidate in that he had name recognition from his father along with the ability to raise money and win endorsements. He was perceived as a candidate who could unite the party, appeal to the independents, and ultimately win the election.

> Step 1—What does the public want? To answer this, the campaign needs to do some market research—polls and focus groups. The campaign responds with a candidate who will appeal to the constituents.

> Step 2—Create the product. In politics, this is the image. It is what you want people to think about you. It is your message. Enter the "Compassionate Conservative," a different kind of politician who will unite both parties and work toward positive change. This was Bush's most outstanding quality. Being a compassionate conservative differentiated him from the other candidates in the Republican primaries. It created his uniqueness.

> Step 3—Implement the message. Create the identity. This captures who the candidate is and what he stands for. His issues were education, social security, budget surplus, tax cuts, and personal responsibility.

> Step 4—Communicate the identity and build the reputation. Identity is the backbone of reputation. In turn, reputation is feedback about the credibility of the identity projected.[3] To win, Bush needed to communicate his message to new audiences (consumers) as well as to the ones he was counting on. For example, he advertised in Spanish and received 49 percent of the Hispanic vote.

Bush's use of political marketing worked to get him elected. Most importantly, he implemented his reputation as a compassionate conservative by what he did once in office. Bush worked with Senator Edward Kennedy and signed the Education Reform Bill. He signed the Campaign Finance Reform Bill sponsored by John McCain, his biggest rival in the primaries. He talked about and encouraged "acts of compassion." His claim was not simply campaign rhetoric, *Bush's acts created his reputation*. He showed that he was indeed a different kind of Republican.

The important point here is to note that whatever form differentiation takes, achieving uniqueness requires actions that demonstrate credibility and earn the trust of key constituents.[4] This uniqueness must be what the public wants, and it must be backed with integrity. No matter what your political views are, or your opinion of Bush, he simply did a better job than the competition during the election in establishing his image and managing his reputation.

However, as Bush's approval ratings have slipped to as low as the mid-30th percentile during his second term, we can also use the model to determine what he has done wrong. Mainly, his uniqueness and his "positioning strategy" are now not what the public wants. He has lost some of this credibility. But, just as product sales go up and down, public opinion polls also shift dramatically. So, let us look at the task of building a reputation or, more specifically, how these same steps can be applied in goods and services marketing.

CREATING YOUR BUSINESS REPUTATION

The translation of the four-step reputation-building process used in politics into a business setting can be accomplished by sitting down with a paper and pen and answering the following questions:

Step 1

Who are my constituents? Employees? Investors? Customers? The community? The point here is that before you can develop your message, you need to know with whom you are communicating and tailor the message appropriately. For example, if we are a manufacturer of small appliances trying to communicate with our customers, we know they are not particularly interested in whether our company is stable and profitable. They want to know that we make a good product and provide quality service. However, our profitability would be of great importance to our investors.

Step 2

What is our image? This is the message our organization is constantly sending to others. *What do we want people to think about us?* What do we want our business to be known for? Credibility? Being responsible, trustworthy, or reliable? Being innovative? As in the political arena, our constituents in business have access to only limited information about us; these images allow the use of only the information that is at their disposal. After an image is formed, it gains a social reality all its own and serves as a reference point—an internal psychosocial anchor —for the evaluation of subsequent communications.[5]

It is important to note that our business's image must have value to our constituents. For example, if we promote our company as one that believes in assuming responsibility for the environment and we are operating in a foreign country that does not share our respect for its natural resources, this image will be of no value to us.

Not only must it have value, our corporate image must have two components: an emotional (feeling) component and a logical component. Both of these are necessary and both are usually experienced simultaneously by others. They fit together to form an overall corporate image. The role of the emotional component is to energize the individual to respond to the company, such as a customer buying a product or an employee working harder. Beliefs without emotions are not effective. Someone or something else has to stimulate action. Likewise, emotions without beliefs may excite you, but leave you not knowing which company is logically the best.[6]

James Dyson, the inventor of the Dyson Dual Cyclone vacuum cleaner, is an executive who understands the value of an image attached to a product. He began producing his first vacuum cleaners in 1993, and his company has since grown to $10 billion in annual sales.[7] Dyson James Limited's company image centers on his personal reputation for vision, leadership, innovation, and quality products. He had a vision of a machine that did not lose suction over time, and he produced over 5,000 prototypes until he came up with a high-quality product. He jumped into the market and took his competitors by surprise, subsequently capturing a large share of the vacuum cleaner market. These other companies, including Hoover, Electrolux, and Panasonic Corporation of North America, have since jumped on the dual-cyclone technology bandwagon with their own versions of the dual-cyclone vacuum. They have recaptured some of the market, but not all. Why not? While they could recreate the Dyson dual-cyclone technology, they could not recreate Dyson's reputation that resulted from the emotional and logical images he created.

Step 3

Is our identity consistent with our image and with the collective values of our constituents? These are your company's traits. Identity captures who your company is and what it does. These identity traits are different for different constituents. For employees, it is important for the company to instill pride in the organization and empower them along with providing an atmosphere of fairness. These identity traits instill the image of trustworthiness. For investors, the identity traits of a company that shows strong, balanced growth along with stable day-to-day operations provides the image of a company that is stable. For customers, being known as a company that provides a high-quality product and good customer service gives the image of a business that is reliable. Finally, a community that sees a company that identifies with it and provides acts of service gives the image of being a responsible business.

Microsoft Corporation is a company that has developed an identity in each of these constituent groups. To its employees, Microsoft is a great place to work. Microsoft has been on *Fortune* magazine's "Top 100 Best Companies to Work For" list for the last nine years. This list is an annual ranking of companies that are highly rated by employees. In 2006, Microsoft was recognized for, what *Fortune* calls, "the most generous health-insurance plan in America," including being the first U.S. corporation to pay for therapy for dependents who are autistic.

Microsoft has rewarded its investors with both consistent growth and stable operations. Its stock has split nine times, and the company continues to grow both through technological advancement and acquisition. In 2005, Microsoft paid $30 billion in both dividends and stock repurchases. Customers rely on the constant updates Microsoft provides free of charge. Not only are they free, Microsoft sends e-mails and pop-ups to its customers telling them these updates are available with the click of a mouse. It does not get any easier than that! Finally,

Microsoft's donations to charities have earned it a reputation for being a "good citizen." In 2005, for example, the company donated $334 million in software and cash. The Bill & Melinda Gates Foundation donated $1.4 billion to causes worldwide. Bill Gates himself leads us to a discussion of another component of corporate identity.

A company's name, logo, founder, or CEO can also become part of its identity. A name alone can also create an identity. And these concepts go so far beyond mere product branding. When an entire marketing effort is coordinated and integrated, then this becomes the company's image. Match.com, The Home Depot, Inc., Foodtown—each name conjures up an identity that speaks to the nature of the business. In terms of logo, who does not think of that red can when they hear the word "Coke?" Every John Deere tractor is that unique green color. It is important to note that this type of identity can be expensive to cultivate as it requires a large investment in media to make the message stick. It also requires time for the logo to be attached to the product or company. Finally, an individual, such as Bill Gates, can become synonymous with the company's identity.

Step 4

Ask yourself, "Are we communicating the company's image and identity and building our reputation through consistent actions? What do others think about who the business is and what it does? In sum, your business's reputation comes into being as constituents struggle to make sense of your company's past and present actions.[8] If these actions are consistent over a period of time and are in alignment with the expectations of your constituents, a good reputation is being built.

IMAGE AND IDENTITY

For some businesses, creation of a reputation has not been a conscious process. Often, it is an evolution that began with the basic beliefs of the founders of the business. The J.M. Smucker Company is one such example.

The J.M. Smucker Company was founded in Orrville, Ohio, in 1897 by Jerome Monroe Smucker when he sold his first product—apple butter—out of the back of his horse-drawn wagon. In 2006, Smucker's reported revenue of over $2 billion and net income of over $35 million.

"Smucker's has a culture grounded upon a basic set of beliefs that are reflected in the behavior of our employees and the business decisions we make," noted Ann Harlan,[9] the Company's General Counsel. These basic beliefs include the following:

1. Quality. This applies not only to Smucker products, but also its manufacturing methods, marketing efforts, people, and relationships.

2. People. Since 1998, Smucker's has been consistently recognized as one of the 100 Best Companies to Work For in the United States in *Fortune* magazine's annual listing.

3. Ethics. These were handed down by J.M. Smucker and include honesty, fairness, respect, trust, and responsibility. (We talk more about this later.)

4. Growth. "Smucker always makes its decisions about growth based upon both the future of our Company and our belief in providing value to our customers and shareholders," noted Harlan.[10]

5. Independence. The Company is publicly traded, but its stewardship is guided by its CEO, Richard Smucker. He is the fourth generation to lead the firm and is committed to the heritage of the business that bears the Smucker name and the beliefs it was founded upon.

The J.M. Smucker Company projects images of trustworthiness, credibility, and reliability through its motto "With a name like Smucker's, it has to be good." The labels on its products and its logo also consistently reflect this integrated message. It has a gingham-checked background in order to create the "down-home" feel.

The J.M. Smucker identity is reinforced by its actions. It does not advertise to children—not even its products that are geared to children like "Smucker's Uncrustables," round peanut butter and jelly sandwiches with the crusts cut off.

"We have strict advertising guidelines. The strictest I've ever encountered," noted Harlan. "Not only does Smucker have rules about the television shows they sponsor, they have episode guidelines as well."[11] While this makes it significantly more complicated for the Company to advertise, this policy is in accordance with Smucker's internal image of itself as a family company.

Smucker addresses the needs of the community and its schools. It plays an important part in Orrville, Ohio, as a sponsor of the Heartland Education Community, Inc. initiative focused on improving educational opportunities within the community. "Smucker does not consciously market an image," noted Harlan. "Instead, through the way we do business and operate in our community, we communicate and reinforce what the Company stands for. This makes it easy to be who we are."[12]

This statement brings us to an important word of caution about your business's reputation. You must be authentic. In business as in politics, the one thing people can spot a mile away is a phony. In the 2004 election, the Kerry campaign attempted to court swing voters with an image usually reserved for Republicans —that of the hunter. The media had a field day with photos of John Kerry dressed in camouflage clothing, carrying a rifle and "hunting" in southern Ohio. This image of the hunting man was not consistent with that of a Democrat. Once again, no matter what your political viewpoint, most would agree that Kerry's biggest downfall was inconsistency. When you are creating an image that is not authentic, it is almost impossible to stick to it, because your true self will eventually shine through. It is just like the old analogy of a lie being like a snow-ball rolling down a hill. You not only have to remember the past lies that you have told, but you find yourself making up new lies to cover up the old ones. If you are being authentic to yourself and there is not a single customer for your "product" or image, it is probably time to come up with a new strategy.

Ask yourself: Is the image your business wants to project consistent with how you view yourself and operate on a daily basis? If it is not, then do not go there.

COMMUNICATING YOUR REPUTATION WITH YOUR MESSAGE

In the beginning, you must work to establish a reputation for one outstanding qual-ity. This quality sets you apart and gets other people to talk about you. You then make your reputation known to as many people as possible and watch as it spreads like wildfire.[13]

A political candidate's message is comparable to a company's vision and/or mis-sion statement. It should be a specific, attention-getting, substantive slice of your soul, delivered with energy, enthusiasm, and conviction. It is uniquely yours and captures your expertise (that is, your unique quality), vision (that is, your image of how you see yourself), and your mission (that is, your identity).

A message has three components, which are a vision statement, a mission state-ment, both of which stress the third component, your unique quality. The vision usually addresses one or more of the following three issues: where an organization wants to go, what an organization wants to become, or what an organization wants to accomplish. Vision differs from a mission statement in that a mission statement focuses on what an organization does, what business it is in, and what product or service it offers. A mission statement emphasizes the here and now, whereas a vision statement points to the future.[14] Finally, it includes that one unique quality that your company possesses that sets you apart from the rest. The primary benefit of a message is that it can focus an entire organization on a common goal, a worthwhile achievement, and the means of measuring when the objective has been reached.

Some corporations have a clear understanding of who they are and that one outstanding quality they see themselves as possessing and projecting. Their under-standing is noticeable even to outsiders.

An organization's message comes from its leadership. It creates an important image to the constituent groups discussed earlier. The message is the idea that rep-resents the image that the company aspires to develop. Your message should not be complicated because it shapes your image and identity in the marketplace. It is not limited by time. It has a broad appeal and an upbeat feeling. For example,

Microsoft's message is "to create software for the personal computer that empowers and enriches people in the workplace, at school and at home." This statement describes a strong, purposeful, personal message to its customers. The message is "our software is going to improve the quality of your life and that of your family."

Likewise, Starbucks Corporation's message is to "establish Starbucks as the premier purveyor of the finest coffee in the world while maintaining our uncompromising principles while we grow." This statement describes a growing company dedicated to providing a quality product while maintaining its ethics.

Some companies can show you their vision or mission statements, but you will not find any evidence of this vision either in their employee, customer, or investor relations. This is a problem with many mission statements. Unfortunately, many times employees do not relate to them because they are too grandiose, and customers do not relate to them because they are not part of the message. For example, think about the following: "To be the world's premiere provider of innovative financial products and services." What kind of reactions from employees might leaders be hoping for? "Gee, boss, I didn't know that. I guess I'll stop writing these instructions and find something else to do." Also, where is that one unique, authentic quality that sets this company apart from the rest that appeals to its customers? A customer is going to read that and think, "Duh, doesn't everyone want to be the premiere provider?"

Most typical mission statements do little more than state the obvious, and that alone is not going to motivate anybody or tell them anything new. What is your strategy for being unique? Being different in business is a good thing. Being different and better is a great thing. The more your company attempts to be different from its rivals, the more the customers you are competing for will attach a strong reputation to your business. Here is an important thing to note: Your uniqueness does not necessarily need to be product oriented. It can be customer, investor, or community oriented as well. Again, it depends on the constituents to whom you are appealing.

So now you have answers to some tough questions asked earlier: you know with whom you are trying to communicate, how you see your company, how you want others to see you, and you have developed a message. This is where a lot of businesses simply get stuck and their reputations do not get off the ground. Why? They fail to live up to their messages, which brings us to another auto shop story. A friend of mine has one of those fancy, imported cars. Besides buying it for the hood ornament, she bought it for the dealership's customer-service program. All she has to do is call the dealership on the phone and someone will come to her house, pick up her car, and leave her another one. Someone will bring it back at the end of the day, fixed and washed. The problem is, she can never get the service department on the telephone. She gets put on hold, at which time she has to listen to the dealership's new showroom description (she bought the car because she did not want to hassle with going to the dealership in the first place) and its new organization, which divided the service departments up according to the types of cars it sold (those with hood ornaments and those without). Unfortunately, the organizational divide resulted in less people answering the telephones, which resulted in lousy customer service. The outcome is not a pleasant experience for someone who was sold on this service-oriented image, which brings us to the next point.

WHEN THINGS GO SOUTH

Your company's reputation comes into being as your constituents struggle to make sense of your company's past and present actions. When you do it right, they do not have to struggle. However, sometimes things happen in your business—you did it, someone did it to you, or it just happened. What do you do then? A poor reputation can cripple your company. Journalists seem to pay attention to companies with poor reputations, customers are more cautious in dealings with less-respected companies, and a poor reputation feeds poor employee morale. From a political perspective, weathering the storm of a reputation crisis depends on the answers to the following five questions:

1. How strong is your reputation? A good reputation will soften the blow when a crisis hits. It buys you the benefit of the doubt and time to recover.

2. How bad is the crisis? This is a tricky question. What may seem inconsequential to your leadership may be a huge problem for your constituents.

3. How do you handle it? Crisis communication should address your constituents' needs for facts, reassure them, and reinforce your business's reputation.

4. What is the media's view? The media view a crisis from two perspectives: your reputation and how you handle the crisis.

5. What else is going on in the news? When there is a lot going on, your crisis may get less coverage. You should not assume that this will be the case and plan accordingly.

How your company communicates in a crisis is a reflection of its leadership. In his book *Creating Corporate Reputations,* Grahame Dowling listed 12 strategies that reflect a range of options that can be used to handle a crisis.[15] Elements from each can be combined to create an effective media strategy.

- *The aristocrat response.* Do not explain and do not apologize.
- *Keep your head down.* Say as little as possible; hopefully if you wait long enough, the media will move on to something else. This is your classic "No Comment" strategy.
- *Call in the lawyers.* This strategy is used when a company is being attacked by hostile outsiders or confidential information has been leaked by employees.
- *ABCD (accuse, bluster, conceal, deny).* It might work...but people will always remember.

- *Blame someone else.* This is risky because this strategy can initiate a bad reaction from the company or person you are blaming. Also, if the facts come out incorrectly, your company's credibility (and reputation) would suffer even more.
- *Counter and disarm.* The company involved counters the claims made by the other party and states its own case. This would be the response to *blame someone else.*
- *Risky business.* No matter what precautions are taken, sooner or later, an accident will happen. Sometimes you can get a higher authority involved in this situation to lend public support.
- *Acts of God or "we were just unlucky."* This strategy appeals to the audience's sense of bad luck. Again, sometimes you can get a higher authority involved in this situation to lend public support.
- *Take it on the chin.* Accept immediate responsibility, implement a disaster plan, and begin planning for reparations.
- *Public sacrifice of the guilty.* Fire someone.
- *Withdraw from the market.* This is what happens to politicians who get caught in public scandals.
- *Give us another chance.* Accept all responsibility and ask for another chance. The bigger the crisis, the higher up the person accepting responsibility needs to be.

Whatever strategy your leadership decides to employ, be ready to speak to the media to show them that you are in control. If you do not, the media will portray you as incompetent, withholding information, and guilty, and then they will go find someone else to interview. The first response is critical in a crisis. It is important to have the appearance of transparency in this situation. This will help set the agenda for future meetings and help to contain the damage to your company's reputation. It is as simple as saying, "We are extremely concerned about this issue" or "We don't know all of the relevant details at this time," or "Investigations are under way." This is so much better than "No comment." And when you come back to them, come back with details so that you can answer what happened, why it happened, and what you are doing about it.

We have come to the part of this chapter where marketing book authors recount the tired tales of the Tylenol contaminations (to illustrate how to properly handle a product crisis) or the Firestone tire/Ford defects (to illustrate how not to handle a product crisis). Instead, I am going to illustrate these points with the examples of a small business owner and a congressman.

Traditions was a high-end furniture store in my community. It was owned and operated by Nick and his wife along with a few salespeople who had been with them since the beginning. When Nick decided to retire, he sold the business to one of his trusted employees. Unfortunately, this individual knew a lot about selling, but he did not know how to run a business. He expanded into a neighboring community that was too small to support a furniture store. Salespeople left and the business took a turn for the worse. He owed Nick money and he used the furniture deposits of customers for payroll and utilities instead of ordering their furniture. At this point, Nick was left with two options. He could let the business file bankruptcy and get about one-tenth of his investment out of it (which would make for a pretty lean retirement), or he could come back and try to save the business. He opted for the latter.

Without the benefit of public relations consultants and image consultants, Nick knew exactly what he needed to do to save his business. He invited the reporters in for a chat. He explained that he was taking the business back, and he planned to contact every person who had put a deposit down to assure them that he planned to honor their purchase deposits or, if they preferred, he would return them. He had been a business man in this community for 25 years and had never taken advantage of a customer. Further, to show his personal commitment to his business, he was changing the name of his business from Traditions to his own last name.

When the news hit the papers, Nick's reputation in the community soared. A few people wrote letters to the editor praising him for his integrity and commitment to the community. Not one person who had placed an order asked for his or her money back. Now business is better than ever. Nick saved his business by saving his reputation. He "took it on the chin" and "asked for another chance."

Now, with the benefit of public affairs consultants, here is what Gary Condit, a former three-term U.S. Congressman, did when things went south for him. On April 30, 2001, this U.S. Representative from the 18th District in California was considered an up-and-coming political player. It was the 100th day in office for George W. Bush, and Condit was considered one of his administration's principal "Blue Dog Democrats" and part of the plan to build bipartisanship in the Congress. Ironically enough, it was also the last day Chandra Levy, a 24-year-old intern from California, was seen alive.

Six weeks after Levy's disappearance, Condit was the center of rumors and intense media interest. Also, it was a slow period in the news. After being contacted by Levy's parents, Condit pledged $10,000 in reward money and described Levy as "a great person and good friend" in a press statement he released. He refused to comment further, and his staff denied a romantic relationship with Levy.

Things got worse for Condit when a flight attendant alleged she had a lengthy affair with Condit who was a married father of one at that time. Finally, Levy's aunt issued a statement that her niece had confided to her that she and Condit were having an affair, and Condit finally admitted to police that he was indeed romantically involved with Levy.

It got worse when Condit was spotted throwing out a gift box from another woman right before police investigators searched his apartment. Despite the fact that District of Columbia police repeatedly stated that Condit was not a suspect, the national media focused their attention on him. This attention continued until

September 11 when terrorists flew airplanes into the World Trade Center and the Pentagon and the media's attention was diverted.

Before this scandal, Gary Condit had been in office since 1989 and was very well liked in his district. He had never been the target of any specific allegation of infidelity, and MSNBC had named him one of the eight legislators in the new Congress who could make or break President Bush's legislative agenda. After the scandal Condit was unable to recover his reputation, and he lost in the March 2002 primary by a wide margin. Two months later, Chandra Levy's remains were found in a Maryland park where she jogged. The events surrounding her death remain a mystery.

Had Gary Condit, with his good reputation and bright future, not lied, but instead publicly confessed to his constituents and asked for their forgiveness as well as his wife's, he would not have been labeled a "liar." His relationship with the flight attendant and the gift box, both of which further eroded his reputation, would perhaps never have come to light. He might have been able to convince his constituents that he should remain in office. Steven A. Smith, who is known for being very forthright on his ESPN show called *Quite Frankly*, recently spoke in a meeting about the Kobe Bryant scandal. The details of the scandal are unimportant. What is important is Smith's advice to Bryant. It is always better to say, "None of your d*** business," than to lie. Lying and failure to be authentic will always get you into trouble. Unfortunately, the ethical component of reputation has long plagued the political arena. "Taking it on the chin" and asking for another chance are rarely considered as good strategies for handling a crisis. The ethical backbone has to exist from the beginning.

THE FOUNDATION OF A GOOD REPUTATION

Not only does Gary Condit point out what not to do when things go south, he highlights another important point about reputation—corporate or otherwise:

A good reputation is founded on an ethical framework!

It is management's responsibility to create a culture where ethics and integrity are rewarded and appreciated. When ethical behavior is encouraged, the sharing of knowledge is also encouraged and threats to your business's reputation can be addressed before it is too late.

In a survey of more than 300 managers completed by the National Institute of Business Management, the behavior of an employee's superiors was ranked as the second-most important factor in influencing decision making. This was surpassed only by a personal code and outstripped the behavior of one's peers, formal company policy, and the ethical climate in the industry.[16]

At the J.M. Smucker Company, ethics are fundamental and deeply rooted in the belief passed down from J.M. Smucker, the Company's founder. This legacy has been carried on by subsequent generations of this Company's leaders who are his decedents. The Company's policy states, "Ethical conduct is vital to ensure successful, sustained business relationships." "Ethical conduct involves more than simply obeying a set of rules. It means being 'ethically fit' in the sense of being ready and able to make the ethical choice in a situation where there is no established rule and where none of the apparent choices are clearly right or wrong."[17] Simply put, the ethics of the leaders in your company play an important part in its reputation.

CONCLUSION: TAKE CHARGE OF YOUR BUSINESS'S REPUTATION

All of the fancy marketing and image consulting a business will ever need can be wrapped up in the sage advice of my Nana Rose. She was a first-generation Italian-American with a common-sense approach to reputation management. She believed that people are lazy, and it is easier for them to judge based upon appearances. Therefore, she always stressed that we must always take care that our attire, words, and actions are impeccable.

She was always beautifully dressed in public, complete with a hat and gloves. She wore a "garment" because "ladies don't jiggle when they walk." She never cursed; she went to church regularly and was pleasant to everyone. Nana Rose developed the reputation of being a lady. It preceded her and created an aura of respect about her that enabled her to navigate through life with ease. It was almost like magic.

Your company's reputation is its most important asset. Develop your own—do not let someone else do this for you. Take control over how the world judges your business. Your corporate reputation is quite possibly more important than employing the top 100 salespeople in the world.

NOTES

1. H.C. Hu, "The Chinese Concepts of Face," *American Anthropologist* 4, no. 6 (1944): 45–64.

2. Robert Greene, *The 48 Laws of Power* (London: Penguin Books, Ltd., 2000), 37.

3. David A. Whetten and Alison Mackey, "A Social Actor Conception of Organizational Identity and Its Implications for the Study of Organizational Reputation," *Business & Society* 41, no. 4 (2002): 393–414.

4. Charles J. Fombrun, *Reputation: Realizing Value from the Corporate Image* (Boston: Harvard Business School Press, 1966), 9.

5. Robery O. Anderson, *A Rhetoric of Political Image Communication* (Ann Arbor: University Microfilms, 1972), 12.

6. Grahame Dowling, *Creating Corporate Reputations: Identity, Image, and Performance* (New York: Oxford University Press, 2001), 20–21.

7. "New Dyson RootCyclone™ Technology," http://www.international.dyson.com/tech/dysoncyclone/default.asp (accessed June 23, 2006).

8. Fombrun, *Reputation: Realizing Value from the Corporate Image,* 729.

9. Ann Harlan, Vice President, General Counsel, The J.M. Smucker Company (personal communication, May 6, 2005).

10. Ibid.

11. Ibid.

12. Ibid.

13. Greene, *The 48 Laws of Power,* 41 (accessed June 23, 2006).

14. Developing Worthwhile Vision Statements http://www.informit.com/guides/content.asp?g=it_management&seqNum=10&rl=1.

15. Fombrun, *Reputation: Realizing Value from the Corporate Image,* 267–272.

16. Dale Neef, *Managing Corporate Reputation and Risk: A Strategic Approach to Knowledge Management* (New York: Elsevier, 2003), 182.

17. The J.M. Smucker Company, *Policy on Ethics and Conduct,* April 15, 2005.

CHAPTER 4

KEEPING YOUR FRIENDS CLOSE AND YOUR ENEMIES CLOSER: WHAT YOU SHOULD KNOW ABOUT YOUR COMPETITOR

Dave Stein

If you know the enemy and know yourself, you need not fear the result of a hundred battles. If you know yourself but not the enemy, for every victory gained you will also suffer a defeat. If you know neither the enemy nor yourself, you will succumb in every battle.

—Sun Tzu, ancient Chinese military strategist and author of *The Art of War*[1]

Who are your competitors? What are they doing, literally at this moment, to take your customers away? What have you done to protect your position so that your competitors' strategies, tactics, approaches, and assertions are met with indifference by your customers? These are tough questions. Depending on how a company answers these questions often determines whether it becomes the leader or laggard in its marketplaces.

It was Sun Tzu, the Chinese general and military strategist (ca. 400 B.C.) to whom the powerful statement "keep your friends close and your enemies closer" has been attributed. In this chapter we are going to discuss the critical importance of competitive intelligence and how to employ that information to your advantage.

WHY IS KNOWLEDGE ABOUT YOUR COMPETITOR IMPORTANT?

Why is understanding your competitors so important? It is so we can, to the best of our ability, predict what actions they will take in a sales situation, allowing us to more adequately prepare and present our business case to the customer at the same time we are preparing and executing our defense against their assertions, representations, and attacks. This is important, but difficult work.

A BRIEF LOOK BACK

Decades ago, selling was much easier than it is now in the 21st century for a number of reasons. One of those was the somewhat closed community of people providing similar types of products and services within a geographic market or a physical territory. There was no Internet and no Wal-Mart. Salespeople working for different companies often knew each other. They belonged to the same organizations; their kids went to the same schools. You were able to size up your competitor (the person, not the company) as a result of that closeness and the ongoing contact in social as well as business situations.

This was an advantage for the competitive sales professional. While never considering negative selling against their competitor, they were very intent on learning their competitor's strengths and weaknesses, because they knew something then that many salespeople do not understand today: In most sales situations your competition is not a company, a product, or a service. Instead, it is a person who is the rival—your competitor—and it is that *person* against whom you will either win or lose a sale. A savvy salesperson would be able to tell you how differently he or she would approach a sale when competing against one rep from a competitor's company versus another. This is an important point for anyone who sells today. Consider the fact that you are competing against individuals first, with their products, services, and companies behind them, as opposed to the other way around. With an oversupply of products and services in some markets, alternative distribution channels, and unprecedented employee turnover among the sales ranks of many companies, we can lose sight of who the opponent really is.

Decades ago marketing had less of a potential impact than it does today in the area of providing competitive intelligence as a critical component of sales support. Today, sales professionals cannot possibly do all the intelligence gathering, analysis, and the positioning needed for success. They need help. That help must come from the output of a carefully engineered, closed-loop competitive intelligence system. We talk more about this throughout this chapter.

A COMPETITIVE STATE OF MIND

Before we go any further, it is important to understand that competitive awareness, positioning, and selling should not be the primary focus of any salesperson, no matter how difficult a situation may be faced. What always comes first is a strong focus on the customer and how your product or service will make a contribution to your customer's ability to achieve his or her business goals and objectives. With that having been said, having the best product or service will not guarantee that you will win—not by a long shot. Winning often is the result of a delicate balance between creating a situation where your customers convince themselves that your offering meets their requirements while at the same time exerting some control over how your competitor's offering (and in fact the competitor himself or herself) is perceived by your customer. If I am selling a product that fully meets all of my customer's buying criteria but my competitor convinces the customer that my company is close to financial ruin, or highlights a weakness in my company's customer care organization, or even lies about his or her own capabilities, my potential sale is at risk. Winston Churchill said, "There is nothing more exhilarating than to be shot at without result."[2]

There is a degree of competitive situational awareness that is required to consistently win business. Think of driving a car. There are generally three mirrors providing situational awareness. Selling without being somewhat in a competitive state of mind is like driving on a busy freeway with no rearview or side mirrors. This is ill-advised and risky at best.

Can you imagine a modern-day professional sporting event where the contestants have not spent hours, if not days, with coaches, consultants, video replays, and chalkboards? The competitor's strategies and tactics are dissected and analyzed. Each player's strengths and weaknesses are scrutinized, assessed, and categorized. A playbook is consulted containing information distilled from past encounters. A series of what-if questions and if-then scenarios is examined, providing the team with a clear plan to win, with multiple alternatives should something not go as planned. The same goes for individual sports as well, such as tennis, boxing, fencing, track and field, bicycling, and others. Of course knowledge of the competition is also required for championship-level play in chess, scrabble, bridge, poker, and other "games."

So selling is not like Yoga, where the focus is inward, and where you compete against no one, including yourself. Nor is selling like jogging or riding a bike for pleasure or even for strenuous exercise. Selling is the toughest kind of hardball, and a good competitor, like a Sumo wrestler, will do his or her best to knock you out of the game.

The same competitive mind-set exists, of course, for organized military operations. Intelligence is collected, assessments are made, objectives are determined, strategies are devised, and tactics are developed. Simulations are done providing strategists with the ability to measure the likelihood of various scenarios until the optimal approach is decided upon, approved, and executed. Many of the largest sales opportunities that are won each year, some many hundreds of millions of dollars in value, are won using this type of precise planning process.

Bear this in mind. Sales are lost for two main reasons: First, the opportunity was never properly qualified and therefore was never winnable in the first place. Second, the person who was doing the selling simply got outsold by the competition.

SALES AND MARKETING WORKING TOGETHER

In an ideal situation, sales and marketing will work closely together to gather, assess, analyze, position, and distribute competitive information to the field. The benefits of such a collaboration are rich. First, more business is won with less price resistance. Second, salespeople are better able to understand how to position their products so there are fewer misunderstandings between buyer and seller. Finally, marketing is able to gather intelligence through the sales organization, which provides insight not only about the competition, but also about customer-buying habits, market trends, common perceptions and misperceptions of its own company and products, and more.

The alignment of sales and marketing is a subject that has been discussed and debated for years and will continue to be. There are a number of touch points between the two functions—in fact the relationship should be symbiotic—as an oversimplified example, marketing generates sales leads, salespeople pursue and hopefully close them, bringing revenue into the company so the company can grow, hire more marketing people to generate more sales leads, and so on.

But we are not discussing lead generation here. We are discussing the fact that among other things, salespeople need competitive intelligence to sell effectively, and it is marketing's job to provide that, willingly and efficiently.

GETTING INTO A COMPETITIVE STATE OF MIND

Many of us are either born with a sense of competitiveness or develop it at a very early age. Certainly you remember children in grade school who were that way, whether on the playground, in social situations, or academically. Later on, competitiveness is apparent in the people who feel the need to earn more money than someone else, pass others while driving on the freeway, or get their children to attend a more prestigious school. Some of us, on the other hand, do not have such strong competitive urges.

What may seem like bad news to those of us who are not as competitive by nature is that we will have to raise our level of consciousness about our competition to be more effective in selling. Upon hearing that news, many are convinced that is not the case. All they have to do, they believe, is know their products better, build better relationships with their customers, and work harder. Sure, all those things will contribute to selling more, but that critical piece is still missing: knowledge of the competitor.

The good news is that getting into a competitive state of mind—gaining competitive awareness—is not difficult. It is a habit (with some supporting skills) that can be learned comparatively easily. Many sales professionals whom I have coached over the years have made great progress in this area by first understanding that competitive awareness is extremely important for their success. Next, they began to understand what competitive awareness is by observing competition in other areas. Finally, they were able to apply what they learned to their own professional selling situation.

Having gone over the importance of competitive awareness already, let me discuss the observation of competitive behavior in other areas.

OBSERVING COMPETITIVE BEHAVIOR

We have looked at how individuals and teams prepare for sporting events, and we have a top-level view of how a military operation is planned. Now let us look at how individuals and teams compete and how we might learn from that.

In this day and age, much of the competitive behavior that most people see is on television. Game shows are what come to mind for many, but that is child's play compared to watching the positioning, spinning, sniping, hyping, and downright nasty business that is the fodder of politics on TV. Just watch a few Sunday morning political talk shows or a critical debate on C-SPAN. If you understand the basic position of the political party that a politician represents, you can see real competition at work. These politicians are selling. They are selling their ideas, beliefs, and approaches to literally anyone who will listen, in order to achieve the goal of securing the listener's support—in campaign contributions, letter writing campaigns, or at the ballot box.

How different do you think the positioning done by a liberal and a conservative on a talk show is from what transpires during the course of a competitive sales campaign? This is not very different, especially when you look at each as an attempt to influence the mind share of the voter/buyer.

Watching some sports is an especially valuable lesson in competitiveness. Think about what is behind that play rather than the play itself. Think about what the overall strategy to win is rather than a single move or individual player's turn. Can you see what the team's approach is? When you are watching a tennis match, can you see how one player is attempting to exploit the weakness of another? In an international soccer match, can you see the culture of the teams coming across in the way they approach the game?

Last, we must focus some attention and thought on competition in the business world. Observing the behaviors (through commercial advertising, for example) of The Coca-Cola Company versus PepsiCo, Mercedes-Benz versus BMW, and which local TV station manages to get you to watch its "News at 11:00" can tell you a lot about those companies and how they compete against each other.

In order to gain competitive awareness—to get into a competitive state of mind —you will have to direct some of your attention to the competition going on all around you. Look over your shoulder, under rocks, around corners, up, down, and sideways. Observe, assess, and then see if what you have learned can be applied to your own competitive situations.

WHAT YOU NEED TO KNOW ABOUT YOUR COMPETITION

Do you have timely, accurate, comprehensive, and actionable intelligence about your competition? You will need to understand your competitor's capabilities and behaviors—not just rival companies, but more importantly, the sales professionals with whom you go head-to-head? You will need to anticipate their future actions so that you can plan more effective sales campaigns to counter them.

It takes a lot of time and energy to gather enough information about your competitor to make a difference. Hopefully the company that you work for sees the importance of this and will provide your marketing organization with the funding and resources so you can have what you need. But if you are not in that situation, please realize that just a little information unfortunately does not provide you with enough of a foundation upon which to build an effective competitive strategy and the related tactics to execute that strategy.

With that in mind, let me provide you with a model and some guidelines so you can determine what information is required in order to make the best use of your time. What follows includes a lot of detail. Do not be concerned. You probably will not need to dive into all of this for every possible competitor. You may already know that you compete against the same three or four companies for every deal. What is most important is that you design your intelligence-gathering activities to suit your situation.

When you are gathering intelligence and assessing your competitor, objectivity is important. Few sales professionals are entirely objective about their competitors. Some overestimate and others underestimate, which is even more dangerous. Learn to gauge the true measure of your competition, and you will plan your sales campaigns more effectively.

LEVELS OF COMPETITIVE INTELLIGENCE

Now we take a closer look at the three levels of competitive information, as shown in Table 4.1, that you will need in order to design effective sales strategies and tactics. Within each level there are examples for each of several different

Table 4.1
Levels of Competitive Information

Level	Content Area	Availability of Information	Value to You
1	Competitor's Company	Easy to find	Low
2	Competitor's Products/Services	Strengths: Easy to find	Moderate
		Weaknesses: Difficult to find	Substantial
3	Competitor's Sales Execution: The Individual Person	Requires an ongoing effort	Very High

categories of information, along with questions you can ask yourself (or others) in order to use that information to your best advantage, ending up with likely sources for specific kinds of information.

Level 1 of competitive information relates to company information. It is much easier to get information about a company with which you compete when it is publicly held compared to one that is private. Thanks to strict government regulations, public companies must disclose information that they would rather not have their competitors know. If your company is privately held and your competitor is a public company, you may have some advantage. A savvy competitive sales professional from the other company will attempt to influence a sales prospect to dig deeply into your company's situation. This cuts both ways, however. Information you would rather not have your competitor know could be readily available on your company's Web site as required by law.

The point here is that Level 1 information is easy to obtain about any company; however, it alone is of little use in devising a winning competitive sales strategy. Clearly, Level 2 information about the competitor's products and services is also needed. There is plenty of Level 2 information available about the strengths of your competitor's products and services. Level 2 information about the weaknesses of those products and services is more valuable to you, but much harder to obtain.

For a complete picture, Level 3 information about the competitor's sales execution is needed as well. Level 3 information, however, is different. It is equally elusive for both public and private companies. And it is the kind of information that winners go looking for: intelligence on the competition's—the person against whom your are competing—sales strategies and tactics. To learn about that which will be used against you can be very valuable.

Level 1: Company Information

Level 1 information is about your competitor's company that is generally available, often because the company provides it on the Internet or as a part of marketing collateral materials. Level 1 information includes the following:

- Company background. Some companies depend on their history in an industry or geography for competitive advantage. Others try to underplay the importance of company background. Learn about your competitor's company background and determine whether it is used as an advantage or not.

- Financial information. Is your competitor's company profitable or is it losing money? Is the company growing or shrinking? Is it gaining or losing market share? What does its financial statements tell you about the company and how it might compete? For example, does its DSO (Days Sales Outstanding) indicate that it has a customer satisfaction problem? How strong is its balance sheet?

- Number of employees. Can your competitor handle the demands of another customer? Or perhaps it has so many available resources that it uses that as a competitive advantage. How large is its sales organization? Does your competitor have the time to be able to successfully pursue this sales opportunity? What job openings are posted? These may signal new product development (Level 2) or regional or global expansion. Be careful here. Companies have been known to advertise jobs that did not exist to mislead a competitor or convince the market that the company is healthier than is the case.

- Office locations. Are they geographically better positioned to service the customer than your company is? Perhaps the reverse is true.

- Their partnerships. Many companies depend on partners to sell or service their products or to add their own products to make a more complete solution. Must your competitor's company bring partners into play? On the other hand, perhaps they have resellers who bring other capabilities that you cannot provide.

- Customer lists. Are your competitor's company's customers listed on its Web site? Does your competitor's company depend on marquee accounts to suggest a level of success it has not really achieved? Who are its customers? Are they happy with your competitor's products? Do you also do business with any of those companies? Is there more information that you might gather about your competitive situation?

- Predominant messages. How does your competitor's company position itself in the marketplace? Does it tout quality, price, performance, or service?

- Key strategies. As you read the annual and quarterly reports produced by your publicly held competitors, what is it that they are trying to accomplish? What are their goals and objectives, as well as their strategies to achieve them?

- Management team members. From what companies did they come? How much experience have they had? How long have they been at this company? From what functional areas do they come—finance, engineering, sales? What is their business style—conservative, aggressive, customer oriented, win at any cost?

- Key markets. What markets does your competitor's company say it is going after? Perhaps you are involved in an opportunity against a competitor whose company is reaching outside its established market, opportunistically.

Where to Get Level 1 Information

- Your competitor's company's own Web site. Again, please remember that publicly held companies are held to a much higher standard than privately held firms. What you read on the Web site of a privately held company must be verified.

- Twenty-first century sales professionals must become adept at reading and interpreting financial statements and reports. Key sources are government filings, such as 10-Qs (quarterly financial statements for public companies required by the U.S. Securities and Exchange Commission), 10-Ks (annual statements), proxy statements, and statements of ownership.

- Analyst reports. What do industry and securities analysts say about your competitor's company? Might this information be useful in planning a sales campaign against it? Might this information provide you with a view that would be well received at the highest levels of a prospect's company?

- Press releases, corporate newsletters, magazine articles. Be careful here. These could provide valuable information, or they could also be propaganda. Information like this must be corroborated before you depend on it as a basis for a competitive sales campaign.

- Press kits and investor relations packets. These can often be downloaded from the company's Web site. Savvy sales professionals will often buy a few shares of stock in their competitor's companies so that they receive whatever information is sent out to shareholders.

- Internet investor bulletin boards. Some small percentage of information you read on these bulletin boards is true, but occasionally an insider or astute observer will provide some insight that could be useful in your sales planning.

- There are numbers of fee-based services and sites designed specifically for gathering and interpreting competitive intelligence.

Level 2: Product or Service Information

There are two subcategories of information about your competitor's products and services. The first is information that is generally available. You will find that the information that is easiest to find is about the strengths and positive aspects of its offerings. On the other hand, what is difficult to find is information about the weaknesses associated with your competitor's products and services. A bit later we discuss how to professionally use information about your competitor's weaknesses. For now, let us look at the kinds of information and where we might find them for both categories.

Information to Gather about the Strengths of Your Competitor's Offerings

- The names of its products and services, including descriptions, specifications, and capabilities.

- Value and benefits associated with the product or service. Your competitor might very well have quantifiable benefits associated with its products. For example, "'XYZ's widget helped us reduce inventory carrying charges by 37 percent during the first year alone, saving us $3.2 million,' said Jane Jones, CFO of ABC Corp." These claims and others like it will be made by your competitor during a sales campaign. You need to know about it in advance in order to effectively prepare. It is very important to understand that you need to look at the value and benefits (strengths) that your competitor's offering provides as the customer sees them, not as you see them. You may know that the competition's software has bugs, but if their sales prospects have a vision of the software helping them compete more effectively, a bug or two has no meaning prior to installation.

  Look for testimonials or case studies. The same customers about whom those were written may likely be reference accounts for your competitor. An important point is necessary here. Make sure you understand your competitor's unique value and how it articulates that to different people within prospects' organizations. And if you learn how that is perceived by the market, all the better. Then you will *really* know what you are competing against. Keep something very important in mind. Everything is always just about perceptions. It is the way the market *perceives* the company's offerings. This may or may not be factual. Perception is everything. Therefore, you need to understand how the customer perceives your competitor.

- Can your competitor provide its product or service when the customer needs it, where the customer needs it, and at the right price? If your competitor can, that is a strength and you will need to record that and be prepared to deal with it later on.

- News. This would include new product announcements, rollouts, upgrades, or enhancements to existing products. One clever sales professional collected three years' worth of new-product announcements his competitor had issued and compared them, in table format, to what was actually delivered. The table became a potent competitive sales tool.

Information to Gather about the Weaknesses of Your Competitor's Offerings

- Product deficiencies, including quality, design, or functional limitations. This is very valuable competitive information that must be used judiciously.

- Service limitations. For example, if a company sells products throughout North America from multiple sales offices, but has only two centers for service, based in California and New York. Were a customer to need service, a service representative would have to be dispatched from one of those two perhaps distant locations.

- Actual selling price. If your competitor's product is unable to stand up to the scrutiny of a savvy buyer because the business value is limited or not unique, it may have to discount regularly to win any business at all. You can save yourself and your company a lot of money if you know in advance how much of a discount your competitor will offer. You may even decide it is not worth getting involved.

- Product life cycle. When was your competitor's product introduced? How much longer will it be offered, serviced, or supported? What technology or intellectual property is it built on? Is that platform at the end of its life cycle? Many companies have learned the hard way not to announce new products if that will freeze purchases of their existing ones. What that means is that in some cases, customers will continue to be sold the "old" product right up until the new one is shipped, leaving them in a difficult position.

Where to Get Information about the Strengths of Your Competitor's Offering

You will find information about the strengths of your competitor's offering on its Web site and from the sources mentioned for Level 1 information above. Also, use a selection of search engines to find product comparisons done by magazines, by independent organizations, or by securities or industry analysts. Some of these may be fee based, so be prepared to make a business case to your management for funds to be allocated to this cause.

Remember, accurate information is often hard to locate and is even more difficult to corroborate. The last thing you want to do is underestimate the capabilities of your competitor's offering based upon wrong information. Here are some sources for this category of Level 2 information.

- It is good practice to be speaking regularly with your customers. When you do, you can, on occasion, ask them for their opinions of your competitor's products or services that they may have used or seen at their current or former company.
- Internet investor bulletin board postings (see above). Again, be careful. Most of what you will find is rumor and innuendo. But there are a few gems now and then.
- When a prospect has your competitor's product and is looking to replace it. If you are called into a sales opportunity where the prospect is using your competitor's product, it is a perfect time to explore the reasons why he or she is interested in switching. Questions of the prospect should include not only what is wrong with the competitor's product, but what the strengths are as well. "Why did you acquire that product in the first place?" is a good place to start.
- Other Web sites. You can search the United States Government Patent and Trademark Office Web site (www.uspto.gov) to find out if your competitor's company has any new patents or trademarks. Although it is becoming more difficult, you can still find Internet domain names that have been registered by your competitor's companies, perhaps helping you predict what its next move might be.

Level 3: How Your Competitor Sells on the Street

Within many marketing organizations you will find a competitive intelligence team. These team members provide their sales organizations with much of what they need to understand and compete against the competition—but not everything.

They deliver, either online or in binders or on CDs, some of the Level 1 and Level 2 information that is needed. With that in mind, a marketing best practice is providing the sales organization with a competitive playbook, with action-by-action instructions for outselling, outmaneuvering, and outpositioning specific competitors' salespeople. For those companies that invest in that level of sales support, the rewards are great. Those companies' salespeople know which battles to fight and when, as the result of a strategic disadvantage, to wait for another day. When they do compete, they are more likely to win decisively.

Level 3 information concerns the particular salesperson working for your competitor's company. What is his or her sales strategy and manner of execution? It is about how to go head-to-head against the opposition and how you both are going to play the game. Think back for a moment to our discussion on sporting events and the deep analysis of the competition. There are referees or judges in most sporting events. There is no such oversight in the world of selling. Are you prepared to compete against someone who might do anything to win a sale? The first step is to learn everything about that person that you can.

Gathering, analyzing, maintaining, and distributing Level 3 information is not easy. It takes time, resources, motivation, and money from corporate executives, department heads, and individuals.

Here are some questions about your competitor that you not only need to consider, but they are questions to which you really need answers:

- What does he generally count on to win? His relationship-building skills? His product? His business savvy or personal capital? Last minute price slashing or slamming the competition?

- When she loses, why does she lose? Does she fail to take the time to understand her customer? Does she sell features and not business value?

- What has his sales performance been? Are you competing against someone who earns a million dollars a year in commissions, or a rank beginner?

- What is her typical sales process? Is your opponent someone who is organized and disciplined, or does she sell by the seat-of-her-pants, counting on good luck to win?

- Whom in accounts does he typically call on? Finance, manufacturing, sales, human resources, the Board of Directors? Does he have the confidence and depth to go right to the highest levels, or is he content hoping that lower-level staff personnel will somehow carry his message?

- How is she measured and compensated? Competing against someone whose compensation consists entirely of commission with no base salary generally means your up against a tough and experienced opponent.

- When does he bring in the management? At a preplanned, logical time during the sales cycle, or when he is in a panic, thinking that he is losing?

- What does she say about your company? Does she employ negative selling tactics? Or conversely does she pretend to ignore you, focusing on her areas of unique business value for the customer?

- Has your adversary adopted any of the well-known sales methodologies? If so, you can anticipate his approach.

- Does she wrestle for control of the evaluation process or decision criteria? Or is she more passive, letting the prospect lead the way?

- What is your win/loss ratio against him? What is your company's record against his company? Is this a person against whom it does not make any sense competing at this time?

- In the past, what tactics have you used that were effective against her? What did you try that was not effective?

- Does he always seem to know and provide your prospects with the names of your least-satisfied customers? If you know that is going to happen, what are you going to do about it?

- What about her business ethics? Does she keep her promises? Does she lie? Does she misrepresent her product, service, or company capabilities? Or is she highly principled, counting on her integrity as an advantage?

- How long has he been employed by his company? If he is fairly new, did he leave unhappy customers behind from his last job?

- Does your competitor always ask for the first or the last slot for her presentations? What can you do to take advantage of that pattern?

- What does your competitor do to hide weaknesses in his product, service, or company? How might you bring that to your prospect's attention?

Where to Get Level 3 Information

- Join any relevant industry associations to which your customers belong. This is not only a good idea for the customer-facing side of your sales and marketing approach, but you may very well run into your competitors there as well. Getting to know them is a good thing. Keep them close, remember.

- Ask someone in your prospect's company with whom you have a relationship to talk to you about the value you are providing during that company's evaluation. Test the waters a bit by leading gently into some questions about your competitor.

- If your industry has bidders' conferences, attend them. Even if you do not ask any questions or volunteer any information, it is a good opportunity to size up your opponent.

- Make contact with someone who knows your competitor. That might be someone who worked with him or her in the same company or for a business partner, for example.

- Recruiters are a good source of information. If you regularly get calls from one or more recruiters, turn the tables on them a bit and ask them to provide you with information about your toughest competitor. They usually have a wide network of contacts and can probably come up with a pretty accurate assessment with just a few phone calls.

- If you work for a larger company, do some internal networking. Pass the person's name around to see if anyone knows or has worked with this person. This is a good practice to start.

WHAT DO YOU DO WITH THE INFORMATION?

Now that you have begun to get into a competitive state of mind and are collecting relevant Levels 1, 2, and 3 information about your competitor, what do you do with the information?

Earlier we discussed the main purpose of gathering competitive intelligence. If you know what your competitors are going to do as well as when and how they are most likely to do it, you have an advantage over them. That advantage increases when they do not suspect you have the information or the skills to do anything with it.

Let us look at an all too common example—your competitor lies when answering RFPs (Requests for Proposals). You know that he does this because you regularly ask customers, colleagues, business partners, and other people in your network about that person who is your archrival.

You receive an RFP as does, you soon learn, your competitor. A quick scan through the document suggests that, according to the Level 2 information you have gathered, there are capabilities the prospect requires that your competition does not provide. You can predict with certainty that he will put checks in all the appropriate boxes representing that he can deliver those capabilities.

What do you do now?

Highly ethical, experienced, and successful sales professionals will probably tell you that they would not likely respond to the RFP since they were not involved in writing it. And furthermore, they will tell you, if they were not involved, it could mean that your competitor was. It is unlikely in this case that your competitor influenced the content of the RFP since, as we said, there are areas within it that are beyond your competitor's capabilities.

You will have to think carefully about precisely when, but at some time you must go to the real buyer—the person whose purchase, project, initiative, or investment this is. Approach the budget holder and say something like, "You and your team have done a terrific job with your RFP. I've been involved in many evaluations, and I understand the time, effort, and complexity involved in defining your requirements and encapsulating them into a document. I can also tell you that not everyone takes the work you have done as seriously as it should be taken. Were I sitting in your seat, I would want to make certain that everyone who responded to your RFP provided truthful answers. In fact, I would randomly check the answers from every vendor and if I found someone misrepresenting their capabilities, I would immediately eliminate them from consideration."

Think of this scenario as setting a mousetrap. Instead of cheese, the bait was the RFP questions that your competitor would not answer truthfully. The trap, if sprung, would be fatal—at least to your competitor's chances of winning the opportunity.

Each strength, weakness, behavior, strategy, and tactic that you know your competitor will exhibit should be accounted for somewhere and somehow in your sales plan. What you do not know, or worse, what you know about but do not take into account, could be your undoing.

SOME TIPS FOR MARKETING ORGANIZATIONS

As we mentioned earlier, marketing has a critical role in helping the sales team learn about, understand, and properly prepare for battle against the competition.

Here are some best practices that will get your team headed in the right direction:

- Everyone in your company should know who your competitors are, and the importance of learning what we can (within the law and corporate principles) about them.
- Marketing must understand that the sales division is its customer in the area of competitive intelligence. Someone in marketing must "own" the competitive intelligence function.
- Sales must understand that marketing cannot provide any worthwhile advice if it does not have reliable, relevant, and timely information. Sales, through one process or another, must provide ongoing information from the field about the competition. Collaboration between sales and marketing on how this can best be accomplished is very important. That approach results in buy-in from both functions.
- Some automated content management software system must be used. There is going to be a lot of information gathered, and it needs to be easily stored and retrieved.
- At least one person on the competitive intelligence team must have been in sales or have a strong knowledge of competitive selling strategies and tactics. In the absence of such a person, strong competitive salespeople from the field should be rotated in and out of the competitive intelligence team.
- Measurement is very important. Benchmarking current performance against certain competitors will serve as the basis against which improvement will be measured.

SUMMARY

As our business environment continues to evolve, selling will get harder. Buyers will have more choices, be more experienced, and have more technology at their fingertips. Your competition will react by working harder, smarter, and even at times doing anything it will take to win, including engaging in unfair tactics.

In order for a salesperson to consistently reach his or her sales targets going forward, he or she must continually improve his or her competitive selling abilities. That is, in this day and age, virtually impossible without accurate, relevant, and timely information about the competition, along with a knowledge of how to acquire it and experience in how to use it.

NOTES

1. Sun Tzu, *The Art of War* (London: Hodder & Stoughton, 1981).
2. "Quote DB," http://www.quotedb.com/quotes/3461 (accessed April 11, 2007).

CHAPTER 5

BUILDING A SUCCESSFUL SALES FORCE IN THE 21ST CENTURY

Daniel J. Leslie

> The best executive is the one who has sense enough to pick good men to do what he wants done, and self-restraint enough to keep from meddling with them while they do it.
>
> —Theodore Roosevelt

According to Don E. Schultz,[1] profits can be increased by 50 percent, 100 percent —maybe even 1,000 percent—if companies would switch just 5 percent of their external marketing spending from things like advertising and sales promotion to increased spending on internal human resource efforts. While this statement seems exaggerated, some studies have shown this to be true, at least to some extent. Greater attention to recruiting, hiring, training, developing, evaluating, and motivating great salespeople can increase a company's profitability. However, creating a successful sales force in the 21st century is becoming more difficult in light of the many challenges that are present today. More competition, more sophisticated customers armed with more information, issues regarding technology, communication issues, meetings, and many other distractions are but a few of the challenges. In this chapter, I talk about what I believe to be the core building blocks of building a successful sales force and building a successful organization no matter what your endeavor. In this chapter, I help guide you to answer the following questions:

- What is your purpose for being in business?
- What are the values that guide your decision-making progress?
- How do you develop these values?

- What vision have you created to share with your people to get them excited?

- How are you using your vision to attract good people, and what selection process do you have in place?

- What are you doing to develop your people and to help them achieve their personal goals as well as your company's goals?

- What program do you have in place to begin to develop leadership within your organization and to develop your second-line management?

In this chapter, we discuss all these topics. This chapter is meant to provide an awareness of the things that will help you to make a good sales force even better. Or if you are starting from scratch, this chapter can provide a road map and an outline for success. This chapter is meant to cover these issues from a 30,000-foot point of view. The details and the work involved will be up to you to explore further. Obviously, all of the aspects of building a successful sales force cannot be covered within one chapter. For example, many important human resource management issues are not included. Most notably, the legal aspects of human resources are not discussed in this chapter. Just as everything else is rapidly changing in the 21st century, so are the laws and the legal ramifications for breaking those laws. As a sales manager or business owner, you must either have a legal department to advise you on such matters or pursue additional training in business law.

This chapter, along with the other chapters in this book, does provide, however, a good starting point to help you address the rapidly changing landscape of this new century. As you read this chapter, one of the most important things you can do is to create an action plan. Think of the outline for this chapter as your action plan for the next 12 months. Get out your calendar and plug in when you and your leadership team will tackle these issues. At the end of 12 months, you will be amazed at how far you have come!

IDENTIFYING VALUES

I believe that in order for a sales organization to be successful, it must firmly believe in a core set of values. Values are those things that are constant, that never change. They provide us direction in times of uncertainty. They are the foundation of any great organization. These values guide us when things are difficult and decisions are not clear. The values of your organization will help you to manage and select good people. They will help you create successful policies and procedures.

In order to determine an organization's values, I recommend taking time away from the office and out of the field. Bring your leadership team together and have a discussion about values. Determine, as a group, the values that really dictate the direction of the organization. What are the things that are important to the individuals and ultimately to the organization. Agree on three to four values to introduce to your business and your personal lives. Here are the values of our sales organization at Northwestern Mutual Financial Network: professionalism, integrity, and excellence. They are the values that guide our organization, and they will continue to guide me as a person. What are your values? How will you lead your organization into the future?

- Professionalism: Professionalism is doing the very best for your client and recommending to your client what you would want recommended if you were in your client's situation. Professionalism means attaining the highest level of competency in your field.
- Integrity: My simple definition of integrity is doing what you say you will do and following through.
- Excellence: Excellence simply means if it is worth doing, it is worth doing the very best that you possibly can and directing all of your energy and resources to accomplish the goal or the task.

Recently, in an effort to merge two of our existing offices, we began to have discussions about our shared values. Our leadership teams met to discuss what values we have in common and what they really mean to us. Out of the discussion came some definitions of values.

One person said values are "those things that guide you when others aren't looking." Someone else said values are "those things that help keep you accountable to what you know are right." Another person said values are "your beliefs put into action." Others said that values really equate to leadership.

I like to think of values as a compass that would guide any person or any organization through difficult times when a decision is not always clear. Would you go sailing out on the ocean without a compass or other forms of instrumentation? Of course not. Why? The potential consequence would be too great. What about your business? What are the consequences for not having clearly defined values and sticking to them?

Think about your current sales force in your business. What happens when a salesperson does not do what he or she says? So, what are the consequences? What happens if all of your salespeople accomplish a goal except for one person? And what if that salesperson is someone that you have a great relationship with and someone with whom you have forged a friendship outside of business? What do you do? Does that salesperson come along for the reward just because he is a nice person or because he has been with the company for a long time? Do your values permit that? If they do, what will that do to the rest of the group the next time you have a goal? Once you have established your core values, there must be consequences. You are doing no one any favors by allowing him or her to fail. A great manager of people has to make tough decisions like this because if you do not, you are actually holding your people back. I believe that holding people accountable will eventually do one of two things. It will either help the salesperson to be the best at his or her profession, or it will help to advise him to get out of the business so that he can find out what he is good at doing. Everyone has something that he or she will excel in naturally, and some do not naturally excel in sales. I have heard it said that only 20 percent of the entire population has the capacity for sales. What kind of impact will it have on your culture to have people on your sales staff who will do anything to make a sale, even if it is unethical? What about borderline unethical? This is where values come in. What are your values? Below are some others that our leadership team came up with that day.

Integrity	Self-Understanding	Desire
Growth	Loyalty	Courage
Intensity	Tenacity	Abundance
Honesty	Follow Through	Accepting Change
Family	Consistency	
Fun	Passion	

Your values will directly impact your culture. Do you have a culture of mentoring? Do you have a culture in which your veteran salespeople help your newer salespeople, or is it a culture of hording ideas and not sharing? Do you have a culture of people showing up to training sessions on time and eager to learn and to grow? Do you have a culture of being professional and doing what is right for the customer? If you do, defining your values will protect that culture. If not and you desire to improve your culture, defining you values will be the first start to turning your culture around.

Now that you have your values clearly defined, communicate and promote them to your organization as regularly as possible. Promote your firm's values by including them in your bulletins; display them in your training rooms. When appropriate, you should also have discussions about how recent actions or decisions were consistent or inconsistent with the organization's values. Having your values clearly defined will help you manage your salespeople to reach a higher standard. Being consistent with your message and actions will help you create a culture of success.

DEFINING YOUR MISSION

Once you determine your values, it is important to create a mission statement. Many times I hear people downplay the importance of the mission statement. A mission statement answers why do we exist and what is our purpose. It defines what your organization or your business brings to the marketplace and your clients. It should communicate what value your business brings to your clients and how you accomplish your mission. These are the three main points to a good mission statement. It should be relatively short and simple and should provide a clear road map for making decisions in good times and bad. My personal mission statement as a financial advisor is as follows:

> My mission as a financial advisor with the Northwestern Mutual Financial Network is to help quality individuals, families, and businesses maximize their true financial potential and gain confidence through the realization of their goals, objectives, and dreams. To achieve this, I will assist them in overcoming procrastination by simplifying the ever changing and complex world of business and personal finance. I am committed to recommending solutions to my clients that I would want recommended to me. My goal is to establish strong, long-lasting relationships of trust that are mutually beneficial. I ultimately believe the greatest gift you can provide to your family is to plan ahead and be prepared.

This is my professional mission statement. This is what guides me on a daily basis. It reminds me of why I am in business. What is your personal mission statement? Why do you exist as a professional? As a salesperson, what value do you bring? What sets you apart from other professionals in your industry? Why are you in business? I firmly believe that it is also important to touch upon this point: I believe that anyone in a for-profit business needs to be in business first and foremost to make money. As I talk to classes at our local universities, I find that a lot of young people are sometimes confused by this. If you are profitable, you will be able to achieve your mission. You cannot accomplish your mission as a sales organization if you are not profitable and if you are not able to be financially solvent. Some may disagree with that, but I feel others put the cart before the horse. As a business, you must be profitable, and by being profitable you will accomplish the mission of your organization or business.

DEVELOPING A COMPELLING VISION

> If you don't know where you're going, that's probably where you will end up.
> —Yogi Berra

Once a company's values are determined and the mission statements have been laid out, the next step is the creation of a vision statement. If a mission statement expresses an idea of where your company is and what it stands for, a vision statement provides clarity for the future. Without a vision statement, how does a company know where it is headed, and in turn, how do your people know what they are striving to achieve? Good leaders are always providing a vision. A vision statement is a written, detailed account of where that business will be in five or ten years. In our organization, we work on a five-year time frame. We believe that you have real control only over what happens in the next five years. The important thing about a vision statement is that it provides inspiration and motivation to the people who are involved. Another important thing to remember is that your vision statement may or may not come true. Circumstances in the future might dictate that the vision that is clearly laid out today might be different two or three years from now based on circumstances outside of your company's control. Your vision statement still provides a target.

Many companies consistently provide good service to their clients, have strong sales, but over time, fail to grow and fail to keep up with the competition. This is sometimes true because they do not have a clear vision of the future. To be a great manager, you need to help your salespeople have a clear vision for their future.

As I suggested when deciding upon your organization's values, the best way to complete a vision statement for your sales organization and each individual salesperson is to have a retreat outside of the office. Take time out of working in the business and spend time working on your business. Many people are afraid to do this. However, you cannot create a vision statement for your business with the phones ringing in the office and with everyone's minds worried about the day-to-day activities of the business. At the retreat, help them and yourself to visualize five years into the future. If this vision statement revolves around your organization, what does it look like? Where are you located? How many salespeople do you have? How profitable is the business? How are you creating value in new ways? You can be as detailed as you want. Actually, the more detailed you are with your vision of the future, the more likely you will accomplish it. Similarly, when helping your salespeople with their personal vision statements, and I highly suggest that you do, ask similar questions. You may even want to include their spouses. Some questions I ask are as follows: Where are you living? Who are your neighbors? Where are you vacationing? What cars do you drive? What is your annual income, and how much of that have you saved to this point? Do you do any community work? Again, the more detailed you are, the better.

Once you have a clear vision statement, it must be clearly communicated to the rest of your sales organization, and you can now use this as a rallying point. People will want to see the vision come true. Update the progress of the vision statement at your quarterly meetings. Follow up on the vision statement with a five-year action plan. The five-year action plan contains the details of what and how the vision statement will be accomplished. It should be a year-by-year account of the progress that needs to be made for the vision to become true. It should include not only what needs to be done, but how and by whom. Deadlines should be in place as targets to accomplish each task. Remember that over a five-year period there may be circumstances outside of your control that may move your deadlines or that could change the objectives completely. You may even make a conscious decision not to follow through on certain tasks because over time it may be apparent they are not needed or may not be as important as you originally thought when creating the vision. In summary, the vision and action plan provide a written, measurable, and attainable goal for your business and for individual salespeople to strive for. You cannot begin the steps of recruiting, hiring, or training until you have gone through all of the previous steps. Remember, strategy should always be your guiding framework.

SELECTING THE RIGHT PEOPLE

Now that we have a core set of values, we know why we are in business through our mission statement, and where we are going with our vision statement, this gives us the basis to select the right people. It is important to recruit people who will fit your sales organization based on the above. In order to attract, recruit, and select the right people, it is imperative to have a clear selection process. Donald E. Kelley, my mentor and Managing Partner with Northwestern Mutual for 27 years, has always told me you must have a clearly defined process that is written and consistent. It should be written in a way that can easily be understood by all levels of your selection team, or any other member of management.

A process for selecting people should include three clear components: subjective evaluation, values fit, and objective analysis. The first part of the process, subjective evaluation, is the relationship part of the selection process. Do you genuinely like this candidate? This could be one of the most important parts of the process. Mike Kelley, a Financial Representative and a member of our Leadership Team, has said selecting good people to him is simply a question of, "Is this a person you would want to go out with and have a drink with after work?"[2] Rather, is this somebody with whom you want to spend time? If the answer is no or you would find yourself not excited about him or her, that should tell you something. Successful managers spend a lot of time with their salespeople. It is critical to know that you will be able to build a good relationship.

The second part of the selection process should be a "values fit." The discussion of values should be an important part of the selection process. Make sure to have a discussion about the values of your organization with your candidate and make sure that he or she understands the definition behind them. Specifically, ask candidates to share examples of times during their lives when they feel they have exhibited the values being discussed. Having an in-depth conversation regarding values will do two things. First, it will give you a truer picture of the character of the candidate, which will help you to make a better decision regarding an offer of employment. Second, you will have formed a foundation for the basis of your coaching process in the event that you do offer employment. We will discuss this more when we talk about development.

Third, develop an objective analysis component to the selection process. What kind of objective selection tools do you use to determine the strengths and weaknesses of each candidate? An important point here is that no salesperson, whatever his or her qualifications, is universally acceptable across the very wide range of all selling jobs. Thus, the sales manager must decide what characteristics a given sales position requires. Selling people-mover systems to airports may call for engineers attired in three-piece suits. Selling manure spreaders to Iowa farmers probably requires another form of dress. The job requirements for an order taker may be quite different from those for an order getter. These requirements must be carefully thought out and matched with job candidates, not only for the sake of the sales organization, but also for the well-being of the individuals hired.

Clearly, the task is to get the right person for the right job. Because selling situations vary tremendously, the analysis of a sales position should include a list of traits that an applicant should have. Some traits and accomplishments commonly considered in recruiting sales personnel are educational background, intelligence, self-confidence, problem-solving ability, speaking ability, appearance, achievement orientation, friendliness, empathy, and involvement in school or community organizations. Having many positive qualities does not guarantee that an applicant will be a successful sales representative, but they may be indicators of valuable attributes that are otherwise difficult to determine. For example, a friendly and helpful personality may be considered a meaningful trait, and membership in clubs and service organizations may suggest that a person has that trait. If the applicant's resume indicates that he or she is a loner, a recruiter may consider that possibility worthy of further investigation.

There are also many computer-based analytical tools to help companies select the right people for the right positions. One example of these is the Harrison Assessments. The candidate is asked to answer numerous questions to help identify personality traits as well as the candidate's strengths and weaknesses pertaining to a specific employment opportunity. An important benefit of these tools is the ability to identify potential challenges that the candidate might have. By knowing these challenges ahead of time, you can decide if you will be able to train this person to overcome those challenges. On the other hand, by using these tools, and identifying the challenges, you will again have a better idea if this candidate fits the job description. This will not only save the company a lot of time and money from not hiring the wrong person, but you also save the candidate from coming into a culture where he or she probably will not fit due to personality or lack of skills to do the job.

Related to this point is the matter of testing. Certainly no personality test or other test proves that a person will or will not be a good salesperson, and this fact concerns job applicants who feel that they have been denied a position on the basis of a pencil-and-paper quiz. Sales managers are willing to admit that no test is right in every case. However, many sales organizations continue to use tests as one form of input in the selection process because the test results have shown some validity over a long period of time. Thus, although tests are not right all the time, they may serve to improve the odds of making a correct choice.

Finally, you must determine where your best candidates come from. Where are you maximizing your recruiting efforts? Career changers? Clubs or professional associations? Career Fairs? The Internet? College campuses? How about within your own organization? The best selection tool you have could be the people in your office right now. Do you have a culture in which your people refer other good people to your company on a consistent basis? Communicate to your existing employees the type of people you are looking for to join the group. Have your Director of Recruitment meet with the salespeople on a regular basis to help people brainstorm. You may even want to put in place some incentives for referring a qualified person who ultimately gets hired. The other sources of recruitment are good, but nothing beats a referral.

Creating a successful internship program is also a great way to identify and select the right people. An internship gives you an early opportunity to identify good people with career potential. You can then mold them into successful salespeople. The second reason to have an internship is to make an impact on young people and encourage them to become a fan and an advocate of your organization for the rest of their lives. I have heard some people say that they went to college to avoid being a salesperson. I find that ridiculous because almost every job involves some form of sales. I make it a point to speak to students at nearby universities to share with them the terrific opportunities in sales. What many young people want is exactly what a career in sales can give them. You can communicate that to them through giving back to the community and speaking to classes and helping young people see the positive impact they can have on their lives and the lives of others.

Another benefit to students participating in an internship is the opportunity to explore a career in sales while they are still in school and in a safe environment. Whether they stay with your company or not, this experience will give them a huge head start, and if they do pursue a career in sales, your organization will most likely be the choice they make.

An internship is also a great way to develop your people early on. It allows young people, through trial and error, to learn the business prior to them making a large financial or personal commitment. They are able to learn without much risk, and we all know that we learn best from our failures. Done correctly, an intern will never forget the experience he or she had while working with your company and whether he or she makes a career with you or not, he or she will always be an ally.

TRAINING AND DEVELOPMENT

Now that you have chosen the right people, it is important to have a system in place to develop your sales force, both from the beginning and in an ongoing format. This is important for different reasons. First, people with a lot of potential want to work in a predictable environment. They want to know that there are consistent ways for them to grow with a support system in place to help them accomplish their goals. People that strive to be successful want to work in an environment where they are challenged. This will help you with your retention. In addition to this, as a manager you want to be assured that there are proven, time-tested ways for your salespeople to advance. Remember that to the extent that you are able to meet the needs of your clients (your salespeople), your needs will be met.

I believe there are three main pillars of development. The first pillar is your formal training curriculum. This is the pertinent information for a new person joining your organization. What information is critical for a new person in your business to know immediately to help him or her have a profitable fast start? I recommend that you break this training up throughout a two- to three-week period. For example, during the first week you might decide to have your new recruits in a classroom setting for the first three days and then out in the field with a mentor for the next two. You may want to continue a schedule like this for the next two weeks. In addition to initial training, what kind of follow-up training is there? Provide at least one or two opportunities a week for your salespeople to learn and to grow in terms of their product development, people skills, and personally. In our office, we do this on a group and an individual basis. We will discuss this more in the section on coaching.

While companies vary in terms of length, location, and even method of the initial formal training, it is imperative that this is done correctly and thoroughly. You may find that formal classroom instruction that is on-site works better than watching videos and running through computer simulations at a national convention in Hawaii attended by all the trainees. What is important is that the formal initial training program covers six basic areas of training. In an effort to rush the sales force out "into the field," some companies forget to cover some of these important topic areas. These six areas are as follows:

- *Sales techniques:* While it is true that some people just cannot sell, or in other terms, people must be born with certain personality characteristics that make them better salespeople, other things must be learned!

- *Product/Service knowledge:* To sell a product, you must understand a product. This includes everything about a product or service: its features, advantages, and benefits, how it is made, how it will be delivered, its accompanying warranties, its price, and everything else about it.

- *Customer knowledge:* 21st century consumers are smarter, have better technical skills, and are more diverse. It is critical to understand everything about customers, including why they buy what they buy and how they buy it. For new salespeople, it is useful to have cross-cultural training since the world of today is so global and cultures can be so different.

- *Supplier knowledge:* Since 21st century relationships are so important, it is just as important to understand the complete value chain. If you are selling a service, and two or three other companies will be a part of this service at some point along the way, you must understand what role these intermediary and third-party firms play in the total product package.

- *Competitor knowledge:* Refer to Chapter 4. Understanding the competition is critical!

- *Individual time and territory management:* Many great salespeople fail because they are so poor at managing their time and territories. You want your salespeople to work smarter, not harder.

In addition to these areas, a study of over 1,000 salespeople was conducted by MOHR Development, Inc., which identified seven "competencies" that salespeople of the 21st century must master.[3] The study concluded that the salesperson of this century must perform like a "mini-CEO," focusing on issues that this book has stressed, like the customer's strategic objectives rather than on tactics, overcoming objectives, or closing. These competencies are listed in Table 5.1.

Training goes beyond the initial training. Also, do not forget about your veteran salespeople. It is sometimes easy to assume that your veterans are okay, and they probably are most of the time. But your veterans need ways to grow and to continue learning as well. Invest in them by bringing in outside speakers or giving them incentives to join study groups or attend industry functions. Make sure they know they are not forgotten. John Ertz, Managing Partner with Northwestern Mutual in Cleveland, Ohio, gives this advice, "Your high producing veteran salespeople want as much as anything to know they are valued and that you care. Investing in their development and spending some one-on-one time with them will help send that message."[4] Another great way to continue to give your veterans an opportunity to grow is to put them in a teaching or training situation. This is consistent with the mantra of "see, do, teach." Sometimes the best way to improve and refine your skills is to teach. You might be surprised by how flattered some people will be by asking them to participate in teaching and training others

The second pillar of development is what that person will learn in the field. As I mentioned earlier, encourage people to go out into the field early on in the training process and to push the limits of what they are comfortable doing. Salespeople will learn the most in the field interacting with clients and watching their mentors. You can put salespeople in training for six months and they will not learn as much as they will one week in the field. Donald Kelley, my mentor and our Managing Partner has always encouraged this. "Doing joint work (doing sales calls with a veteran salesperson) is like getting paid tuition to go to school."[5] Encourage your salespeople to go out and implement the things they learn in training and to partner with a veteran to maximize their learning. If this is not already a part of your culture, find a veteran salesperson who is inspired by helping others and pair him or her up with a new salesperson. If done right, you will see the production of the new sales representative go up as well as the veteran's production. Once others see the results, they will want to pitch in and help out as well. Again, is giving back a value within your organization? Is it part of your culture?

Table 5.1
Competencies of Successful Salespeople in the 21st Century

Competency 1: Aligning Customer/Supplier Strategic Objectives by identifying new opportunities and applications that add value to the customer organization and enhance the value of the relationship with my organization.

- Gathering information to understand customers' business strategies and view of market opportunities.
- Staying up-to-date with new developments and innovations in customers' markets.
- Keeping current with emerging trends and initiatives of customers' competitors.

Competency 2: Listening beyond Product Needs by identifying business process improvement potential and opportunities to add value to my organization and our customers.

- Keeping the customer regularly updated with information and changes that might be important.
- Suggesting ways that the salesperson can bring added value to the customers.
- Helping customers think differently about their future needs.

Competency 3: Understanding the Financial Impact of Decisions on the customer's organization and on my organization by quantifying and communicating the value of the relationship.

- Looking actively for ways to contribute to the customer's profitability.
- Searching actively for more cost-effective ways to serve customers.
- Focusing on the financial consequences of approaches to meeting customer needs.

Competency 4: Orchestrating Organizational Resources by identifying key contributors, communicating relevant information, and building collaborative, customer-focused relationships.

- Communicating customer needs, suggestions, and concerns to appropriate resources in the organization.
- Working cooperatively with people in other parts of the customer organization who can be useful sources of ongoing information, resources, and support.
- Ensuring that product, sales, and service units work together to deliver value.

Competency 5: Consultative Problem Solving to create new solutions, customized products and services, and paradigm changes while being willing and able to work outside the norm when necessary.

- Anticipating possible problems and inviting discussion about how they can be overcome.
- Determining the cause of a problem and identifying constraints before recommending a solution.
- Proposing innovative solutions that go beyond the immediate application of the product or service.

Competency 6: Establishing a Vision of a Committed Customer/Supplier Relationship by identifying value-adding produces, processes, and services.

- Creating a relationship that supports the goals and values of both organizations.
- Developing relationships that recognize the needs of all contributing functions in both organizations.
- Communicating objectives for the relationship that are achievable and challenge the creativity of both organizations.

Competency 7: Engaging in Self-Appraisal and Continuous Learning by securing feedback from customers, colleagues, and managers.

- Demonstrating an understanding of what is working, what is not working, and how salespeople can do things differently.
- Staying up-to-date in their field of expertise.
- Asking for and welcoming feedback to assess a salesperson's performance and the degree to which he or she is meeting expectations.

The third pillar of professional development is what salespeople do in their spare time. Are they using their spare time effectively? Encourage your salespeople to utilize their spare time. Direct them to the learning resources you might have on your intranet or direct them to sales tapes and CDs or product information so that they can learn and fill in the gaps on their own. Some companies pay the membership fees for their sales force to join local organizations. This creates not only a culture of continued learning, but also opportunities for networking. In summary, your salespeople should always be striving for continuing education. If this is available to them in your industry, then that should be a priority. Is this a value? Is personal growth and excellence a value of your organization? If not, it should be or your development initiatives will not reach their full potential.

I find that these three pillars create a stable foundation for the development of a salesperson, creating almost a vortex of learning that builds up steam and momentum. Taking away one of the pillars will hold a salesperson back from achieving his or her potential. Managers should be able to expect that your salespeople will go the extra mile to learn, to develop themselves, to improve their product knowledge, and to further enhance their people skills. Do this and you will have salespeople who are growing as people as well as making sales for your organization.

ACCOUNTABILITY: CREATING A CULTURE OF SUCCESS

A casual day in the office is nothing more than a day off in the office.
—Harry Hoopis, Managing Partner, Northwestern Mutual Financial Network

Once your values and mission and vision statements are complete, and you have recruited and developed people consistent with those values, you now have the building blocks of creating your culture of success. We now need to take action. I believe the culture of success has three primary areas that need to be developed thoroughly to have a successful sales force. They need to be clearly defined and communicated expectations of professionalism, activity, and production. They must be consistent in every situation, and there must be a strong system of accountability to those expectations. What is your culture? Is it based on your values? For instance, Harry Hoopis's statement above is an example of a culture. Over the past decade or so, it seems that many organizations' cultures have begun to be eroded or dictated by the casual dress that many companies now promote. Harry, obviously, feels a little differently about that, as do I. What is your culture? Is it okay for salespeople to come in wearing polo shirts and wrinkled khakis? Or does it make sense to create a successful environment with people that are dressed and look the part? My wife, for instance, has always said that you dress to pay respect to yourself and for the people you meet that day. Is that going on in your office? What impression are your salespeople giving your prospects and clients? Are they paying respect? This, of course, is just a small example of a culture. Again, I am not suggesting that everybody in every sales situation wear a suit and tie or that it would even be appropriate, but it might be more appropriate than you might think. It all comes down to this issue that you must consider: What culture have you created regarding sales activity in your office? Remember, everything else will filter down from the overarching strategy, culture, and values.

> The secret of Success of every man who has ever been successful lies in the fact that he formed the habit of doing things that failures don't like to do.
>
> —Albert E. N. Gray

The above quote from Albert E. N. Gray is one of my favorite quotes as it relates to success. I firmly believe in his theory. Habits are the key to success, and creating a culture of success means creating an environment that promotes good habits. What does a good environment look like and what are the specific activities that should be in place on a daily, weekly, and monthly basis to develop successful salespeople? First, remember successful people make habits out of doing things that unsuccessful people do not like to do. Successful people also have a strong desire to succeed. Having a system of accountability in place will build on the strengths of your people and will help them succeed.

It is important to meet with new sales professionals every day. This should be done by a mentor, a coach, or someone designated to hold your salespeople accountable every day. If not, the new sales professional will quickly fall into bad habits and ultimately fail. Remember, it is all about setting goals and objectives (which we covered in the beginning), and salespeople must be held accountable to their individual goals just as corporations should be held account-able to their corporate goals.

In order to instill the habits of a successful salesperson, there must be daily accountability in the first 90 to 180 days. These meetings should be brief and ideally held first thing in the morning. Hold the meetings between 7:30 A.M. and 8:00 A.M. every day. During that time, record the activity of the salesperson from the previous day and then compare that to the expectations set by him or her and the organization. In addition to that, discuss the present day and make sure that he or she is properly prepared. Allow for no more than 15 to 20 minutes per person. Remember, these morning meetings should be moderated by some-one who has a leadership role, but not someone in senior management. It is important that the moderator hold the salespeople accountable. This is not an easy job. It is important for the moderator to ask the tough questions and help keep the salespeople on track. Eventually, if the salespeople are successful and stay with the organization, they will realize that having the moderator do his or her job is one of the many reasons they are so successful. Pair these brief morning meet-ings with a weekly one-on-one meeting with the sales manager or mentor. Between these two meetings you will create a high-touch atmosphere and head off any problems or bad habits. You must have accountability to help in develop-ing the habits that will make the new salesperson successful.

Once the new salespeople have succeeded in their first 90 to 180 days, do not think that they will fly all on their own. Move the accountability to a weekly basis or at a minimum, for your very senior salespeople, monthly. Remember, if you are selecting highly motivated, driven people, they want to be held accountable. Even the most motivated people can get distracted by all the noise and issues on a daily basis. Having the opportunity for the sales manager to look at the weekly activity from an objective point of view should often identify what is holding them back.

COACHING

This, then, leads us to having a good coaching process. You have the right peo-ple based on your values and mission statement. They have gone through initial training, and they have had a successful 180 days in the business. Now what? This is when the one-on-one meetings become even more important. Depending on the success of the salesperson, we may end the daily morning meetings and begin one weekly individual meeting and one group meeting. Having group meetings provides an environment of accountability. Individual meetings allow the new or veteran salesperson to discuss more personal issues. If you eliminate the one-on-one session, you are putting yourself and your people at a disadvantage. During these individual meetings you may discover the real reason that the sales-person is struggling. It could be problems with his or her marriage or issues with his or her children. You just do not know prior to this, and group meetings will not bring these to attention.

One of the biggest challenges that companies of the 21st century face is having a span of control that is simply too large. This is partly due to the rampant downsizing and layoffs of the 20th century. But, whatever the cause, the result has been that some managers are now managing double-digit, if not even triple-digit, numbers of salespeople. Most scholars feel that the appropriate span of control is anywhere between 6 and 18, depending on the type of work and type of employee. It is a lot easier to manage veteran salespeople than it is to manage new salespeople. Whatever the case, the coaching step is critical to the success of each salesperson and then ultimately to the whole company. A first level supervisor must be able to spend adequate one-on-one time with all subordinate employees.

The most difficult and most important part of coaching is holding people accountable. As we discussed earlier, we are not doing any favors when we help people fail. In your own business, do you currently have a process in place of consequences to implement when people do not do what is expected? Now is when we refer back to your organization's values. By having clearly defined values, your second-line management will be able to coach to those values. For example, let us pretend that a salesperson is not doing what he says he will do, and it is in direct conflict with our definition of integrity, which is one of our values. So, instead of your manager spending time on the actual activity that was not done, the manager could have a conversation about integrity and how his actions do not reflect your expectations. The employees should also know that they are not living up to the values of your organization. Find out how they feel about that. Of course, the salesperson is not going to feel good about letting down his or her manager or mentor, let alone being in conflict with the values that helped bring him or her to you in the first place. This kind of a discussion is much more productive to be able to go back to the values and to coaching versus using strong-arm tactics.

As I mentioned before, this is not an easy job for the second-line management. These managers will build great relationships with the sales force and will most likely be friends. It is a difficult job to hold your friends accountable. It is impossible to do without being able to fall back on the values. Your second-line management will be much less stressed and your salespeople will understand that their performance is measured not just through the eyes of their manager or through potential forms of punishment, but they actually are not living up to the values that they agreed on when they joined the organization.

Ultimately, if a salesperson does not come through and does not follow through on the clearly defined expectations, then it is the values that are not in alignment. It is not a personal situation; it is just a values discussion. That way, if that happens, that person will leave knowing that, for whatever reason he or she did not live up to the values and it was nothing personal. This creates the culture of not letting people who should not be around, hang around any longer and erode your culture. How many times have you seen a situation where people lingered in an organization, eroding the culture because nobody had the guts to let them go because they have a personal relationship? Define your values, communicate them, and then coach to them. That is how to treat your salespeople like clients.

Helping people work through what they really want and dispelling any fear of failure will help your salespeople push and strive to do bigger and better things. One of the things I think we do so well in our organization is to get our younger and newer salespeople exposed to what the possibilities are. We have picnics and get-togethers at some of the veteran financial representatives' homes to see the level of success they have. Some of our salespeople have homes down on a lake for the summer, and they have our young interns or our new salespeople down for a weekend just to see what it is like and what the possibilities are. I find that so many people that want to be successful sometimes actually have a fear of success, and if you fear success, how can you create a culture of success? Give them the ammunition they need to learn about themselves and to learn about the possibilities, and your salespeople will go above and beyond and not only accomplish your company's goals, but accomplish their own as well.

Invite your salespeople to sit down and have dinner with you and your spouse, and get their spouses involved. The more the spouses are involved in the career of your people, the more in harmony their families will be, and ultimately the more productive your salespeople will be. By treating your salespeople like a customer or a client, you will create a culture of success. It will help you deliver on the promise of your mission and achieve your vision for the future. Not only will this help the company, but it will help you attract and retain your good people, knowing that there is room for them to grow in the future.

DEVELOPING YOUR NEXT LINE OF MANAGEMENT

> There is no limit to what a man can do or how far he can go if he does not mind who gets the credit.
>
> —R. W. Woodruff

As I work to continue to build a successful sales force, I am reminded of these words. Great managers surround themselves with great people. By doing this, whatever task is at hand will be done efficiently and done well. Bad managers surround themselves with less effective people. The reason they do this is to make sure that the manager always looks good in comparison. They are threatened if someone is more intelligent or a better people person. It is critical when building a successful sales force to keep this in mind. We must surround ourselves with people who do not always think alike but have the same core organizational values.

One of the biggest challenges that many companies face is developing leadership for the future. Attracting good people to your organization and helping your people create a vision for themselves means giving them an opportunity to become leaders. What kind of leadership development program do you have in your company? Are you identifying people early on and teaching them about leadership? Are you giving your people leadership responsibilities and having them learn from those responsibilities and positioning them for future—do not make the mistake of not developing your second-line management. If not, the success you have today will soon come to a screeching halt, and your people will be looking for direction and will go elsewhere to find it.

Invest in leadership development. You can buy leadership books and schedule weekly or monthly meetings to discuss them. Hire outside consultants that you get references from that promote leadership. Spend time going to other successful sales organizations inside or outside your industry to get perspective and to share ideas. Build a special relationship with your leadership team by going on retreats away from the office. Invite your up-and-coming leaders to your main leadership team's meetings. Pair them up so your senior leaders can mentor your emerging leaders. Whatever you do, investing in leadership is a tax-deductible investment in your company's future success.

CONCLUSION

Building a successful sales force in the 21st century is an incredibly challenging and rewarding endeavor. It is my hope that this chapter will better enable you to build a successful sales force for your organization. By following through on the outline of this chapter, and implementing this as part of your action plan for the year, it will force you to spend time working on your business and on your sales force. Take time out of working in your business and work on it. The basics of sales have not changed over the past 50 years, but the backdrop has changed dramatically. Salespeople are more sophisticated, as are our customers and clients. Dealing with the large amount of information can become distracting, and the amount of time spent in meetings and communicating and follow through can be daunting.

Remember to run your business based on your values, use these values to select the right people, and then manage and coach them to their fullest potential. A plan for developing and coaching and a strategy for developing second-line management will allow your company and your sales organization to thrive, not only today but into the competitive and ever-challenging future. Your sales force is your best client, so treat it as such. Yes, it takes time and a lot of patience, but most of all, it takes great leadership.

All of these things will allow your salespeople, and your organization, to be highly rewarded beyond your wildest dreams. These rewards will not only be financial, but you also will have built incredible relationships. Best of all you will have made a lasting impact on the people you work with and your community. Good luck. I hope these ideas prove to be helpful and add value as you embark upon your future success.

NOTES

1. Don E. Schultz, "Studying Internal Marketing for Better Impact," *Marketing News* October 14 (2002): 8–9.

2. Mike Kelley, Financial Representative and Leadership Team member, Northwestern Mutual Financial Network, personal communication.

3. Bernard L. Rosenbaum, "Do You Have the Skills for 21st Century Selling? Rate Yourself with This Exercise," *American Salesman* 45, July (2000): 24–30.

4. John Ertz, Managing Partner, Northwestern Mutual, Cleveland, Ohio, personal communication.

5. Donald E. Kelley, Managing Partner, Northwestern Mutual, personal communication.

CHAPTER 6

It Is All about Money and the Bottom Line: Creating and Measuring Sales Effectiveness

Ingrid J. Fields, Michael F. d'Amico, and Linda M. Orr

An acre of performance is worth a whole world of promise.
—William Dean Howells

So, you have managed your reputation, you have built long-lasting relationships with your customers, you know everything there is to know about the competition, and you have hired and trained the best sales force in the world. What is left? You have to know if you truly did achieve these goals. And how will you know? Measurement is one of the hardest tasks of all the sales (or any marketing) manager's jobs. It is the infamous concept of Return on Investment (ROI). Obviously, strategy is only half the battle. The other half is knowing whether or not the strategy worked well, and then, if useful, figuring out how to adjust that strategy for the future. In terms of sales, you need to know if your overall organization was successful as well as knowing if each individual salesperson is meeting his or her potential. And to get to this point, it is important to understand how to motivate your sales force to achieve more. As human beings, we tend to think that money is the primary indicator of performance and the primary tool to motivate and to utilize to get the sales force to achieve more. Money does make the world go around, and will be discussed in great detail in this chapter, but it is not the only tool and indicator of success. This chapter discusses all of these issues associated with measuring, evaluating, and motivating the sales force and their effectiveness.

PLANNING SALES OBJECTIVES

It always comes back to strategy, does it not? All good managers, before setting out to accomplish a task, first give considerable thought to what that task should or must be. In other words, they plan and set objectives. The reason a statement of sales objectives is so important is that much of sales management involves the assignment of resources. How can the manager know, for example, how many salespeople to hire unless the manager first understands the tasks that need to be accomplished?

Sales objectives should meet the same criteria by which objectives are generally evaluated in the marketing world. They should be precise, quantifiable, include a time frame, and be reasonable given the organization's resources, its overall promotional strategy, and the competitive environment in which it operates. If the objectives are not precise, managers will not know what they are trying to accomplish. If they are not quantifiable, managers cannot know when an objective has been reached. If no time frame is included, the manager has "forever" to reach the goals. If the sales objectives are not reasonable, the manager can waste time and effort in a pursuit that was doomed to failure from the start.

Sales objectives can be expressed in many ways—as sales totals in dollars, as sales totals in units of products, as percentage increases over previous sales totals, as market share, as number of sales calls completed, as number of sales calls on new customers, and as dollar or unit sales per sales call made. An example of a sales objective stated in terms of sales volume is "expand annual sales revenue in the Virginia/West Virginia sales territory by 10 percent over last year's dollar volume." A market share objective might be to "increase market share in our region by 1 percent every year for the next five years." The sales forecast, which may or may not be the responsibility of the sales manager depending upon the organization, strongly influences decisions about sales objectives. And keep in mind: you cannot measure what you do not collect data on in the beginning. Thus, if your initial sales call objectives involve market share, then it should be much easier to measure market share to evaluate performance.

CREATING SALES EFFECTIVENESS: MOTIVATION

As previously discussed, there are many variables that influence effectiveness. Some are in your control and some are not. For example, you cannot control your competition and environment, but you can become more knowledgeable of them to better assist with strategy development. Then, while you cannot control your salespeople in some ways, in other ways you can. First, you must hire the right salespeople. Furthermore, you must give them the right tools and resources to do their jobs properly. And then, you must constantly monitor and evaluate their performance, provide adequate and effective feedback, and then select your "motivation tools" to encourage them to always strive for more. We tend to think of money as the primary motivator for salespeople. In this section, we explore how important money is to the success equation, but also note some of the other important variables that enhance motivation.

Sales forces of the 21st century include many unique situations that did not exist previously. While it has always been the case that many salespeople work alone in the field, often at great distances from their home offices and far from direct supervision, this has been amplified in this century. Huge *Fortune* 500 companies like IBM have all their salespeople work directly out of their homes. This unique situation, this feeling of working for oneself, and the lack of strict schedules, and even the ability to show up to work in your pajamas, draws many talented individuals into selling. But it can also create problems and thereby strongly influence and affect the role of the sales manager.

Because of the nature of the job, many salespeople are high achievers and seldom require supervision from sales managers. For these people, selling itself is highly motivating. There is a challenge intrinsic in the selling process, and a related challenge is trying to understand and solve customers' problems. Despite all this, most salespeople need at least occasional support from management. Sales personnel are often subject to broad fluctuations in morale and motivation, ranging from the lows that accompany a string of customer rejections or a sense of being alone on the road to the highs of obtaining major orders, enjoying peaks of success, and earning substantial commissions and bonuses. Sales personnel, especially young trainees, may become discouraged if they do not receive proper help, supervision, and attention to morale. Because sales personnel do need a "listening ear" as well as direction and advice, telephone contact can help the sales manager supervise the sales force, but face-to-face communication is even more valuable.

While experienced sales managers may know how, by words and actions, to properly reward and encourage salespeople to keep them fresh and interested in the job, others need to learn how to motivate members of the sales force. Many corporations use various forms of sales promotions to help with motivation. Sales contests, bonus plans, prizes and trips, and sales conventions in exciting cities can help a sales manager keep motivation high among the sales force. Periodic sales meetings are also useful for creating a feeling of group support and mutual interest, as well as for providing training and transmitting information to members of the sales force.

Sales organizations, such as Tupperware Brands Corporation, rely on sales meetings as the primary means of motivating the sales force. Every Monday night, for example, Tupperware distributors hold a rally to announce sales successes with considerable hoopla and celebration. At another company, the field sales manager of a New Jersey territory rented Giants Stadium. Corporate executives, family, and friends were assembled to cheer as each salesperson emerged from the players' tunnel. The electric scoreboard bearing the salesperson's name and the cheering crowd motivated the salespeople to keep excelling at their jobs. That was a night to be remembered by all involved.

There are a few key points to consider when determining the optimal mix of incentives for a company's reward system. First, sales managers must balance the needs of their salespeople, the organization, and the customer. All three of these groups are going to have very different needs, but the most successful reward model will attempt to achieve an optimal mix of the three. Of course the salesperson wants to make a sale, the customer needs the product at hopefully the best price, and the organization wants to be profitable. Given that in the 21st century relationships are more important than transactions, many companies are redirecting their efforts to include this new emphasis on partnering. For example, companies are realizing that a strict focus on getting as many sales as possible may erode customer satisfaction because it forces salespeople to be "pushy." All policies must be tied to organizational and strategic objectives.

Additionally, managers need to realize that it is not necessarily about the almighty dollar to all salespeople. Different forms of compensation are discussed later, but at this point it is very important to stress that all people have varying degrees of intrinsic and extrinsic needs. Some salespeople really do just want the money (extrinsic), and some people are more satisfied with a combination of money along with recognition and opportunity for advancement than money (intrinsic).

Another key point that seems almost self-explanatory is that motivation systems must be financially sound. The 21st century is one of increased accountability and less margin for error. Just as marketing intermediaries must demonstrate their ability to add value, salespeople must pull their weight. Motivation, compensation, and reward systems should not be designed to let poor performers slip through the cracks. Likewise, systems need to be designed so that top performers are rewarded. Top salespeople are a rare gem and need to be paid what they are worth. When people are undervalued, they usually figure it out very quickly and can just as quickly find someone who will value them more.

Compensation systems must also be easily understood by all those who must adhere to them and must be flexible to adapt to the rapid changes that can occur. I have seen some incentive systems that are so complicated that it takes a brain surgeon to figure them out. Face it: if you cannot understand how you are going to make money, you are likely to just give up. Also, everything about the 21st century includes rapid changes; therefore, a compensation system must be able to adapt to those changes. The Dun & Bradstreet Corporation (D&B) plans to leave about 70 percent of its compensation the same every year, which also allows for about 30 percent of it to change from year to year.[1]

A few other issues must be considered when thinking about motivation that are unique to this century. First, many companies are now realizing the need for global alignment. It would not make sense to pay exactly the same all around the world for obvious reasons like different standards of living. However, managers are realizing that the sales compensation plans need to be designed to reflect common objectives, principles, and performance metrics. Likewise, as employees are more readily transplanted all over the globe, companies need to learn that sales forces are becoming more similar than different and compensation programs need to reflect that.

The late 20th century had a huge push toward sales teams. A trend toward team compensation quickly followed. While teams are not disappearing anytime soon, team compensation does seem to be. Let us review what was just discussed. Salespeople by nature tend to be very intrinsically motivated. They do not want to rely on a team of other people to get their deserved credit. Salespeople tend to be so intrinsically driven. Consequently, individual efforts must be rewarded. Some companies have found that even though revenue accrues across the team, customer surveys and 360-degree feedback systems can determine who is doing the most and the best work. And the good news of the 21st century is this: new forms of software are emerging every day that make these processes even easier. Software such as Callidus can handle payments for thousands of sales reps for even the most complicated compensation system with ease. An added bonus is that it makes sure that everything is compliant with 21st century regulation, such as the Sarbanes-Oxley Act of 2002.

COMPENSATING THE SALES FORCE

Now that we have examined some of the issues associated with motivation, it is important to understand the tried and true nitty-gritty details of designing compensation systems. Working in sales, unlike certain other professions such as accounting and personnel management, is often highly visible to people from outside the company. It involves attempts to achieve clearly measurable results, such as the following:

- Did sales go up or did they fall?
- How many new accounts were opened?
- How much gross margin on sales was achieved?

For this reason, most sales managers believe that salespeople who achieve the highest performance in terms of some specific measure should receive the highest compensation. As described, financial incentives are not the only way to motivate salespeople, but they are important and deserve the sales manager's close attention. The other forms are discussed later.

What is the ideal compensation plan for salespeople? It should be simple so as to avoid disagreements over the size of paychecks and bonuses. It should be as fair as possible to avoid arousing jealousies among the sales team members. It should be regular so that salespeople will be able to count on a reasonable reward coming to them steadily. It should provide security to the salesperson and yet provide an incentive to work harder. It should give management some control over sales representatives' activities. Last, it should encourage optimal purchase orders from customers. For example, a heavily incentive-based plan might encourage salespeople to engage in unwarranted hard-selling activities. It might result in selling customers items that they really do not need at the present time. This is not optimal ordering. Ordering should promote the development of a profitable long-term relationship with clients.

Unfortunately, no compensation plan completely satisfies all these criteria. Based on the desires of the sales manager and his or her salespeople and also on the nature of the selling job, management must select from among the available compensation plans described below. The range of compensation plans used in selling situations represents a continuum. At one end is the straight salary approach. At the other end is the straight commission plan. All other possible compensation plans are trade-offs between these two extremes in that they attempt to borrow the good points from both salary and commission approaches.

Straight Salary or Hourly Wage

The straight salary method or an hourly wage plan offers the salesperson compensation that is not directly tied to sales performance. Instead, the payment is a function of time. It can be based on an amount of money that was previously agreed upon for a certain period of time (for example, weekly, biweekly, monthly, and so forth). Under this condition, there is an assumption about how many hours per week will be worked and then no added payments are made for working more hours within a certain time frame. Alternatively, and more likely to occur within a business-to-customer setting, the salesperson and the sales manager can come to an agreement about the pay per hour. Then, the input metric could be hours worked during some time period.

Under the straight salary or wage plan, management has the greatest control over how sales personnel spend their time. This system also provides management with the least uncertainty about selling expenses because each salesperson's earnings are not tied to sales results. As a consequence, many highly successful salespeople dislike this plan, preferring to accept the risks of a commission plan in the hope of achieving high earnings.

There are some selling situations, however, in which the straight wage or salary plan makes the most sense. The common denominator among these situations is management's desire to control a salesperson's time and activity. Straight salary is most likely when the job requires the salesperson to engage in a considerable amount of nonselling activities. For example, retail sales personnel may be expected to arrange stock, clean up spills, feed the fish in the display tank, and fill in whenever an extra worker is needed. Paying these people on anything other than a straight wage or salary plan would reduce management's control over what they can get these salespeople to do.

Straight Commission

Unlike the salary plan, the straight commission plan rewards only one thing: generating sales revenue. The prime advantage of the straight commission is that salespeople are highly motivated to sell more sooner. On the surface, this plan would seem to have considerable appeal to most managers. However, the plan also has a number of disadvantages. As previously suggested, salespeople paid this way cannot be expected to perform additional activities that do not lead directly to sales. In other words, their activities are difficult to control. Furthermore, they may be reluctant to try to sell to new accounts that may develop slowly or to sell merchandise that is difficult to move, preferring instead to raise their short-term compensation by concentrating on products they know they can sell easily and quickly.

Management may decide to discourage this understandable behavior by lowering the commissions on easy-to-sell goods and raising them on hard-to-sell goods. This, however, destroys one of the straight commission plan's key advantages, namely, its simplicity. In addition, salespeople will resent changes that are likely to reduce their incomes. Straight commission has other shortcomings, too. The salesperson has little security. If the economy slows down or if sales fall off for some other reason beyond the salesperson's control, the incentive in the plan may be lost if the sales representative fails to achieve a satisfactory income over a period of a few weeks or more. Finally, when managers do not know exactly what commission expenses will be, they cannot accurately predict selling expenses with complete accuracy.

Commission with Draw

Management, seeking to keep the incentive of the commission plan while softening the blow that a run of bad luck might deal a salesperson, can move toward the middle of the compensation continuum. One possibility is the plan known as commission with draw. Under this plan, the salesperson is still on straight commission but can dip into a "drawing account" to increase his or her pay during slack seasons. This pay plan is especially common when demand for the product being sold is seasonal, as it is for certain construction materials. The important thing to remember about commission with draw is that it is, at base, a true commission plan because the amount taken as a "draw" must be paid back into the drawing account once the sales representative's commission returns to higher levels.

Quota-Bonus Plan

Under a quota-bonus plan, each salesperson is assigned a sales quota, which is a specific level of sales that should be achieved over a specified period. In addition, though, an incentive is built in because salespeople who exceed their quotas receive bonuses. The base salary is related to the quota total, while the bonus provides a commission-like incentive. This plan, like others in the compensation continuum, provides aspects of both straight salary and straight commission.

While the quota-bonus plan has a good deal of appeal, inherent in it are possibilities for friction between salespeople and management. For example, expert sales representatives may find that they can make their quota very quickly. If some flat bonus amount is offered for any number of sales over quota (regardless of amount), the salesperson may be tempted to take it easy for a time and then make just enough sales to earn the bonus by exceeding quota. This behavior will make many sales managers very unhappy. As a result they may raise the salesperson's quota. This makes the salesperson unhappy, and the cycle continues. In contrast, if more and more bonus money can be earned for more and more sales over quota, the salespeople may be motivated to maximize their bonuses by selling more than just enough to exceed quota.

Salary Plus Commission

As the name suggests, the salary plus commission compensation plan combines the two pay methods at each end of the continuum by granting the salesperson both a straight salary or wage and a commission on sales. Typically, because a salary is provided, the commission rate is smaller than would be expected in a straight commission pay package. In addition, because a commission is provided, the salary is smaller than would be expected in a straight salary pay plan. The intent of the salary plus commission plan is to allow management to ask salespeople to engage in nonselling work (since they are on salary), but also reward them for successful sales efforts (with a commission). For example, increasingly sales representatives are being asked to collect data from customers and then to enter that data into their laptop computers for use in the company database. When a salesperson must give up selling time to help the company build its system files, the compensation system of salary plus commission makes a lot of sense.

Other Forms of Motivation

As most sales managers of the 21st century know, there are many forms of incentives. The nonfinancial types are opportunity for promotion, sense of accomplishment, and opportunity for personal growth, recognition, and job security. No matter how motivated by money we may be, we all need some degree of some of these other variables. In a recent study of more than 100,000 employees at 11 large companies and 13 small companies, it was found that for a motivation/

incentive plan to be successful, it must include elements of three broad categories.[2] These categories were (1) equity in treatment and wages, (2) achievement available on the job and in terms of company pride, and (3) camaraderie, which refers to being part of a productive and cohesive team. Employees who worked for companies that had all three of these variables present reported being "enthusiastic about their jobs."

However, as with everything else in sales, managers must treat individuals differently and realize that even though treatment should be equitable, no one wants to be treated with a cookie-cutter approach. We want to be recognized as individuals and have managers treat us that way. Some of the individual difference variables make logical sense. For example, someone who is 60 years old will probably place a great deal of importance on job security. He or she wants to live out his or her last few years of work without needing to worry about changing jobs and learning something completely new. Meanwhile, the fresh college graduate probably cares more about opportunities for promotion than job security, unless of course he or she has a baby on the way or some other life-changing event like that occurring.

Sales contests have become one of the most popular incentives in the 21st century. They can vary in reward offered from money, to travel, to merchandise. Contests have become controversial because some feel that they lead to short-term gain with no long-term results. Likewise, in the increased era of accountability, contests are much harder to link to return on investment. However, contests remain quite popular and show no signs of decreasing in frequency. One benefit of contests is that they can strengthen the internal organizational culture, especially when branch locations are competing against other branch locations. A little competition is always good for motivation.

A guideline that must be followed anytime contests are used is not to overdo it by having too few or too many winners. To be effective, several people need to have a chance to receive prizes, but it is not really a contest if every participant "wins." Many times sales contests have become like elementary school sports. In an effort not to destroy the precious self-esteem of young children, everyone that competes gets a participation award. If everyone wins, then no one really wins, and the contest loses all its value. The same applies when they are run all the time like furniture store sales. Why should you rush right out and buy when you know there will be a "Second Tuesday of the Month Sale" right after today's "Sweetest Day Sale."

The key to all these "textbook-like" lists and various approaches to motivation and compensation is to realize that we are all unique individuals and have very different needs. The 21st century has brought us an even more diverse workforce with an even broader range of needs. In a survey of almost 41,000 salespeople across that globe, only those in the United States, the United Kingdom, and Singapore rated money as their number one motivator.[3] Thus, the job of motivating has become more difficult because everyone is so much more different. However, sales managers must take the time to get to know each one of their employees and understand what motivates each one of them. The 21st century is too competitive even in the job market to not treat all top salespeople the way they want to be treated. While we want to think we are all completely self-motivated, we know this is not the case. We need a reason to get up and go to work everyday, and we need a reason to reach our full potential. That reason may be the paycheck, but it also may be something much more psychological, like self-worth. Managers in the 21st century must take the time to get to know each of their employees to understand what makes each of them "tick."

EVALUATING THE EFFECTIVENESS OF THE SALES FORCE

At the end of the day, ultimately, the most important question is, Did we make money? You have to have a system in place to evaluate the effectiveness of both your organization and your sales force. To do this, an organization's overall marketing plan must be translated into a series of sales plans that specify regional, district, or territorial goals. Evaluation of a sales manager's performance or a sales representative's work is based on whether or not the predetermined and hopefully appropriate objectives have been met.

Objectives, especially those that the sales manager and sales representative work out together, should be specific and measurable if they are to form the basis for reviewing the salesperson's performance and progress. Because salespeople are often a bit leery of how objectives are set for them, the evaluation system must be fair and be based on a mutual understanding of the performance standards and how they were determined. Note that the person's actual performance should be measured against predetermined standards, not standards set after the fact. It does little good to tell the sales representative that his or her performance this past year was "not too good" if the salesperson had been given no indication of what was expected at the start of the year. To minimize misunderstandings, the salesperson often is assigned a sales quota. During progress reviews, actual sales can be compared with the achievement of quota to date.

To do their jobs properly and meet their own objectives or quotas, sales managers must develop control metrics to provide feedback to salespeople in the field. This feedback is not always expressed in terms of sales generated but may involve measures of effort, such as increases in the number of sales calls made per week, increases in the number of orders per sales call (the sales "batting average"), or reductions in selling expenses. Feedback tells managers if they should proceed with plans as scheduled, change course, look into particular problems, or check in with local sales personnel to take corrective action.

For example, a simple but fundamental aspect of the sales manager's job is to make sure that each salesperson is calling on an appropriate number of customers.

In most companies, therefore, sales representatives keep a log, a call report, or an activity report that must be filed weekly or monthly with the sales manager, which indicates the number of calls made and other requested information about each account. Increasingly, salespeople enter these call reports directly into a computer and e-mail this customer information directly to their company's database. Sales managers should periodically evaluate this "paperwork" to determine whether the sales representative is working at an appropriate level of intensity.

An evaluation of the sales representative's paperwork might indicate to management, for example, that several of the salespeople enjoy calling on old standby accounts but seem to avoid trying to develop new accounts. This could indicate a need for additional motivation or for training on approaching new prospects. Alternatively, sales management could consider that a change in the compensation plan in which there was an increase in the commission rate for new business but a decrease in the rate for existing accounts would be useful. Below are some of the commonly used bases for evaluation of a given salesperson's performance.

Activity

Evaluation of the selling activities performed by a salesperson is especially useful for those who are paid by the salary only method. This is often described as an input approach to control of the sales force. The idea is that if enough sales effort is made, then eventually orders will be the consequence of these sales activities. Examples of these types of sales activities include sales calls, customers contacted, presentations made, written proposals submitted, or displays constructed. The idea is that orders will follow effort. We can generate sales by asking enough people to buy our goods or services, and then we will meet our targets. A more scientific approach uses the same concept, but traces activities through the steps necessary to bring a prospect to a point where orders are likely. This is sometimes called a funnel system, and each necessary activity within the sales cycle is measured along the way. Individual performance at each level of the sales funnel is tracked, examined, and rewarded.

For example, Account Manager Jenny is good at prospecting, and she adds additional potential clients to her funnel every week. She does not like to "close the deal" by asking for the signed contract and sometimes needs a sales manager or peer to come along on sales calls to do the paperwork with her at client meetings. Account Manager Joe, on the other hand, is reluctant to start the new conversation with prospects, so his funnel does not often get refreshed with new opportunities. Joe has excellent financial knowledge, however, and that can be very persuasive, so clients usually buy his products because the ROI is favorable for a positive decision. He closes a very high percentage of his prospects. There are a lot of salespeople like "Joe" working in sales.

Many of the current software tools attempt to measure sales effectiveness by examining the four stages in the sales funnel. Often a probability of closing the sale is assigned based on movement through the sales cycle, for example, a 10- to 20-percent probability of closing is assigned to new relationships, 40 percent is assigned if we have written a proposal or presented an offer, 60 percent is the assigned probability when we have qualified the financial impact of the proposal, and, of course, there is a 100-percent probability of closing when the project has moved to the closed or sold stage in the sales funnel. This is a good forecasting tool for sales managers, but it must be checked for its linkage within a particular business's results.

Units Sold

It is easier in some industries to simply measure the number of products manu- factured and shipped because of the company accounting methods. This, then, may become the metric that management uses to evaluate the effectiveness of each member of the sales force. It is common for smaller business sales forces to use this approach because of limited product offers and less complex relationship needs. Transaction selling and limited need for an ongoing customer service is also typi- cal in this transaction-oriented selling environment in which success is measured by units shipped. The linkage of the sales effectiveness metric to the business plan is easy to understand in this case. Ultimately, this is what the previously men- tioned activity metrics are intended to produce.

Revenue

A slight variation is to track dollar amount of revenue per salesperson rather than just the number of units sold. This has added precision and takes into con- sideration the price at which each product is sold. Of course, if many different products at a wide range of prices are sold, this method enables a much better determination of sales effectiveness across members of the sales force. It also links to the business plan in more obvious ways and can discourage counterproductive behaviors like discounting. One challenge with this method is that it does not encourage salespeople to provide better client service after the sale. Once large orders have been shipped, there is no incentive in other time periods to continue providing excellent service if future deals are not possible due to having fulfilled a client's current demands. Another constraint resulting from using this evaluation method is that small client orders that are needed to establish a business relation- ship in a certain time period are not valued highly even if there is huge potential for future growth of revenue.

Profit

Ideally, of course, the perfect metric for measuring each salesperson's success is his or her impact on profit. The challenge here is to be able to accurately calculate this indicator of sales effectiveness. When many different products and services are sold with a wide range of margins and when the costs of the sales efforts needed to achieve the sale are difficult to track, the profit model is difficult to implement. Furthermore, often there are many overhead costs and other complicating factors that make tracking profits by salesperson and even by customer very difficult. Attempting to do so is more common in the services environment where margins are higher when managed correctly and when each sale represents something of a "project." This approach to determining sales effectiveness does encourage members of the sales organization to consider which clients represent attractive business relationships and which ones are likely to become problems to serve over time.

Client Satisfaction

Customers who buy again and again are also indicative of either good sales and service satisfaction or good products or both. Surveys are used after a large order is fulfilled or after a sales transaction is complete. Surveys can offer valuable input if it is convenient for the customer to complete, but does not substitute for excellent relationships with customers.

Organizational Effectiveness

In addition to examining how each individual salesperson performs, a sales manager must understand how the sales force as a whole contributes to the organization's bottom line. Keeping in mind that everything must be linked back to the initial strategic objectives that were established, overall organizational performance must be assessed as a part of the evaluation procedures. Organizational effectiveness and performance can be examined in many different ways. Performance is a multidimensional construct encompassing financial, customer-related, organizational, and learning processes. Valuing any component over another would lead to an incomplete picture. Robert S. Kaplan and David P. Norton present a story that serves as a metaphor to the dangers of an unbalanced performance measure.[4]

Imagine how you would feel about flying in a plane after having this discussion with your pilot:

Q: I'm surprised to see you operating the plane with only a single instrument. What does it measure?

A: Airspeed. I'm really working on airspeed this flight.

Q: That's good. Airspeed certainly seems important. But what about the altitude? Wouldn't an altimeter be helpful?

A: I worked on altitude for the last few flights and I've gotten pretty good on altitude. Now I have to concentrate on proper airspeed.

Q: But I noticed you don't even have a fuel gauge. Wouldn't that be useful?

A: Fuel is important, but I can't concentrate on doing too many things well at the same time. So, this flight I want all my attention focused on airspeed. Once I get to be excellent at airspeed, as well as altitude, I intend to concentrate on fuel consumption on the next set of flights.

This story illustrates that just as you would not want to be a passenger on that plane, you would not want to be the manager of a company that had a narrow focus. Overreliance on financial measures can be just as detrimental as over reliance on "fluffy" measures like customer satisfaction. Firms must take a balanced approach to both management and measurement of their organizations.

Businesses must take a two-pronged approach to their measurement, just as they did in their initial strategy-making processes. First, measures must be set and measured from an internal perspective. Second, indicators must be assessed against external indicators through methods like benchmarking. Benchmarking seems like a relatively straightforward concept. Look at who does it best in the industry, look at what they are doing and how they are doing it, and then see how you measure up. However, as simple as this seems, the value of it cannot be underrated. Industries are so different across the board from margin to sales cycles. Some industries have extremely high margins, and some have very low margins; some are likely to use large discounting procedures, while others do not; some have sales cycles of a couple hours, while sales in other industries can take over a year from the first sales call until the close.

As mentioned, the more measures that are used to assess organizational effectiveness, the better. An organization cannot have too much information. The only caveat here is that, of course, gathering information takes time and money. There is a careful balance between having enough information to be beneficial and spending too much time and money to collect that information. Luckily the 21st century has brought us wonderful technology that makes both information collection and analysis much easier. Chapter 13 will discuss some of these technologies in more detail. There are four large categories of variables to measure organizational effectiveness: (1) sales, (2) cost, (3) profitability, and (4) productivity.

Sales analysis can be analyzed on many types of categories, such as product type, account types, type of distribution, or order size. These data can then be compared against the forecast, the quotas, previous periods, or competitors within the industry. Then an effectiveness index can be created by dividing actual sales by predicted (or actual competitor) sales. Cost analysis is very important in order to compute actual profitability. As mentioned many times, the 21st century is one of increased accountability for managers. ROI is a very important concept of the day and will likely remain that way. Managers must calculate their total costs is terms of all selling activities such as salaries, commissions, bonuses, travel, and even administrative costs. These costs must be compared to overall profitability —$1 million in sales is a terrible accomplishment if you have $2 million is expenses. Managers of the 21st century must understand for every dollar put in, how much you are you getting back out. And then, what is your bottom line? These are critical questions for this century. Productivity analysis is very similar, but must also be analyzed for the same reasons discussed earlier. What if you find out your top salesperson is wasting half his or her time on sales calls and could be even twice as productive? What if you find out from an overall organizational perspective that you simply have too many (or too few) salespeople? These are the facts that must be analyzed that lead to decisions that must be made.

Data should be collected on all types so that a true picture of effectiveness can emerge. Of course, in order to have something to compare these data to, sales forecasts need to be set in the beginning when strategic sales objectives are made. From this initial forecast, everything else can then be formulated, from quotas to sales territories. The "math" involved with a sales manager's job that is needed to calculate these things is outside the discussion of this book. However, at this point a few key factors are noted. The 21st century involves more changes that are occurring more rapidly than ever before. The key factor to success when determining the forecasts, the territories, and even the quotas is as much information as possible. Information must be taken from external sources as well as internal sources. Some studies have shown that 21st century sales forces want to be included in most of these decision processes. Only the frontline salespeople know how their territory is changing, how customer tastes are shifting, and what trends may be occurring in the environment. Salespeople are likely to be more motivated and enthusiastic about reaching their goals if they were involved in the initial processes.

CONCLUSION

It really all comes down to the bottom line. Even with great salespeople, you must pay them right, which will motivate them to do better. Then you must have a measurement system in place to make sure you are meeting your strategic sale objectives. All measurement methods send a message about what is important to the sales force. They all provide good information and blind spots. You must have enough information to make sure you can continue to make good decisions, but you do not want to have so much that you are wasting your time and money both getting that information and sorting through it. There are two good rules of thumb to remember with all compensation, motivation, and measurement systems: Keep it simple and keep it consistent!

NOTES

1. Henry Canaday, "Dollar for Dollar: Prune Your Compensation Plan into Perfect Shape," *Selling Power* 26, no. 3, April (2006): 60–63.

2. Sirota Survey Intelligence, "S&MM Pulse," *Sales & Marketing Management* 158, no. 6, July/August (2006): 20.

3. John F. Tanner, Jr., and George Dudley, "International Differences: Examining Two Assumptions about Selling," *Baylor Business Review* Fall (2003): 44–45.

4. Robert S. Kaplan and David P. Norton, "Using the Balanced Scorecard as a Strategic Management System," *Harvard Business Review* 74, no. 1, January–February (1996): 75–85.

CHAPTER 7

LEARNING FROM YOUR CUSTOMERS: BUILDING MARKET FEEDBACK INTO STRATEGY AND INNOVATION

Jason DiLauro and Linda M. Orr

> People will sit up and take notice of you if you will sit up and take notice of what makes them sit up and take notice.
>
> —Anonymous

If we make products or offer services that do not fulfill our customers' needs, sales will suffer. In most companies, research and development (R&D) and product development are separate departments. This separation was brought about by the creation of functional silos that were created in many organizations in order to operate more efficiently. By the very definition of the name, R&D usually has its own research function, which possibly forms focus groups, looks at last year's sales and products, or looks at what the competition has done. This set of processes, many of which were created in an attempt to be customer driven or emerged out of "customer relationship management" (CRM) strategies, have unfortunately resulted in being anything but customer driven. However, we know that in the competitive landscape of the 21st century, businesses that do not employ CRM strategies will probably not be as successful as those that do.

Given CRM's great potential, some have been disappointed with the results to date. There are many reasons for the fact that the implementation of CRM strategies has not resulted in a greater focus on the customers and their needs. The very people who understand customers the most, who deal with them every day, who understand their needs, and who make daily attempts to find products and services to fulfill these needs are frequently the last ones consulted in the product development processes. Salespeople, who are serving on the front lines, are excellent sources of knowledge for improving and upgrading product and service offerings. Involving the sales force in the product-development process indirectly brings the customer directly into the process through the sales force's daily associations with the customer. Companies that truly can bring the customer into the product development process will benefit from greater customer satisfaction and loyalty. Thus, even though sales forces of the 21st century are finding greater responsibilities, across broader functions of the organization, one of those added responsibilities must be a strategic involvement in the CRM and product-development processes. Figure 7.1 demonstrates the customer relationship and product development processes.[1]

CRM is a set of business processes, strategically embedded within a company, that create the value propositions and linkages between the firm and all of its

Figure 7.1
CRM Processes

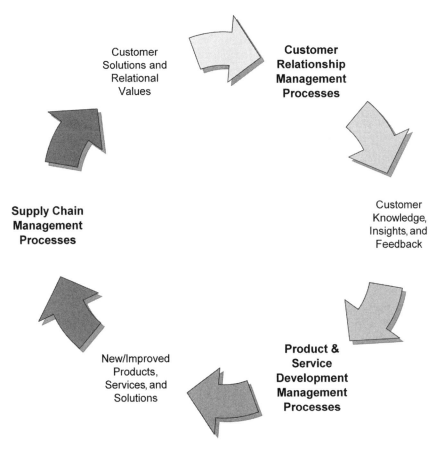

external stakeholders. As shown in Figure 7.1, companies must first gain customer knowledge and insights. One of the easiest and most accurate ways to do this is through a company's sales force. After a firm gathers knowledge, it must then relate that information into ways to upgrade and adapt new products and services, if that is what the market wants. Additionally, it is important to note that new products and services may need consistent adapting to appeal to the needs of all stakeholders, including suppliers. Thus, 21st century salespeople must be gatherers and distributors of customer information, and they must be entrepreneurial in order to understand how to best utilize this information in terms of providing solutions to customer needs. Saying that 21st century sales forces need to be entrepreneurial, or creative, or innovative, means more than just utilizing information to provide customer solutions. Salespeople must be innovative across many parts of their jobs, from more innovative prospecting methods to even finding out more creative ways to gather information from customers.

Customers today are busier and more distracted. Many times, customers do not even know exactly what they need, and good salespeople can help find the right products and services for customers to fit these needs. This chapter first discusses the process of gathering feedback from the marketplace from the perspective of the "ideal client." Some of the topics covered are how to identify your ideal client, how to then understand why he or she is an ideal client, and then learn how to replicate your ideal client. We do this by analyzing your existing clients, categorizing them, asking them questions based on the service you provide and how you can improve this service, making changes based on analysis to improve your relationships, and changing and becoming adaptive in terms of product and service offerings. Finally, we examine working with your clients to help grow your business more effectively and efficiently. But first, we need to understand why adaptability is so vitally important in the 21st century.

ADAPTABILITY AND INNOVATIVENESS

Salespeople do more great things for a company than merely listening to and understanding the growing and changing needs of the customers. Contrary to the typical way in which businesses are set up to have functional silos, salespeople can be the best innovators in a business. Not only do they listen to the customer, but studies show that salespeople share personality variables that enable them to be more innovative and creative than some other employees.[2] These common characteristics are that salespeople tend to be achievement oriented, persistent, persuasive, assertive, more likely to take the initiative, versatile, perceptive, energetic, self-confident, independent, more likely to have an internal locus of control, have a tendency toward risk taking, creative, resourceful, an opportunity seeker, comfortable with ambiguity, hard working, and well organized. These types of personality variables enable salespeople to think of the most innovative creative solutions to business problems. In the 21st century, innovativeness is imperative.

Several significant changes have occurred recently in the business arena that have caused a true realization in the statement—change is the only thing that remains the same. Some have termed the 21st century as "the next industrial revolution." Some of the changes are (1) the pace of economic change is accelerating, (2) there is an explosion of innovation and new knowledge generation, (3) competitive pressures are intensifying, (4) manufacturing can now take place almost anywhere, (5) new organizational structures are emerging, (6) international trade is being liberalized through trade agreements, and (7) company actions are becoming increasingly visible.

In light of this environmental turbulence and competitive intensity, many feel that the only way to succeed today is through learning and adaptation. The simple process of listening to and learning from the customers can be a sustainable competitive advantage that cannot be easily imitated or eroded away by competitors. The ability to learn faster than competitors may be the *only* real source of sustainable competitive advantage in the 21st century. Organizations that are adept at learning are more adaptable to change and are better equipped to undertake the processes of strategic renewal. Strategies can no longer be designed without allowing for and capturing what is emergent in contemporary situations as they unfold.

Innovations, whether they are small changes to products or services or radical innovations of new products or services, better enable businesses to fulfill customers needs. Studies have shown that returns on innovation can account for as much as 50 percent or more of corporate revenue.[3] Continuous innovation is a necessary condition for a focus on total customer satisfaction. Innovation creates new processes, both administrative and technical, that can create and produce products and services in more efficient means.

Some innovations can take a firm to the position of market leader. For example, The Gillette Company's innovative Mach3 and Venus razors, introduced in 1998 and 2001, respectively, currently account for 80 percent of the total blades and handles market.[4] For the first time, a company really studied women and how women view the symbolic act of shaving differently than men (as a necessary evil instead of a symbol of the progression to manhood). Through this attention to the diverse needs of women, Gillette succeeded in distinguishing itself from the competitors in a very mature industry. In contrast, innovations can also occur through new ways of thinking. By taking the focus off of target marketing and putting it on product attributes, Google has revolutionized the advertising industry. Advertisers pay only when their ads (or searches) are clicked. The more that companies spend on their ads, or listings, the more likely their listings are to appear on searches; and the more carefully they define their product attributes, the more likely the consumer will be to find their products online. This innovation in thinking provides Google with over $6 billion annually in total revenues.[5]

The need and the impetus to be innovative have emerged from more than just a desire to create new products that will sell better, therefore increasing profitability. Even in the most low-tech situations, it would be essentially impossible to find an industry that is not engaged in continuous or periodic innovation and reorientation due to the dynamic nature of most markets. Further, intensifying competition and environmental uncertainty has made innovation increasingly important as a means of survival. Innovativeness shows a strong, positive link with performance because innovations serve to accommodate the uncertainties (that is, market and technological turbulence) a firm faces in its environment. Innovations set companies apart from their competitors in turbulent environments. The differentiation that can arise from innovations provides firms with competitive advantages.

Unfortunately, in this era of hypercompetitive and mature markets, most *marketing* programs fall short in terms of innovation and creativity, which results in markets overflowing with very similar "me-too" products and even downright failures. For example, 80 to 94 percent of all new grocery products are outright failures.[6] No one seems to understand all the elements of innovative idea generation. One of the nation's largest health care and beauty aids manufacturers found that almost 95 percent of all its innovations were minor package changes, line extensions, and other incremental improvements. These simple improvements were mostly me-too products that had relatively little effect on the company's bottom line.[7]

Thus, in light of the importance of innovation in the competitive marketplace, it is vital that business owners gain an understanding of how to increase innovative thinking that can lead to a competitive advantage. A solid competitive advantage is one that cannot be easily eroded away by competitors. As companies like the ones used in the previous examples have found out, the innovation of each individual new product or product improvement by itself is not the most important component of the successful business model. Single new products or new product improvements, whether they are tangible products or improvements in services, may easily be copied by the competition.

The key to developing innovative programs does not lie in each single innovation, but instead lies in a company's ability to be innovative on a consistent and continual basis. Firms that have a customer-focused vision realize that their success lies in the processes or capabilities, not specific resources. Once a firm becomes adept at the capabilities or processes that are utilized to create each innovation, they can then use these processes to create other forms of innovative products or services. Thus, the firm's competitive position is not dependent on each single innovation that may succeed or fail. The firm instead builds and attempts to become proficient at the capabilities of the firm, which can then create and consistently renew the firm's strategies and products and, therefore, create constant innovation.

Thus, the firm's competitive advantage becomes the processes or capabilities that create innovation, not the innovations themselves. So, what are these processes? What can we do as a company to find out our customers' needs? How can we fully utilize the full potential of our sales force? As mentioned, adaptability is crucial for a sustainable competitive advantage and success in this century. Salespeople by nature have personality characteristics that make them more likely to be the great innovators of the firm. The following sections explain how salespeople can very specifically first identify the ideal client to provide feedback and then the steps a salesperson must take to get this feedback and ultimately interpret it to help provide better products and services.

THE IDEAL CLIENT

In the early stages of your sales career you are usually forced to grasp onto any piece of business you can get. No matter how small or large the client is, you open it without a single thought about the long-term consequences. What tends to happen is that the first accounts you open receive all of your attention, all your best effort, time, and service. What happens over time is you develop a larger group of clientele with larger average client sizes. When the larger clients start to eat most of your time and the smaller ones no longer receive the service they once did, you start to lose them. This is not necessarily a bad thing, but it is not the ideal situation. You would ideally bring on a partner to continue to give good service to the lower tier of clients or create a team structure so they are provided the attention they deserve. The point is, your ideal client will grow and emerge and change as your business changes, so it is vital that we realize this and learn how to develop a business plan that accommodates this change. The ideal client for any business is a nice person who needs you, appreciates you, is willing to pay for your service, and can make decisions. This is the same for all businesses. Of course we want to deal with only nice people, but we want the customer to need us. If customers need us and we provide the product or service they need with reasonable service, then they will appreciate us. If they appreciate us and feel that we provide a good value, then they are willing to pay for our service or product. To be able to provide excellent service, the person or business has to be able to make decisions in a timely manner. Add to these traits one more very important quality and you have the perfect client: a person who is willing to refer you to other potential clients. If we can replicate this person or business over and over again, this creates opportunities to grow at a more rapid pace than ever found before. The steps to segment accounts are discussed in more detail in the two following chapters.

INTERVIEW YOUR CLIENTS

So how do you ask your clients to help you? What are the different ways of gathering this information? The conservative way is to send out a survey. The most efficient way is to conduct an interview over the phone. The most *effective* way is to sit down with them and conduct a face-to-face interview. This is not to be taken lightly. When important clients take time out of their busy schedules to help you, you owe them the courtesy of sitting down with them, giving them the respect of going to a place they are comfortable, and showing them the appreciation you have for giving you this opportunity. There are many reasons this is so very important; we name a few: First, the client needs to understand how important this feedback is to you. If you send a survey it is very easy for a client to discard it and, quite honestly, view it as a nuisance. If you conduct the interview over the phone, while it saves you time, the same amount of sincerity will not come through over the phone as it would in a face-to-face meeting. Second, the face-to-face interview gives you the opportunity to express your gratitude to the client for being with you.

How do we set up this meeting? By using your segmentation look at all of your "A" clients. Which of them think you are wonderful? Which clients have sent you referrals in the past? Which clients have told you how much they appreciate you, and the service you provide? These are the ones we talk to first. It will make this difficult process a little easier starting with the people who really like you. We can work on tougher challenges later. Now that you have identified a few of your favorite clients, it is time to make phone calls. When you call your clients, tell them you need a favor. "You would like to have their opinion on the service you are currently providing them. As a matter of fact, you are in the process of making your service model more efficient, and you would like to have input from your best clients." Let them know they are one of the best; after all, a little flattery never hurts. Then say, "Would you be willing to share some thoughts with me?"

By doing this, you will get many different responses, but the most typical will be, "ABSOLUTELY!" As you make this call to your lesser clients who do not get as much of your attention, you will receive a different response, which will typically be a pause, with a "why me?" type of comment. There are many ways to look at this. You can shut down, get nervous, and not push the issue, or you can look at this as an opportunity to find out what you have been doing wrong. Spend time with the client to learn what you can do better, and then reestablish the relationship, and make it stronger. The reason your best clients will react favorably is because they have a bond with you on a higher level. They trust you, they understand you, and they appreciate what you offer them, and more importantly, they *know that you appreciate them.* Simply put, people stay where they are appreciated; they go where they are invited. The reason lower-tier clients will not act favorably to this type of questioning is because they do not have this comfort level with you. They do not necessarily feel appreciated; they definitely do not feel important. This is where we discover an opportunity. The client wants to feel important. Clients want attention just the same as we do individually. Give it to them and let them know we hear what they are saying, verbally and nonverbally.

WHAT DO WE ASK?

The answer to this question depends on which response you get to the initial call. The positive response leads to a very direct line of questioning. The negative response offers a challenge in that you need to initially find out what is making the client uncomfortable.

Let us first look at the positive response. When together remind the client why you asked him to meet you. He is here so you can ask questions about the service you have provided him in the past. Not only that, but what changes would he recommend to make it even better. Ask him what he feels differentiates you from your competitors. What you are really asking is why he is doing business with you, but doing so in a way that tells you your competitive advantages. When he offers his suggestions, and opinions, ask him what they mean. Why is it important to him? What we really want to find out is, *Where does he see value in the relationship?* You will hear answers that will surprise you. You will hear answers that will upset you. Either way, we are learning what your clients like and what they dislike about your offering.

Of course answers will differ dramatically depending on your industry, but some of the most common positive responses in financial services include the following: you return phone calls in a timely fashion, your office staff is very supportive, you are consistent in delivery, you help my organization run more efficiently, your prices are better than others, and the consistency of your service allows us to focus on other things that are more important. While all of these are nice responses, which ones carry the most power and meaning? Returning all of the phone calls and a nice office staff should be a given in today's business, but surprisingly this is not the case. Answers like "you help us run more efficiently," or "your consistency allows us to focus on more important things" are much more meaningful. The reason they are so important is that the client is telling you where she sees value in your relationship, she is telling you where you help her the most. She is telling you loud and clear the strongest characteristics of your service model and what it is that makes her stay with you.

A small caveat about comment on price is warranted. Price is a double-edged sword. It is positive from the aspect that you have earned the client's business. But it is a negative from the aspect that he or she will be gone the next time someone offers a better price. Be careful. Instead of stopping on these comments, push a little deeper. Just as in a sales situation, when a prospect starts making price objections, there is usually a much deeper hidden objection that you must find. Also, keep in mind from a competitive standpoint, 21st century strategic business models that have a sustainable competitive advantage are much more likely to be successful if there is a differential advantage. Just having a lower price is not necessarily something that will enable a competitor to keep clients in the long run. If you are truly seeking to learn from your clients, going beyond price and money will almost always enable you to reap richer information.

When a client tells you that you have freed up time for him to concentrate on other things, ask him to give you an example. This is important. It is just like the saying "a picture is worth a thousand words." Stories and examples provide clients the ability to elaborate. When they start elaborating, you have a better chance of uncovering deeper needs and concerns. Also, by digging deeper into the details of each example the client is reinforcing in his own mind how important you are to his business. When he answers a few questions like this, he is ready for you to press forward. This is when you ask if there are other businesses or people that share the same need for a service like the one you provide. Off the top of his head, he may not be able to think of anyone, or any organization, immediately. Give him a moment, and interject by asking, "Do you *feel* it would be a good idea for me to offer my services to others in your field?" He knows the answer is yes, but is he willing to share you with anyone else? You have to ask. If clients are not completely satisfied with your offerings, they will not refer you to someone else. Most clients will say yes and will tell you that it is a good idea that you pursue more opportunities in that field, as long as it is not at their expense. After they have told you about their own field, ask them if there are any related areas that would benefit from your service as well. You will be surprised that many clients at this point put on their thinking cap and start to become your marketing department. They will come up with suggestions you have never thought of. They will come up with specific names for you to call and maybe even make the calls for you to make the introduction.

WHAT HAVE WE LEARNED FROM THIS EXAMPLE?

We have definitely discovered that our clients are willing to help us. They want us to learn. We have learned that our clients have a good understanding of what they need from us. We have found where they see value in our relationship with them. We have found that clients appreciate what we do for them. And finally, we have found that if given the opportunity, our clients may send us referrals based on the service we have provided to them in the past. The key is you have to EARN the right to get the referrals. Remember that 21st century selling is all about the relationship. Referrals are not to be expected; they are to be earned. Clients will give you the opportunity to meet their peers if they feel you will not embarrass them, and if they feel you can truly help others. When you develop the relationship at this level, you know you have a client for life. This is the ideal situation.

LET US NOW TAKE A LOOK AT A NEGATIVE RESPONSE TO OUR INITIAL QUESTION

Keep this in mind. It will be rare that a good client will turn down the opportunity to give you feedback. If a client tells you that she would rather not have this conversation with you, you must do a quick self-analysis to see if this is the type of client who has always been withdrawn, which is all right. Or is this a client who is unhappy, one who feels unappreciated, or mishandled? If this is a client who just truly is not a person who will typically share her opinion, thank the client and move on. If you feel that there is a possibility the client is not happy, this is your opportunity to take a step back and ask the client, "If there is one thing about our relationship you could change, what would it be?" This gives her the opportunity to speak her mind and give you some feedback that will allow you to repair the relationship. There is a good chance the client will tell you there is nothing wrong. But you have to have the courage to push and find out if there is the slightest issue. If there is, and you do not uncover it, eventually another organization will come along with something better, whether it is price, service, reporting, and so forth...and you will lose the client. You must discover what the issue is. Many times, in going through this process, the client will appreciate your effort and will rediscover why she chose to work with you in the first place. This type of communication will repair the relationship and maybe even give you the chance to do more business than what you did in the past with this client.

On the other hand, you may also learn that the client just does not fit your profile anymore and that it may just be best to part ways. This is a tough pill to swallow, but what you will find, in time, is that the sales industry is difficult enough on normal days. If you add to your typical day angry clients, unappreciative clients, clients who are not willing to make decisions, clients who are unwilling to pay, or clients who do not see the value you provide, you will soon be miserable in your position. The point is, work with nice people—people you want to work with, people who are willing to pay for your service, appreciate your time, and are willing to make decisions. We all have had to open accounts and do business with people we do not necessarily like, but if you can minimize this type of person, your days will be better, with much less stress. Chapter 9 will discuss the problem of when to get rid of certain customers in much greater detail.

What have we learned from the negative response? We have learned that negative responses can sometimes create an opportunity—an opportunity to ask the questions about what has happened in the past, and what we can do to fix it, or make it better. We have learned that an unhappy client can be brought back to positive status with proper handling. In fact, sometimes the most loyal customers can be those who had a problem that you corrected. These opportunities can create very strong, long-lasting relationships. We have learned that some clients will just not give feedback. They may just want to keep their opinions to themselves. From them, you must learn by their behavior and reaction to the way you work with them. This may be a big challenge, but it is a skill you must develop to be successful in sales and marketing.

WHAT DO WE DO WITH THIS FEEDBACK?

The reasons for segmenting clients, asking difficult questions, and challenging them to give us detailed answers are to learn more about what will make our business successful, what makes our business vulnerable, and, most importantly, what helps us take better care of our clients. By interviewing each level of client we gain a better knowledge of our service model on all levels. If we were to look only at our top-tier clients, we may get a false sense of reality. Our top clients will typically love us because they are getting all of our attention. Our lower-level clients will typically share their displeasure with us, because their experience is not quite as positive. With the positive comments, what we want to do is obvious. Continue to do it! With the negative comments, correct them! This is not a quick fix. We cannot just flip the switch and be done with what we have done for the entire time it has taken to build a business. We will have to take baby steps. Find the most common complaint and start from there. Once we have solved this issue, we move on to the next common, and so on. By doing this we will gradually improve the quality of service we are providing to each and every client.

THE FOLLOW-UP

The best way to find out if it is working is to go back to the interview section of the process. Go back to the same people we interviewed in the past. First, ask them if they have recognized any of the specific changes we implemented. Then ask if they like these changes. Since they were the ones who suggested the changes, typically the answer will be a resounding yes. If it is not, we have to go back to the interview part and ask what needs to be adjusted. For the most part you will hear many positives. The few negatives you do receive will be from people who just want something to complain about. Most of our clients will be so happy we listened to and executed their suggestions, they will feel closer to us and will appreciate the fact that we care enough to listen. This will prove to be invaluable as the relationship continues to grow—no matter the level of client. They will respect us for listening and for making the effort to follow through.

HOW DO WE IMPROVE OUR BUSINESS BY IMPROVING OUR BEHAVIORS?

Remember that old motto of the 20th century? It is all about location, location, location. There should be a new motto for the 21st century: listen, listen, and listen! Our clients will tell us what we need to do. Listen to their needs, listen to their suggestions, listen to complaints, listen to their compliments, and we will find what it is that they really want. The sales and marketing representative who understands the "gift of gab" is nice to have for social events, but the true art of sales starts with a better understanding of silence. The ability to ask open-ended questions that give clients the opportunity to *share* their thoughts is what will help us understand their true needs. If we ask the right questions, and our line of questioning is leading, we help clients discover that they need us. They realize that we are asking all of the appropriate questions helping them understand that we have the product or service that solves their issues. This allows us to be an advisor, or a valued salesperson, instead of a vendor. Vendors may get business a few times, but they will never be able to hold a candle to a consultative advisor, who is appreciated by the client. Our ability to listen to clients, and interpret clearly what exactly is needed or wanted, gives us the ability to analyze the situation and respond in a more appropriate manner. This behavior creates a better atmosphere for our clients.

Our ultimate goal should be to make our customers feel important, to treat them like no one else will. If our clients feel appreciated, they will stay with us and continue to introduce us to more people who can benefit as well. By taking the measures discussed in this chapter, you will be able to create a business structure that will allow you to be efficient, effective, and successful. We can do this only by learning directly from our clients. And then it is that learning that can help us provide better, more innovative solutions to the needs of our customers. The 21st century is one of rapid change, and we must learn to listen to customers, find out their needs, and incorporate these changes into our business. The independent, creative, risk-taking salesperson is best suited for this job. Successful 21st century companies will realize what a gem they have in their sales forces and utilize this gem to learn from the customer in order to constantly improve their businesses, business models, products, and services.

NOTES

1. The Sales Educators, Strategic Sales Leadership: Breakthrough Thinking for Breakthrough Results (Mason, OH: Thompson Higher Education, 2006).

2. Ibid.

3. Jin K. Han, Namwoon Kim, and Rajendra K. Srivastava, "Market Orientation and Organization Performance: Is Innovation the Missing Link?" *Journal of Marketing* 62, no. 4 (1998): 30–44.

4. Christine Bittar, "Brand Builders,"*Brandweek* 43, no. 5, February 4 (2002): 16–18.

5. David F. Carr, "How Google Works," *Baseline* no. 61, July (2006): 31–47.

6. Robert M. McMath, "Kelloggs Cereal Mates," *Failure Magazine* July (2000) http://failuremag.com/arch_mcmath_kelloggs.html (accessed September 21, 2006).

7. George S. Day, "Feeding the Growth Strategy," *Marketing Management* 12, no. 6, November/December (2003): 15–21.

CHAPTER **8**

KEY ACCOUNT MANAGEMENT IN THE 21ST CENTURY

Ingrid J. Fields, Jason DiLauro, Michael F. d'Amico, and
Linda M. Orr

> The difference between involvement and commitment is like ham and eggs. The chicken is involved; the pig is committed.
>
> —Martina Navratilova

Do you want all of your relationship marketing efforts to pay off with "involved" customers or totally "committed" ones? How loyal are these customers? What value can you gain from identifying these committed customers and excelling at managing them? One of the most rewarding leadership jobs is the management of the firm's largest accounts and the people who handle these. There are several ways to describe these large customers: national accounts, global accounts, complex team selling, solutions delivery sales organization, Top 10, Top 100, and so forth. To simplify this discussion, the term "key accounts" will be used. With so much on the line, this is not a job for the timid in any corporation!

The real work here is to decide to build the firm's offering around the unique needs of these important clients, whether they represent your top revenue, your top profit, or your best new opportunities. No industry seems to have handled these tasks of serving key accounts perfectly, which is amazing because some studies have shown that key accounts can account for more than 95 percent of a firm's total revenue. Many companies do have professional sales organizations and a differentiated service as well as a support program for these accounts. This chapter will outline a few considerations for segmenting and working with key accounts, along with some complex issues related to organizing and managing the salespeople who deal with these accounts.

DETERMINING KEY ACCOUNTS

The first step in key account management is to classify your customers into categories or a ranking system. Most books will outline a list of varying characteristics to do this classification, but the key is that even though classification can be done in many ways, the actual method that you choose depends on what is most important to you and your organization. Remember how important strategy is? It always has to go back to that. What are your goals and objectives, and what do you feel makes the most important customers? Some key criteria used to categorize or rank your clients are (1) how much they pay you, (2) the volume of business they do, (3) the profit margin they are paying, (4) the amount of referrals they have sent to you, (5) the industry type, (6) the demographic characteristics, in terms of individual or organizational buying characteristics, (7) the type of relationship they want, (8) geography, (9) functions and levels and how the businesses handle their purchasing, (10) outsourcing and propensity to involve or not involve you in their key strategic relationships, and even possibly (11) price sensitivity. Keep in mind this list is not exhaustive; it always depends on your organizational objectives.

No matter what the criteria may be, we are trying to discover who our best, and least favorite, clients are and rank them as an A, B, C, or D level client. In this example, we classify by purchase size. We use a business that has annual sales of $1,000,000.00, 100 clients, and has an average client that produces $10,000 in business per year. It is doubtful that every client does precisely $10,000 per year. Realistically, there are a handful of clients who produce $20,000 to $50,000 in business annually and many others who produce $1,000 to $3,000 annually. Using this example an "A" rated client may be any client who produces more than $30,000 per year. A "B" rated client would be a client who produces more than $10,000 to $29,999 per year. A "C" rated client would produce $4,000 to $9,999 per year, and a "D" rated client would be one who produces less than $3,999.

Once we have ranked our clients, we look to see how many fall into each category. Using the same 100 clients as above, let us make the assumption that 8 of the clients are A clients producing a total of $500,000 in sales, 12 are B clients producing $300,000 in sales, and 25 are C clients producing $110,000. the remaining 55 are D's, giving us our remaining $90,000 in sales production. What this tells us is that 80 percent of our sales are coming from 20 percent of our clients, supporting the "80/20 Rule."

There are many things we can do with this information from segmentation. We can modify our service model. We can modify our account minimums. We can look at each category of client and recognize how we landed the client and what the characteristics or traits of the client are. What is the makeup of an "ideal client"? We can exercise this research to help make our sales process more efficient and help us locate more ideal clients. Let us look deeper.

Service Model

What does each client expect and what exactly do they deserve? Every business has a maximum capacity. What we mean by maximum capacity is the point where the business can no longer service, or produce, any more while still remaining effective and providing optimal service. Since we all have the same number of hours in a day, another thing we have to do is establish a service model that provides proper service to each category of client. We cannot provide an A client the same level of service we offer to a D client and expect the A client to be satisfied. While the D client would be enthralled, the idea is to make your business efficient by having less small clients and more big clients. The result of having fewer clients is the ability to give more time to each client and also to free up more time to go find the larger, more ideal client.

Account Minimums

When establishing a business plan there are many components that make it up. One of the components often overlooked is the value of our time. By taking the amount of dollars earned in a year and dividing that by the number of hours worked, we come up with a wage per hour. If we earn $100,000 and worked 2,000 hours, this means we earned $200 per hour. To find out what our account minimum is, we must apply this to the number of clients we have and how much business each client does with us. We then need to calculate how much each client has to generate in sales to pay our hourly wages and expenses. If we use the example from before, making the assumption that we now know what our average client produces and what our top category client produces, we need to establish production minimums for new clients to come on board. If our existing average client produces $10,000, we should make every effort to open accounts only with clients who intend or commit to producing more that $10,000 annually. By establishing a production minimum we continue to raise the average production of our clients.

Marketing

How did we land these clients? When we look at each category of client, it is important to recognize how each category was brought into our business. Was the client a cold call, cold walk, seminar attendee, social prospect, or a person or business that was referred to you? This is all vital information when we are trying to identify key accounts and hopefully replicate our ideal client. Looking at category A, let us make the assumption that of the 8 clients, we discover that 2 of them were cold calls, 2 of them were met through trade shows, and the remaining 4 were introduced by a referral source. In category B we find that out of the 12, 6 are referrals and the others where found in trade shows and a few cold calls as well. We see that the strongest way to land *big* accounts is to be introduced to new prospects by a friend, colleague, or some other center of influence. If we look at categories C and D we may find they were brought in by mailings or some other source that may not have developed the same level of trust and comfort that would earn a larger share of their business. Many professionals will share that when they find a method of marketing that works, you should continue to do the same thing over and over until it does not work anymore. This is definitely true.

Segmentation Shift

This is when you prospect the lower categories to search for more business. By giving them more attention and service, you may create the opportunity to earn more business bringing the C or D client to A or B status. This is a very efficient form of marketing that is effective due to the fact that it is inexpensive and just requires that phone calls are made, follow-up is executed, and a bit of pride is swallowed to get back in front of them. Some clients will be responsive to the newfound attention, some may push back, but the bottom line is that an effort is being made to take care of the customer. The segmentation shift takes place after you start over with the C and D clients. Learn what is important to them and what they want out of the relationship. Then execute by increasing the amount of business they are currently doing to a higher level. When they do more business the status of the clients is increased to a higher level, then justifying a higher level of service.

THE MATH: CALCULATING CUSTOMER LIFETIME VALUE (CLV)

Although we want to think this is all about the relationship, we are not going to be stupid here. Yes, we are creating relationships so that we can make money. One of the most important things that a sales manager can understand is the monetary value of customers. These principles can be applied in unison with key account segmentation strategies to gain a more complete understanding of accounts. As we briefly touched on in Chapter 1, the cost of servicing customers declines over the lifetime of those customers, while purchasing quantities generally tend to increase. Thus, creating loyal relationships with customers increases profitability in two ways: pay less and make more. From a managerial standpoint it is critical to understand this concept in a strict dollar sense. Basically, how much money are you going to make from one customer, for the life of that customer? This is as simple as CLV gets. You analyze the total financial contribution of a customer over his or her lifetime. To calculate this, you take total revenues from a customer minus total costs of that customer.

Unfortunately, as simple as this sounds, and as easy as the math is, coming up with the total revenue and costs can present a challenge. You are required to make certain assumptions about the quantity the customer purchases and the typical life-time of each customer. Then, you have to make assumptions about the total cost of goods sold, the cost of acquiring the customer, and the reoccurring costs to service that customer. CLV is very different from the return on investment (ROI), and it is important to understand this. Many astute salespeople will turn away from an account by looking at ROI, whereas CLV shows a very different picture.

Consider the owner of a local restaurant. He knows that Mr. and Mrs. Jones come to eat at the restaurant every Monday night and spend an average of $30 at each meal. Mr. Jones was the type that was hard to satisfy. Usually, the servers just made jokes about his not-so-pleasant demeanor and took the necessary efforts to placate him. But, on one particular evening, Mr. Jones sent his meal back to the kitchen to be recooked five times. After realizing that the five recooked steaks cost the restaurant an average of $10 a steak, thus representing a loss of $50 for that eve-ning, the manager went to Mr. Jones, explained that the restaurant just simply could not satisfy their needs, and maybe it would be better for the Joneses to not return.

At the time that this occurred, the couple had already spent approximately $11,000 ($30 a meal * 52 weeks a year * 7 years = $10,920) at the restaurant over the course of the last seven years. The manager did not consider the fact that the average couple living in the community tended to frequent the restaurant for about 15 years. Thus, refusing to lose $50 in steaks that one evening caused the company to lose an added $12,570 in revenues over a period of the remaining eight years.

This is not a black-and-white situation though. How often does Mr. Jones send his steak back? Do they often eat meals that have a high margin or a low margin? If the Joneses are water and entrée people, they are probably causing the restau-rant to lose money in the long term. If they are heavy drinkers or frequently order appetizers and dessert, they would more likely be worth keeping. The point is, the good sales manager looks at customers over the total lifetime of customers, not just each unique sales transaction. Likewise, good sales managers also consider the referral chain. Maybe the Joneses are not profitable customers. However, maybe they tell their entire church of 2,000 members every Sunday that the best restaurant in town is this particular restaurant. Then, does it become worthwhile? Managers must collect and consider all this information when making key account decisions. Once you have determined the CLV for an account, you can then go about making key strategic decisions, such as the ones listed below.

1. How much should we spend to acquire new customers?
2. How much service should we give each customer? The answer to this question also incorporates the question, how much should we spend to maintain each customer in terms of time and money?

3. Should we be more concerned about retention or acquisition? In some industries, or during certain times, it actually may be more profitable to spend more efforts on acquiring new customers.

4. How long are we keeping customers? And on that note, how long are our competitors keeping their customers?

5. What is the true picture of our referral chain?

Once these key strategic issues have been addressed, now we can examine some of the 21st century rules about key accounts. Being a key account manager or deciding how to organize your sales force across key accounts takes some special consideration. Before we cover this, let us review the basics of organizing the sales force.

ORGANIZING THE SALES FORCE

Just as we organize accounts, we need to organize our sales force to best suit the needs of each customer. Calling regularly on the same organizations and individuals leads to a better understanding of their problems and needs and provides sales representatives with an opportunity to develop personal relationships with clients. Further, some form of organization is required to prevent several company representatives from calling on the same customers where this is unnecessary. Duplication of calls is a waste of resources and may annoy clients.

The specific accounts and prospects assigned to a salesperson comprise the sales territory. A sales territory is commonly thought of as a geographical area. Territories are not always so defined, however. In addition to geographically defined sales territories, they may also be determined according to customer type, product line, or selling task. Every method of creating territories has advantages and disadvantages. Whatever the method employed, the characteristics and needs of the customers served should always take precedence over the convenience of the sales force.

Geographically Based Sales Territories

Sales personnel are frequently assigned to particular geographical sales territories. District sales managers and regional sales managers, who are held accountable for the activity of sales personnel operating within specific areas, are referred to as *field* sales managers because of their direct concern with salespeople out in the field. Their primary concern is management of the field sales personnel who report to them. Much attention has been given to the design of geographic sales territories. A number of variables must be considered as the market is being "cut up" into sections for assignment to individual sales representatives. Clearly, even though each company's situation is different, all companies must weigh similar factors when determining geographic sales territories. A major concern is creating territories that are roughly equal in terms of physical size, number of current and potential customers, general economic condition, current sales volume, and future sales potential.

Personnel problems result when one salesperson gets a "bad" territory and another gets the "best" territory. Plus, this method does nothing to integrate the goals of our key accounts. Thus, equality and fairness are important goals in establishing territories. A related goal is the development of geographic territories that allow the sales manager to maintain as close a working relationship with the sales representatives as necessary. In some cases, the relationship may primarily involve telephone conversations and the filing of reports rather than actual face-to-face meetings. For example, in sparsely populated portions of the western United States, consumer goods companies such as P&G-Clairol, Inc. typically have very large territories, which may include Montana, Idaho, Wyoming, the Dakotas, Nebraska, and parts of other states. When a sales territory is that large, the opportunity for close personal contact between supervisor and salesperson is small. Personal encounters may be limited to occasional meetings at the home office. To encourage closer contact between sales manager and sales representatives, some firms require that the manager periodically travel with individual salespeople. This time together traveling and calling on accounts provides great opportunities for sales managers to serve as role models.

Sales Territories Organized by Customer Type

When a sales organization specializes by customer type, two or more salespeople may cover the same geographical area. For example, a chemical manufacturer may have one sales representative call on users of petrochemicals in the Southwest and another representative call on users of other chemicals in this region. Similarly, a textbook publishing company may cover Georgia with one sales representative who calls on business and engineering professors and another who deals with professors in colleges of arts and sciences. In both cases, more than one representative of the same company may call on a single organization, and the representatives may call on different individuals within this organization. Obviously, decision makers at both the chemical company and the publisher believe that their customers are better served by dealing with a salesperson who is a specialist rather than a generalist. Yet even when salespeople are assigned by customer type, the matter of geography still enters the picture. The bookseller specializes by buyer type within a specific area, as do the chemical company's representatives. Thus, the sales force is organized through a combination of geography and customer type. In fact, the inescapability of the geographic factor makes a combination approach the most commonly employed method of assigning sales territories.

Sales Territories Organized by Product Line

Within large, multiproduct companies, it is not uncommon for each division or product line to have its own sales force. As with organization by customer type, the emphasis is on specialization. Multiline organizations often find that their salespeople must know a great many technical details about their products and customers. The need to remember too many details about too many products will almost certainly reduce the salesperson's ability to sell a product effectively.

The net result of specialization may be a situation in which several sales representatives from a single company call on the same client organization. However, as with organization by customer type, the specialized nature of the products may be reflected in a similar specialization by the buyers. Thus, a single purchaser may not have to deal with several representatives of the same firm.

Sales Territories Organized by Selling Task

Sales forces can also be organized according to selling task. This method has a big potential upside and some potential problems as well. The logic for organizing by selling task is that not all salespeople are good at doing the same things. Some salespeople are judged to be best at sales development. They are pioneers who specialize in bringing in new accounts and could be described as especially proficient as "hunters." Others seem to perform best at sales maintenance and account management. That is, they are really good at calling on existing accounts and making sure that these customers continue to purchase the products being offered. In contrast to the previously described hunters, people who are good at account maintenance might be described as "farmers." Individual attitudes, aptitudes, and personalities play a part in determining who fills each of these important roles.

The potential problems here include poor hand-off between salespeople and a lack of knowledge transfer across the two groups of salespeople. There is also usually a different compensation method across the two different markets, and this can cause potential morale problems, especially since the size of the average sale is usually large for the hunter and often smaller but more frequent for the farmer.

TEAM SELLING ASSIGNMENTS

There has been a recent trend of the 21st century to form teams to handle key accounts, instead of making individual territory decisions. Why would it make sense to put highly competitive Type A players together on the same selling team? Because it is possible to get more from them: sometimes one plus one equals three. In other words, if you can take people who had individually produced say $2,000,000 per year in revenue and put them together to serve on a key account selling team that produces far more than $2,000,000 per team member in sales revenue, then there is a good chance that a team approach to key account selling would be a good way to use their skills.

How is this best done? Picking the right players and leader/managers with access to company support is the key to success. Big expectations are important right from the beginning, but so is access to company executives and a company-wide respect for what these teams are trying to do for the company. When the senior author was in the technology field, she worked as a key account manager and had access to anybody doing research in our research and development group. If her firm's direction on a new product development area was important to the client, the product manager and development team would get involved to do a nondisclosure briefing if the client was willing to sign and honor their nondisclosure agreement. They were not selling a new product. Instead, they were strategizing with an important customer to help plan a mutually beneficial course of action. The customer did not "bid out" its next generation of equipment purchases; we were already developing its next generation for it. What a great benefit for both companies!

Generally the typical structure of a key account selling team is one senior account manager along with a junior account executive or two who are assisted by a supporting engineer or other form of technical resource that is shared across a few teams. Each member of this group reports to the same executive who leads several teams about this size. Multi-level sales teams can be so very good for developing customer relationships, in revenue growth, and also as a way to help develop members of the sales force.

This is often part of the value-added program components for a customer designated a key account. When the senior author worked in technology sales, one major employer in her sales territory clearly informed her that one of its expectations of us was to be served by this kind of account team. Its chief technology leader often told her that he paid our prices because she saved him headcount. As long as her team delivered the help and support he needed, he could justify buying from the market leader and paying our company for the products, services, and maintenance support he needed across the country. As their locations expanded through organic growth and an aggressive acquisition strategy, she enjoyed $3–$6 million more each year from this account, plus a very nice residual base, which also grew every year. It was a win-win situation for everybody involved.

Another differentiating question relative to the development of a key account strategy would be if your customers need centralized project management for your products, logistics, delivery, or other offers. For example, there are several financial services companies that insist on standardization. Every branch has to have the same technology, security, Internet connections, furniture, and so forth. You have probably also been to these places, such as a branch office, as a customer and you have seen the brand identification that these standards reflect to customers.

Several times, these key vendor battles were fierce for large deals because so many locations were involved, and the winning company received all the location orders as a single "deal." The winning strategy can be to include exceptional project management with status meetings, branch office templates, and a specific and customized ordering process with project manager oversight. For me, many times this has been a winning strategy when selling to large, multilocation key accounts. Again, we were trading our headcount and experience for a price decision. *Please realize that this does not always work!* But even an occasional success can represent large amounts of sales revenue and profit.

Some clients want to prove their personal worth to their employer by squeezing the breath out of any vendor, getting a real deal from a starving vendor, or generally buying the most stripped-down version with no support from your staff. They probably do not merit key account status. That is okay; just know what the customer's buying behavior is and decide to bid or not bid for his or her next project ahead of time. You have time and talent and worth as a knowledgeable industry player. Decide and implement your sales strategy; understand which accounts to open and develop and which accounts to fire. See Chapter 9 in this volume for more discussion on this topic.

TEAM OR INDIVIDUAL QUOTAS AND PERFORMANCE MEASURES

This is trickier than it appears. Good compensation practices could be the subject of an entire book. The problem with giving everyone on the team compensation tied to the "big" number of the entire account is that within six months human behavior will drive salespeople to comment on who is most responsible for bringing in the results and who is not. Pay is very personal, is is not? For example, the complaints can include the following: "my spouse will notice if I earn less," "my bills will be a problem," and so forth.

If there is a strong respect for the role each member is playing and for the skills and leadership of the team, then the problem is smaller and can be looked at more in terms of the timing and performance needed to produce revenue over the years for mutual success. From a measurement perspective it is hard to select one weak team member at times if only one quota is used. The opposite problem is that individual quotas do not encourage sharing and building positioning for the common good of the business results.

There are many ways to make compensation so complex that it does not provide any motivation. Often, the combination of individual performance and team quotas is not dealt with very well. Pay can include an ongoing services revenue reward for encouraging longevity of client relationship and a new business component measurable by all team members individually. In addition, a team bonus can be offered if the team hits the numbers.

It is rare to find such a clear yet comprehensive plan. When management finds a good compensation plan that works in a multiplayer team environment, it should be kept. Changing plans every year is silly if the business is meeting its goals while account managers and clients are happy with the situation. On the other hand, to bring other people under the motivational umbrella, most plans do need to be reviewed for changing business goals every two to three years. Look at poor results as an opportunity to review compensation. As a wise CEO once told me, any compensation plan that is not linked to business strategy is a waste of paper.

Another consideration should be the provision of incentives throughout your business, with a special focus on all customer-facing positions. Again back to our favorite CEO and his strategy concepts, make sure that a cohesive program motivating and rewarding the right behavior is directly linked to the business goals and is strongly communicated to everyone. A favorite example comes up for discussion every year or two as a really hot issue.

Should the engineers who do presale design work be paid an incentive? One view is that they do not have direct control of the client relationship is one view. On the other hand, the engineers have very little risk. Yet a third perspective is that they might overbuild the needed design. How about the contracts and pricing teams, would they look the other way if they had a personal incentive at stake?

While all these issues are valid points to consider, we encourage working through the details for equity and contribution but get everyone in an incentive program tied to the key initiatives of the company. From a personal growth and satisfaction perspective, the "best years" in a sales career occur when there is a clear vision, when everyone understands the mission, and performance indicators like pay are leveraged to reward this performance. There should also be a clear set of cultural values shared among a diverse, energized workforce pulling in the same direction.

As described in the previous chapters, shareholders receive value when employee satisfaction leads to and is additive with customer satisfaction. When everyone has clear performance objectives that are reviewed on a structured and a predictable basis, and when compensation incentives are an upside result for us personally, groups usually meet business goals. It is worth considering the introduction of these concepts into your business. There are many good books and available articles in this area. One of our favorites is *Recognizing and Rewarding Employee Performance* by R. Brayton Bowen.[1]

BUSINESS ACUMEN NEEDS

Higher-level skills are needed for selling in a large, complex key account environment. That does not mean that key account teams are better people or even better salespeople. It means that each aspect of their work with clients is more complicated and they have to focus on performing fewer activities, each with more time and effort being required in order to succeed.

A priority area in terms of skill improvement for members of key account teams is the development of business acumen. The ability to understand a client's business strategy and the associated financial position will enable members of the key account team to better partner with the buying organization. If you can have a meaningful discussion with the CFO at the key account about his or her pain points, then you will stand out from competing vendors.

Let us review a few basics that are needed when dealing with any strategic account. First, what is the client's organizational structure? This will provide information about how to pair employees of the selling team to members of the buying team. Second, is this a privately held business with family or investor backing, or a publicly traded corporate organization with shared central services such as human resources, purchasing, and information technology? The type of ownership can have a huge impact on how best to help members of the buying team move forward in the purchasing process. Other ownership structures that can complicate the selling process include limited partnerships such as an LLC (limited liability company), which is common among large law firms, not-for-profit holding companies such as hospitals and other medical delivery organizations, or a charitable organization with or without agency affiliation, such as the United Way or a religious organization.

A third issue that needs to be determined is the client's decision criteria for making major purchases. For example, is an internal payback period calculated for this type of a decision?

Is an IRR (Internal Rate of Return) computed and expected for a positive decision? What is the customer's internal cost of capital? Does the organization's board have a mandatory voting process on decisions over a certain amount? What are the hurdle rates or other necessary measurements for its internal evaluation of major purchases?

Some other important questions revolve around how internal processes work in the customer's business and include the following:

- What and where is the fulfillment or manufacturing of goods and services?
- Are sales done directly or through channels and what segments are targeted?
- Have the revenue and profit goals been met over some historic view?
- Do operations teams deliver customer support?
- How do they retain clients, and are clients identifiable in a database?
- Is cash flow and billing a metric for this organization? Profitability?

Systemic thinking about these processes within a client's business is absolutely required to automate, improve, or differentiate your interactions with them. Your key account team will reap tremendous rewards from a better understanding of the client's operations.

SALES CYCLES AND OTHER DEADLY DISEASES

A real problem that many key account teams often face is the tendency to focus all efforts on making the single "big deal" without earning smaller revenue streams on a more frequent basis. This is a huge but common mistake that is often made by key account teams. It is not okay to avoid analysis of sales funnels and other activity management tools because the customer is sizable or because one proposal has really large revenue potential.

Please consider the following. We learn that a large replacement of current equipment is scheduled to be discussed with senior-level decision makers, and we are told that decisions can be expected in about 12 months. Our account team members consider themselves to be well respected by the users and middle managers in the customer's organization, but few transactions have been actually occurring. We do not know our share of the customer's available spending. These middle managers make it known that they will be most influential in all evaluations and recommendations and that they would not look kindly on any vendor's attempts to bypass them and directly contact senior management. Repeated attempts to engage in systematic planning with the client and invitations for them to meet your senior managers have are not been successful.

In this scenario, if the account team members are waiting, hoping, or even praying that the big deal will be theirs and are therefore not focused on smaller wins in this account along the way, the funnel will produce no sales for a long time and possibly never. This does not have to be the case. While it takes a lot of the selling firm's resources to support a major revenue opportunity, there are many ways to ensure ongoing sales and consistent revenue over time. There are many books that detail methods for moving a sales opportunity forward in small but measurable ways to help the team determine if it is making progress understanding the client needs and if it is in a position to win the big deal. We particularly like the book titled *Customer Centric Selling* by Michael T. Bosworth and John R. Holland.[2] Continuing to work toward achieving these small wins will help to develop a better understanding of the client's processes and to further develop the relationship with the client's staff. Working with more than one account will help generate income from other sources just in case the big project is not funded by the client or your team is not the one selected. In any event, sales cycles and sales funnels should be reviewed across all sales territories and account sizes.

KEY ACCOUNT MEETING FORUMS

Outside of the key account context, most firms employ a marketing strategy emphasizing advertising. For key accounts, however, the marketing strategy should be somewhat different from the firm's more broadly based general advertising plans. Often, marketing to key accounts includes potentially a number of different types of meetings. Part of the process for building a key account program as something special and unique with a particular client is to share information in a way that is relevant and desired by the customer. The best way to get what you need is to simply ask the customer. We get into very detailed positioning discussions about this process in the next few pages and determining who within the customer organization should be asked would be relevant as we think about positioning. Information sharing by your firm and its key accounts can occur in a variety of ways, and there are many different approaches to this important activity. Here are a few examples that often seem to meet with some success.

User Groups

Whatever it may be called, programs known as user groups or another similar name provide an opportunity to have executive speakers and industry leaders speak to large groups of customers about the future in terms of the big picture. This forum can also provide direction by offering small group specialty education topics about the uses, benefits, or service of key products, especially new ones. Usually an attractive location and a few good meals or refreshments help attract a good audience and make this a useful communication forum with key account personnel.

Many customers learn from other customers, and this can provide an overall positive influence on buying behaviors among customers. Some companies struggle with services or product delivery issues, and these become a focus for some customers at such meetings and they appreciate the opportunity to be "heard" by senior leaders in the vendor organization. There are many benefits from hosting a national event such as the chance to get all of your customers together. Such meetings can also diffuse dissatisfied customers because you have a productive mechanism for listening to their feedback.

Executive Briefings and Product Seminars

An executive briefing can be an effective way to communicate a higher level of partnering with large customers. Executive briefings should be used to set the direction and facilitate a more strategic discussion with your customers about what your company offers and why it is relevant to the business initiatives of those customers. This should be a highly customized meeting with advance planning and heavy input from the key account team. Product seminars, on the other hand, are not usually tailored to a single customer and its situation but could still be highly informative for the right customer personnel, such as administrators and purchasing and procurement teams.

Shared Expectation Meetings

These forums can be very good for the relationship between an important customer and a strategic vendor. Generally these meetings are more effective when held periodically as part of the routine sales process and not as a sudden or one-time venting meeting. There are consultants, facilitators, and coaches who can be retained to moderate these meetings. Henson and Associates, for example, based in Dayton, Ohio, specializes in this field.[3] At least one customer has even written a book on how to partner with Henson and Associates. The tri-service committee of the Air Force, Army, and Navy prepared a book titled *Partnering Guide,* which even includes an explanation on how to organize and run a "partnering workshop."[4]

STRUCTURING THE KEY ACCOUNT TEAM

There are many good approaches to organizing the people who will work together to serve a key account. The two most important methods include what has come to be called the ladder and the account ownership models.

The Ladder Model

As previously described, several people from the selling firm are likely to be involved in servicing a key account. One major skill needed is for the senior account manager to be a team leader for his company. Part of this leadership of the team involves assigning roles and responsibilities for each person who works to serve the client. Using a ladder model means that every functional person in the selling firm's organization has an equivalent contact in the customer's business. For example, the sales engineer has a relationship with the buyer's technical staff. Another example would be for your back office or sales administration person to develop a relationship with someone who works in purchasing within the client organization. To continue this line of reasoning, your sales manager would meet with the influencers within the customer organization and your top executive would get to know his or her counterpart within the client's business.

There are several advantages of the ladder model as a way to organize these relationships. For example, the major players should have empathy for each other. In addition, useful and valid information about decision processes, budgets, and allegiances can more readily be exchanged. If personnel problems develop, they can be identified quickly and resolved. Another outcome of this approach to organizing the efforts is that your organization should develop a culture that is customer focused because everyone has a linkage to his or her equivalent in the other organization.

Of course, the laddering concept is not without its drawbacks. One disadvantage is that the role of the account manager is not as prestigious as in the account ownership model. In addition, customers can become confused about who within the selling organization should be contacted when a concern arises. Furthermore, accountability can become a problem when revenue declines or the relationship sours because it is hard to pinpoint who within the selling firm dropped the ball.

Many companies do not have a local customer-service person assigned to each customer because these functions have been centralized at the firm's headquarters or at a call center. Sometimes, there simply is no customer support provided at all. The account manager still needs to have ownership of the quota and the overall quality of the account relationship even in the ladder model. It is important for success of the key account manager to discuss these issues with his or her internal team even at the interview stage if appropriate. In addition, there needs to be a match of the selling firm's culture with customer expectations and culture.

Account Ownership Model

A different approach to structuring the key account management team is to use the account ownership model. We prefer a culture in which all levels of the client organization consider the account manager as the "go-to person." That does not mean the account manager is responsible to actually perform all of the work by himself or herself. Rather, it means that all functional areas in the selling firm that touch base with the key account and provide deliverables understand that the account manager is the central coordinator of this buyer-seller interface. As the central coordinator, the account manager needs to communicate his or her expectations of being informed of all opportunities and concerns.

Let us look at Sally and her strategic account leadership for a financial services customer, which is also one of the largest employers in her town. She has worked with the buyers of her product for years and knows the client organization's buying criteria as well as its financial decision processes for large and small purchases. Her team is pursuing revenue opportunities in several business units of the key account, and in team meetings the members share information and update Sally so she can direct strategy and keep her main contacts informed. She also is seen as the resource manager by her company and when Sally has specific needs she is able to articulate the type of resources needed and for what duration. For example, if an extra engineer or a product specialist for an emerging technology is needed for her client's project from design through installation at ten different locations, then Sally's management can see a payback for such staffing for the account compared to needs elsewhere within the selling firm.

Sally would introduce her senior-level executives to the people on the top floor at the customer's home office. She has specific business goals for these meetings and takes the time to identify key concerns for each executive and also ensures the personal compatibility across the players within this environment. Schedules are discussed and meetings are booked on both sides for the various forums such as dinner meetings, executive briefings, and golf or other sporting event of common interest.

Every executive gives feedback individually to Sally on how the client's needs are being met and where they see an opportunity to further serve this client. These executives also are Sally's internal escalation point should a serious problem occur in serving the customer. Let us further explore an example since this scenario is very common.

Sally has a need for operational improvement in customer support to a key account. The selling firm's invoicing system has developed an accuracy problem and billing cycles are out of step as a result. Overdue notices and fines are being delivered automatically without justification. The customer is unhappy about its current need to expend staff time simply to prove to the selling firm that the invoices it has received are not correct. Furthermore, it is, of course, also concerned at the potential for negative consequences to their credit ratings or reputation.

Unfortunately, this scenario is a very real example that happens far too frequently in the real world. In this case, if Sally cannot pull together the internal billing managers and quickly persuade them to fix this internal problem, it will hurt Sally's credibility at customer meetings. Maybe the billing managers can also host update calls on clearing the list of issues, maybe Sally wants to have a temporary customer-service person dedicated to the account until this problem is fixed, or maybe Sally wants her boss to be sitting at the table for discussions with the customer. There are many ways to handle an issue affecting customer satisfaction that puts your revenue at risk. The account manager and the team need to support each other in communicating these dissatisfiers, but ultimately it is the account manager as team leader that has to own his or her employer's response to the problem. Occasionally grumbling can be heard from members of the account team that they should not be held accountable when someone else within the company "messes up," but when the customer is not well served, all team members of the selling firm suffer the consequences.

There are a number of advantages to the use of the account ownership model. First, this is a highly effective way to run an account program because there is clear ownership and responsibility or accountability. In addition, if the account manager is highly persuasive, members of the selling team can be influenced to provide excellent customer service. Furthermore, there is often better and more frequent executive positioning on a consistent basis, which leads to a better understanding of the client's needs. This leads to more opportunities for moving from a commodity to a differentiated type of selling situation. Last, there is the opportunity for clear communication and information exchange within the relationship.

Disadvantages of the account ownership approach include the fact that sales resources can get tied up in operational or delivery problems. Unfortunately, the key account manager may be perceived as being linked to his or her employer's problems even when this is not the case. That can harm the relationship between the key account manager and members of the buying team. Another disadvantage is that of free riding. Weak players can hide on a successful team, which can make performance review difficult. Finally, recruitment of key account managers may be difficult because the firm will need to recruit account managers who are effective leaders with high-level business management skills.

CUSTOMER SATISFACTION AND RELATIONSHIP MANAGEMENT FOR CAREER SALES

The authors have heard some of the best motivational speakers in the business. At sales conferences we have learned about great programs on expectation management, customer satisfaction, and many other related topics. Some of these presentations were performed in huge auditoriums on several digital screens at once with music and other visuals as a part of the show.

The very best speech we have ever heard on customer satisfaction, however, was short, very direct, and delivered without any audio or visual support. A very wise Business School Dean who used to work in sales gave a powerful talk on the reasons why selling is one of the highest calling professions. He outlined several examples of building a territory leading to building a business leading to building a life. He had a room full of stuffed suits on the verge of tears as he described customer service that will keep your relationship intact during the rough years with some customers. He shared how a competitor had developed better physical products than his employer offered within a key niche, how legal fussing almost ruined a long-standing revenue stream and professional relationship. He had worked under managers who did not seem to understand or want to have customer contact at any level. Some did not see marketing or sales as strategic, but he outlasted them.

He coached more than one account executive who just did not understand his role in customer service. "Why else are WE HERE?" his voice boomed with a stern and questioning look at our group. Our job is to humbly serve our clients, manage and mentor our salespeople fairly, and to develop winning strategies with our employers. It is that simple and the Dean made a compelling case that this hard work is also the most rewarding financially as well as personally due to the relationships that we can develop. We are sold and hope that you are, too.

NOTES

1. R. Brayton Bowen, *Recognizing and Rewarding Employees* (New York: McGraw-Hill, 2000).

2. Michael T. Bosworth and John R. Holland, *Customer Centric Selling* (New York: McGraw-Hill, 2004).

3. Henson and Associates, "Services," http://www.hensonassoc.com/services.asp (accessed July 21, 2006).

4. Tri-Service Committee of the Air Force, Army, and Navy, *Partnering Guide,* http://www.p2pays.org/ref/22/21476.pdf (accessed July 21, 2006).

CHAPTER 9

WHEN DO YOU GET RID OF THE CUSTOMER?

Jay Prakash Mulki

All customers are equal but some customers are less equal.
—Adapted from George Orwell's *Animal Farm*

Marketing is about managing profitable customer relationships. The basic premise of marketing is to identify a segment of customers, to identify their needs and wants, and to supply the goods and services that match those needs. It is about meeting the needs and wants, but also exceeding their expectations in order to create satisfied customers.

Managers believe that when customers are satisfied, they are more likely to return to the firm. They will continue to buy goods and services and thereby develop an ongoing relationship with the company. Satisfied customers are also more likely to recommend both products and the company to others. The firm thereby grows its business by supplying products and services to existing customers, as well as to new customers. Thus, the marketing activity is an exchange process.

This exchange process contributes to profit when the supplier collects payments. As a result, the company's market share grows and the number of customers increases. This in turn should cause the firm to experience higher revenues and higher profits. In view of this, managers put premiums on strategies that lead to both new customer acquisition and higher market share, which thereby positively contributes to business growth. The underlying assumption is that more customers mean higher profits.

Unfortunately, this is not always true. The reality is that all customers do not necessarily contribute to profit. Having more customers does not necessarily mean more profits. In fact, some customers can create losses. For example, maximizing market share may not lead to higher profits if this increased market share was achieved through large price reductions. So, while providing great service and creating satisfied customers is considered a good strategy to grow business, trying to please all customers may not necessarily be a sound business decision. Firms are finding that some of the customers who are being wooed by great products and service promotions are, in fact, distracting from profit.

Recent industry reports showed that while the top 20 percent of the customers generate most of a firm's profit, the bottom 20 percent may actually be taking it away.[1] A recent analysis of customers in a major bank in Australia revealed that 12 percent of its customers contributed to the bulk of the profits, 60 percent were at a break-even level, and the remaining 28 percent cost the bank money.[2] In the case of one of the largest banks in the United States, only 6 percent of the customers were the most profitable. On average, they produced $1,600 in revenue and cost $350 to serve. Compared to this, 14 percent of customers contributed to loss and produced only $230 in revenue while costing $700 to serve.[3] The percent of profitable customers varied from a mere 7 percent of the customers for a software company to 16 percent for a media company.[4] Unprofitable customers are present in almost all industry segments.

The previous chapters have discussed various strategies used by the companies to increase market share and grow the business through successful sales and sales management strategies. These strategies include programs such as relationship marketing and key account management programs with views on how to acquire and retain customers. These processes require companies to make resource allocation decisions in order to implement these programs. Firms have to differentiate themselves in providing customized solutions to their target markets. Good marketing is about selecting target segments based on need and potential value, then aligning segment needs with specific offers that can be profitably delivered.

The effectiveness of managers and their sales strategies is ultimately reflected in the profitability of the firm. However, if the company's cost of serving the customers exceeds the margin from that sales revenue, then increased retention will decrease the value instead of adding to the profitability of the firm. Keeping this in mind, in order to be effective, it is not enough to have a sound customer acquisition policy. Managers should also consider dumping unprofitable customers as a viable strategy for improving profitability.

In this chapter we take a closer look at customer profitability and its impact on business results. We also examine why getting rid of some customers is a practical option for improving overall profitability of the business. This closer look at customers should help marketers realize that to be effective, they have to be selective about whom they serve. In order to be more selective, they will need to implement a number of initiatives to ensure this selectivity. They have to be able to group customers by profitability. They need to identify and separate profitable from unprofitable customers. They have to devise programs to convert unprofitable customers into profitable customers. They also have to develop programs to get rid of customers when they cannot be made profitable. They have to devise strategies to make unprofitable customers voluntarily walk away from the firm and its products without creating negative publicity.

In particular, we explore the following questions:

- Why do some customers not produce any or adequate profits?
- Who are these unprofitable customers?
- What should the managers do with unprofitable customers?
- What are the strategies to convert unprofitable to profitable customers?
- Is getting rid of unprofitable customers the only option?

THE ABC'S OF CUSTOMERS

As described in the previous chapters, the focal point that drives the idea of segmentation is that not all *customers* are equal. *Customers* have to be different in order for segmentation to work. As a general practice, businesses divide their customers into A, B, and C categories by the amount of business each of these customers generates. Firms build their marketing plans and resource allocation decisions based on this grouping. Group A customers are a few very large customers that contribute significantly to company sales. Group B customers are a more substantial number of customers that contribute moderately to sales revenues. Group C customers are very large in number, but with very low per capita purchases. The pie charts in Figure 9.1 show the number of customers and their contributions to the revenue in 2005 for a company that supplied energy products to customers in a city located in the western United States.

In this company, customers in Group A account for less than 1 percent by number, but contribute about 49 percent of the sales revenue. These customers deserved and are provided with special treatment by the firm. The marketing

Figure 9.1
The ABC's of Customers

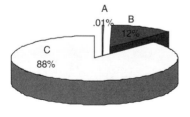
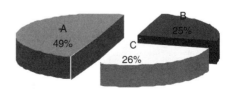

Number of Customers   Contribution to Revenue

department develops special programs and offers for them while assigning their top salespeople to these firms in order to provide the best service. Group B customers account for about 12 percent of total customers and contribute about 25 percent of sales revenue. They are generally treated well, but are allocated less senior salespeople and are dealt with only on an as-needed basis. Group C customers account for about 88 percent of the total number of customers and generate about 26 percent of revenue. While not entirely ignored, these customers get the minimum necessary amount of attention.

While we just saw this approach explained in the previous chapter, there is a missing piece of the puzzle. The above approach overlooks one important criterion: profitability of the customers. This grouping just by sales revenue or by size alone can represent misdirected attention. While large customers and higher revenues are generally associated with higher profits, this is not necessarily the case. This is especially true if these big customers are more demanding, insist on onerous levels of service, or are chronic late payers. It is also possible that some of the very large accounts may require heavy sales support with experienced account managers, participation by high-level executives, and custom design services. Each of these demands can contribute to erosion of margins if not managed properly.

To address this, in addition to grouping customers by revenue, some firms have now decided to further differentiate between profitable and unprofitable customers within each of these groups. Then managers can customize services in an effort to provide a higher standard of quality to their best and most profitable customers to preempt their defection. They also have to understand why some of the customers are unprofitable in order to possibly convert them into profitable customers. If such efforts do not succeed, then managers have to decide how and when to let unprofitable customers go.

CUSTOMER PROFITABILITY

I run my company with this saying: volume is vanity, and profit is sanity.
—Brad Skelton, Managing Director, Skelton Tomkinson,
a shipping, earthmoving, mining, and construction machinery company

Customers differ by the size and number of orders, the number of required sales visits, and the use of customer service, returns, and follow-ups. Even when they are buying the same product, at the same price and volume, and generating the same overall margin, two customers may provide different profitability due to differing costs. Research showed that at the individual customer level, the cost of selling can vary from 3.6 percent to over 300 percent of the revenue. At the same time, customer profitability can vary from about −260 percent to +60 percent of sales revenue.[5]

Profit is the difference between the net revenue realized and the total cost of actually providing and serving the customer with the product or service. At a broad level, total cost includes cost of goods sold and selling costs.

$$\text{Profit} = \text{Sales Revenue} - \text{Total Cost.}$$

We define gross margin as sales revenue minus the cost of goods sold (COGS).

$$\text{Gross Margin} = \text{Sales Revenue} - \text{COGS.}$$

Profit margin is calculated as the difference between gross margin and the selling costs.

$$\text{Selling Costs} = \text{Sales Costs} + \text{Service Costs} + \text{Cost of Credit.}$$

$$\text{Profit Margin} = \text{Gross Margin} - \text{Selling Costs.}$$

Suppliers make a profit when the net sales revenue realized is more than the total cost. Profit becomes negative or the firm loses money when the total cost exceeds the sales revenue. Generally, firms set a selling price above these costs in an attempt to generate a profit.

Let us illustrate this with a simple example. Take the case of customer A in the illustration below. The sales revenue from the customer is more than the total of cost, which includes COGS and selling costs (sales cost + service cost). A transaction with this customer produces a profit for the company because the overall margin exceeds the selling costs. Thus, customer A is a profitable customer. In the case of customer B, the sales revenue is less than the total of COGS plus sales plus service costs. Because of this we can classify customer B as an unprofitable customer. While COGS is the same in both transactions, the second transaction loses money because of higher selling costs. These could be due to any number of reasons including too many service calls, bad customer credit, customer delinquency, and so forth. Therefore, depending on the customer, a firm may make a profit on one customer and lose money on another.

For example, let us assume that customer A and customer B both have a contract with the firm providing revenue of $100,000 per year. Let us also assume that the estimated overall margin is the same at 15 percent or $15,000 from each of these customers. Customer A negotiates this contract once a year, requiring one sales call and one presentation and contract negotiation in a year. Customer A also pays on time. On the other hand, Customer B makes you bid every three months and requires four contract negotiations per year requiring four sales calls and four sales presentations. In addition, customer B never pays on time, requiring a somewhat lenient credit policy. If we assume that each of these sales calls costs about $4,000, then the sales and service costs associated with this contract exceed $15,000. The costs of sales calls and the extra cost of credit result in negative margin from customer B. While the company can have a good control over COGS, its ability to manage sales costs, service costs, and cost of credit will depend on how well the target customer segment is chosen, how well the customer transactions are managed, and the soundness of its credit policy.

UNPROFITABLE CUSTOMERS

> You can not make on volume what you lose on margin.
> —Anonymous oil trader on the Chicago Oil Trading Floor

In general, marketing is centered on the concept of managing profitable customer relationships. To achieve this, the supplier identifies the target customer segment with the needs and wants as well as the resources to pay for the provided goods and services. Marketers spend resources in qualifying customers to make sure that they have the money, the authority, and the desire to buy products and services before focusing their sales efforts. However, in spite of these strategies to ensure profitable business through qualifying and screening customers, industry sources estimate that on average about 15 percent of all customers are unprofitable.[6] Banking industry sources state that on average banks make money only on about 20–40 percent of their customers.[7] Unprofitable customers are a drain on the firm and can suck the firm's resources dry like parasites.

Customers can be considered not profitable when they either pay late or do not pay at all. These are customers who want lenient credit terms. They never pay on time. Their checks bounce. They are chronic complainers and take undue advantage of the return policy. They are bargain hunters with minimal loyalty, buying only those items on sale or waiting for even better deals later. They tend to "nickel-and-dime" the firm to death with every transaction. They tie up the salesperson's time and make last-minute changes to the product specifications or to delivery schedules.

Transactions with these customers can become not only unprofitable but also unpleasant. Then, a lot of time and effort may be necessary in order to attempt collecting payment. They create negative margin to the firm's operations and are rude and disrespectful to a firm's sales and service people. This in turn can cause low employee morale and higher turnover of employees. Many of these customers often have unrealistic expectations. This causes them to have lower customer satisfaction and thereby causes them to generate negative word-of-mouth advertising.

Take the experience of a clothing retailer in any city. A customer picks only those clothes that are on sale and writes a check for that amount. The check is returned and a collection agency must be involved in order for the firm to collect its payment. Another variation to this situation is one in which the customer returns the merchandise. The retailer senses that the clothing has been worn by the customer and has no choice but to mark the item down substantially, repackage it, and place it on the "sale" rack. This contributes to losing profit margins as well as potential sales. In addition, there is an opportunity cost in terms of lost sales to more profitable customers.

A customer can also become unprofitable because of the lower volume of sales and/or the lower frequency with which purchases are made or the services are used. At some point, the margin does not justify the service demands of these customers. Imagine that you work for an airline company. You have customers with frequent flyer cards; however, they fly only once a year at best, at the lowest price offered. Yet they expect a statement every month concerning their frequent flyer status. This adds to your overall cost without corresponding revenue benefits. This is not limited to small buyers. As we discussed before, a large buyer may also become unprofitable, based on too many demands on a salesperson's or firm's time, schedule changes, delivery frequencies, or for nonpayment.

In spite of these kinds of experiences, companies are reluctant to cut loose from loss-making customers. It is interesting to note that companies will often implement budget cuts or fire employees in order to improve profitability, while not addressing the problem of no-profit customers. While customer acquisition is a constant mantra, dumping customers is seldom considered a viable option. In fact, in a world where the customer is considered the king, getting rid of an unprofitable customer is considered a sacrilege. Companies bristle at the idea of getting rid of a customer as an option to improve profitability. Managers generally make the mistake of equating revenues or the number of customers with success and/or profit. They believe that if the revenues are increasing, then the profits should follow. This theory can be attributed to the lack of individual customer profitability information that could have helped to determine the folly of continuing to serve customers contributing to loss.

ALL CUSTOMERS ARE NOT EQUAL

> We will no longer conduct operations that don't produce profits.
> —Toshimasa Iue, President, Sanyo Electric Co.
> (quoted in *International Herald Tribune*).
> The company said that in a break with tradition,
> it would put profit before market share.

Sanyo, like many other companies, has painfully awakened to the one corporate strategy almost guaranteed to lead to failure—the quest for market share at any cost. Other companies have also learned that seeking market share as a strategic goal can hurt profitability. General Motors Corporation is probably the best-known example of a firm that suffered from pursuit of this strategy. A recent *Fortune* article[8] on unprofitable customers illustrates such dismal experiences. Gap, Inc. went on an aggressive campaign to acquire new customers by opening new stores and lost money. Telecommunication companies have offered so much in cash incentives to attract new customers that many firms have failed. Some of these customers just took the cash incentives and switched again and again to an alternate provider, leaving the companies with negative returns on their investments.

Using a simplified example, the article provided the following scenario:

> Imagine a company that launches a big push for new customers and acquires 5,000 of them at a cost of $1,000 each. That amount is what the company spends on advertising, promotion, sales calls, and so forth to get those customers in the door. To keep things simple we'll assume that the new customers don't produce any business in the year in which they're acquired, so the company's operating profit is $5 million lower than it otherwise would have been. That is, it has invested $5 million in the hope of realizing much more than $5 million in future profits.[9]

Now let us see this from another angle. In the above example, the firm has to recover $1,000 from a single customer just to break even in the next five years, without considering the time value of money. (This revenue requirement will be higher if the cost of capital is considered.) In other words, this customer has to be a *profitable customer* for at least the next five years with a profit margin of at least $200 per year. Assuming 10 percent as a typical margin, this company then expects that this customer will spend a minimum of $2,000 every year for the next five years for the firm just to break even. If the customer spends less, makes too many returns, defaults on payments, or switches to another firm after the second year, then there is a net loss for the company. In the face of this customer acquisition cost, a firm's hope for profitability rests on the probability of customers spending more than $2,000 every year for five years or more. In the current competitive environment, this would mean that the company has taken steps to make sure that each and every customer it has acquired has not only the need and the desire, but also the resources to pay. In addition it has to ensure that the value provided by its goods and services continues to keep the customer loyal to the company.

Firms are beginning to take a closer look at the impacts of market share when the real cost of serving customers exceeds the margin generated. They are also coming to the realization that all customers are not equal. As firms juggle their resources to maximize profitability, they are beginning to sense that they will not be able to serve *all* customers equally. They understand that an undifferentiated service strategy can reduce the service level quality for the profit-producing customers, thus making them vulnerable to defection. The realization that all *customers are not equal* is leading to the strategy of selective acquisition and the provision of an extra level of service to a select group of customers in hopes of achieving long-term profitability.

MBNA America Bank is well known in the industry for its ability to retain customers in a very competitive credit card market and remain profitable. It does so by carefully choosing a segment of customers based on their excellent credit histories and who demand above average service. Interestingly, these MBNA customers do not have the most favorable interest rates. Their loyalty to MBNA is not because of lower rates, but because of the excellent service. They stay with MBNA because they get customer service that is based on fairness, respect, and appreciation of their business by MBNA. These customers know that their phone calls will be answered on the second ring by a polite and helpful customer-service agent who is able to solve the problem.[10] MBNA on its part can afford to maintain this service level to its profitable customers by being selective about its choice of customers. This selective strategy has meant that its resources are not tied up serving unprofitable customers.

IDENTIFICATION OF UNPROFITABLE CUSTOMERS

In a recent *Fortune* article,[11] top executives of the largest U.S. retailers responded firmly that they did not have unprofitable customers even while these firms were reporting huge losses. They were unable, however, to explain how millions of all these profitable customers led to such financial losses. The truth was that some of their customers (unprofitable customers) were destroying shareholder value, and yet the retailers were continuing to spend money serving them. This clearly indicates the some executives lack the information needed to make better strategic choices.

The first task to improve profitability is to identify unprofitable customers. But most companies cannot do this because traditional accounting systems are centered around product profitability, which does not provide customer contribution. Profitability by broad aggregates of customer segments or average margin by customer type is not very useful. Identification of unprofitable customers requires margin analysis at the individual customer level. This is because using an average margin on a customer type can be deceptive and misleading. The average margin of customer groups masks the difference between profit-making and loss-generating customers. In the aggregate, the margin from the profit-making customers usually (hopefully!) covers the loss incurred from serving unprofitable customers.

A manager's use of this average margin or margin by customer groups to make resource allocation decisions would lead to an undifferentiated allocation of resources that can be counterproductive. Firms will end up spending the same amount to attract and serve a profit-producing customer as they do for a customer who is contributing to the companies' losses within each segment. While the average margin across a customer group may be positive, taking this analysis to the individual level displays the wide difference in margins across individual customers. This is because companies make higher profits on some customers, lower margins on others, and negative margins on yet others.

To understand customer profitability, it is important to examine customer revenue and the breakdown of the costs for serving each of these different customers. Thus, when the margin is analyzed at the customer level, there is a sudden realization that a higher market share or larger number of customers does not necessarily mean higher profits. This is because the cost of serving some of the customers may be very high. As stated before, reasons that could increase the cost include a higher number of sales calls, too many small or low-margin orders, high service costs due to wrong use of products, time-critical operations, and high cost of credit due to lenient credit terms. Customers can also differ in terms of service demands, paying behavior, and so forth.

Thus, understanding the profitability of individual customers is important because it helps understand how to identify the impact of problem customers, as well as helping to make decisions about resource allocations. Once identified, the firm should "demarket" to its low-margin and unprofitable customers by seeking lower cost methods for fulfilling their orders. If defection to the competition occurs, count your blessings and refocus resources on serving your profitable customers. This elimination of unprofitable customers can help margin in three ways. First, it eliminates loss-making transactions. Second, the redirected resources toward more profitable customers can improve their service satisfaction and thus prevent their future defection. Third, the resulting increase in inelasticity of demand also enables price increases.

NEW APPROACHES TO CUSTOMER GROUPINGS

To be effective and to avoid inappropriate allocation of resources, firms should develop customer lists organized by profitability. This listing ranks customers from the highest to the lowest based on the amount of profit each customer has generated. At the bottom of the rung are customers with negative margins. The profitability grouping can be based on margin percentage or on absolute dollars. This customer profitability ranking helps the firm to focus efforts on the right customers to improve business performance. This listing helps to identify heavy hitters in terms of contribution to the bottom line and those who are average contributors. It also brings to light those customers who cost rather than make you money with every transaction. This listing can also be used to help differentiate services, decide on which customers to retain, decide which clients will be directed to lower-cost forms of services, and decide what strategies can be used to encourage some customers to seek alternative suppliers.

FedEx Corporation, General Electric Capital Corporation, Bank of America Corporation, and Hallmark Cards, Inc. all group their customers by profitability and vary their services to their customers based on how much each of these customers contributes to their bottom line. Customers of FedEx are grouped as the Good, the Bad, and the Ugly.[12] Good customers are provided with special privileges and benefits. They discourage unprofitable customers by withdrawing special privileges that are given to good customers. Thus, for example, while a "Good" customer may see her late fee waived for a missed payment, an "Ugly" customer would face a hefty penalty for his bounced check.

Separating customers by the 80:20 grouping is also a well-known and useful practice. This grouping is based on the observation that 80 percent of the sales or value often come from only 20 percent of the customers. This two-tier grouping is a valuable categorization, but it overlooks the dissimilarities of the customers within each group. To address the inadequacy of the 80:20 two-tier scheme, a prominent research group suggested a customer pyramid that groups service to customers into four levels: Platinum, Gold, Iron, and Lead.[13] Factors used in this grouping include profitability, difficulty or ease of doing business, time and effort requirements, the associated returns for these efforts, and potential for spreading positive word-of-mouth advertising about the company. Using these factors, the four categories of customers can be described as follows:

- *Platinum* customers are the company's most profitable customers. They use large quantities of product, are less price sensitive, are willing to try new offerings, and remain loyal customers.

- *Gold* customer profitability is not as high as it is for platinum customers, but they are heavy users of the firm's products. They are not quite as loyal and look for price discounts. These customers would like to have alternate supply sources to minimize risk, as well as to use this to negotiate price discounts with the company.

- *Iron* customers buy enough products to utilize the firm's capacity, but their purchases are not large enough to warrant special treatment. Like the Gold-tier customers, they have multiple supply sources.

- *Lead* customers produce negative profit and are a drain on company resources. They can be chronic complainers and demand more resources than they are worth. They can also be a source of negative word-of-mouth advertising about the company and products, thus causing the company to lose potential business from better customers. Companies are generally better off finding a way to get rid of Lead customers.

Consider the following hypothetical example of this grouping. A Platinum customer for a real estate company could be one who is planning to sell a home of $500,000 or more, willing to pay full commission, has purchased more than two homes in the past, plans to buy a home within the next six months, and is part of the personal network with similar characteristics. Most likely, this customer will refer the real estate company to other Platinum prospects within her network. Compared to this, a Gold customer may sell and buy in the same price range but is likely to negotiate with the company to lower his selling costs. Iron customers would be selling a less expensive house, but have the potential to become a member of the Gold group. Lead customers, on the other hand, are seen as shoppers who generally tie up an agent's time looking for houses in different price ranges, but are most likely to buy in the $100K range. Lead customers are difficult to upgrade to higher levels, can reduce profitability, and tie up resources that could be used on Platinum or Gold customers. The strategy for Lead customers is obvious: discard them or avoid them.[14]

Banks generally consider customers who do not have a home loan or the potential to own a home as unprofitable customers. Some of the other characteristics of these "questionable" bank customers include lack of access to the Internet, no regular income, no assets, and no savings. Interestingly, these customers seem to prefer the more expensive face-to-face teller transactions in banks over ATMs. Another example involves insurance. Agents try to stay away from home owners in high-risk areas (hurricane, flood, or burglary), as well as car owners in high-theft areas and other frequent claimants.

DEALING WITH UNPROFITABLE CUSTOMERS

What should the company do with unprofitable customers? Say good-bye? Can you afford to lose these customers? "Firing" customers is still considered bad even when firms are losing money on unprofitable customers. However, this mind-set of "can never lose a customer" is changing. Companies are finding that by culling unprofitable customers, they can better serve the remaining customers, thereby growing the business and increasing shareholder value. Survival in a competitive market requires businesses to understand who their customers are, what their needs are, and how they can best meet those needs. Furthermore, they need to decide whether or not they should continue to serve all customers. When a customer is not profitable in the short run and does not show the potential to be profitable in the future, then the company has to consider its options. One of the options clearly is firing that customer. Culling the customer base to get rid of unprofitable customers is a viable strategy and should not be ignored if the manager is interested in maximizing shareholder value.

Firing the customer should not be automatic nor should it be done without considering its overall impact on business operations. For example, firing an unprofitable customer is a better option when this customer can be replaced with a profit-making customer. Take an example of a customer who accounts for a large portion of sales, but is not profitable. While this unprofitable customer may not be covering its total cost, this customer may still be contributing to the firm's fixed cost, thus allowing the company to stay price competitive.

When a firm decides to fire an unprofitable customer and is unable to replace it with another revenue-producing customer, the firm is losing the ability to recover some of that fixed cost. In the absence of a customer to recover this fixed cost, the firm may have to spread the fixed cost over other remaining customers. This can result in raising the price for all customers, thus becoming uncompetitive on price. The other available alternative would be to reduce some fixed costs in proportion to the contribution of the lost business. If this cost reduction leads to deterioration of service quality for the remaining customers, then the firm faces the possibility of defection among its best customers. Thus, company action to get rid of an unprofitable customer (based on total cost) without first reducing the fixed cost or without finding a customer to replace the lost one can lead to lower total profit.

In addition, before firing a customer, things beyond immediate profit need to be taken into account. Firms have to include strategic considerations in making customer firing decisions. Managers should evaluate both financial measures as well as nonfinancial values in assessing customer worth. For example, a customer could generate additional income by bringing in other more profitable customers. This could also be based on customers' ability to serve as a reference for the product or service. Given the importance of word-of-mouth promotion and the critical role of early adopters, these criteria could be particularly important when a company is entering a new market or when a company is in the process of introducing new products or services. Of course, there can also be legal, ethical, or regulatory issues relating to firing a customer that must be considered.

Most firms instead first explore opportunities for improving profits with the loss-producing customer by way of raising revenues or by lowering costs to serve them. On the revenue side, actions could include traditional price increases as well as cross-selling and up-selling. If the margin cannot be increased on the revenue side, then the firm should explore options for reducing costs or minimizing loss-contributing transactions. This can be done by adjusting the service level downward or by taking out some of the product or service features. Finally, directing customers toward alternative solutions may also be an option.

ROUTES TO PROFITABILITY

There are two primary routes to profitability for a company faced with loss-making customers. These are (1) converting an unprofitable customer to a profitable customer or (2) firing the unprofitable customer. As stated before, conversion strategies mainly focus on price increases or cost reductions. Here are some additional and more detailed ways to succeed.

1. Increase Revenue by Raising the Price

This is the best option since it increases profit by increasing the overall margin. Price increases can be direct or indirect such as eliminating discounts to unprofitable customers.

Unprofitable customers who refuse the new price will walk away. This is an indirect way to off-load them without overtly firing them. Industry experts estimate that a 1-percent increase in price could lead to an 11-percent increase in customer equity. Most customers accept price increases and continue to do business with the seller. Price increases can also be accomplished in an indirect way by eliminating discounts based on purchase volume or order size. The seller could also implement price increases by tightening credit policies or eliminating grace periods.

For example, many customers place a lot of small orders and then ask for a price discount based on the total volume. Since several small orders can increase total processing costs, it would be beneficial to eliminate discounts under this condition. The elimination of discounts could be explained by the increased costs of frequent deliveries and the processing costs. Generally, most customers understand this logic, accept the elimination of the discount, and will continue to do business at the increased prices.

As a case in point, an owner of a small company was supplying a large international conglomerate with key component parts. The seller was losing money because the buyer kept changing the delivery dates and product specifications. Even though these changes were increasing the supplier's cost of meeting this order, the seller did not raise prices for fear of losing this large chunk of business. After several months of suffering losses, the supplier finally met with the buyer and explained the situation of increased costs associated with product specification changes along with the last-minute demand for deliveries. The buyer was sympathetic and agreed on a minimum order size, regular delivery schedules, and surcharges for any changes. This resulted in the hoped-for increase in the seller's profitability.

2. Reduce Costs by Changing Packaging, Shipping Policies, Credit Terms, and So Forth

A firm's policies should be differentiated across profitable customers and unprofitable customers. This differentiation helps the firm to provide treatment that is appropriate and expected by the profitable customers while discouraging unprofitable customers. For example, while profitable customers may be forgiven for a late payment, unprofitable customers could be charged very high fees. Profitable customers get discounted shipping while unprofitable customers are charged normal prices to recover full costs. Prices can be restructured by offering a la carte services at higher prices so less profitable customers can pick what they need at a price that reflects the full cost to serve them as well as providing reasonable profits.

3. Lower the Costs to Serve/Plug the Profit Leak

This is a very popular strategy adopted by several investment brokers and financial institutions such as Fidelity Investments, The VanguardGroup, Inc., and the Charles Schwab Corporation. These firms use automated phone systems to identify unprofitable customers and then direct them to their Web sites or to longer queue phone lines. This has lowered the costs of serving them and has resulted in positive margins. Banks found that tellers were the most expensive way to service customers and encouraged online banking and ATM systems to turn around unprofitable customers. Banks, such as First Chicago Bank and Canadian Imperial Bank of Commerce, found that they increased their return on customers after some were directed to ATM and online banking options. Airlines such as Southwest Airlines and American Airlines have lower fares when tickets are bought on line.

Recently, a wholesale distributor of HVAC (heating, ventilating, and air conditioning) and plumbing systems in Connecticut found that many of its customers were unprofitable because of the associated inside selling expenses. This distributor also realized that converting its unprofitable customers to profitable customers offered the greatest opportunity for improving the firm's bottom line. The supplier strongly encouraged these customers to place their own orders on the firm's Internet order entry system. This change resulted in a 90-percent reduction in the firm's inside selling costs, and these customers became profit makers for this distributor.

4. Stay with Core Offerings and Strengths

At times, a profitable business starts losing money when it steps outside its area of strength based on special requests from customers. This may result in increased activities and expenses because the firm lacks the skills to provide these other products or services. Firms should resist the temptation to accept a customer request that is outside of the firm's area of strength and expertise. It may be possible to improve profitability by eliminating products/services that are outside of core competencies.

5. Encourage Customers to Fire Themselves

Firms should offer different levels of service and assign worst customers to the lowest level of service that can be offered. For example, while the most profitable customers are pampered with senior sales representatives and face-to-face technical help, the worst customers can be directed to phone-based support. Even with the phone-based support, the worst customers can be allowed a certain number of free calls. Beyond this, each additional call results in a fee for services provided. This should either reduce the number of requests for service or result in customers leaving the firm.

A bank in the southeastern United States adopted this strategy. Like many other banks, it was suffering from the high costs associated with customers who come in frequently and kept tellers busy with small transactions. The bank was reluctant to cut these customers off for fear of bad word-of-mouth publicity. The bank implemented a tiered service plan, including a $2 charge for every in-person transaction. The least-profitable customers voted with their feet and left the bank. Bank tellers were then able to focus their time on the more profitable large accounts, thus improving service levels to these customers as well as increasing profitability.

CUSTOMER CULLING AS AN OPTION

Just as one manages a business or a stock portfolio, firms should manage their customers like investments because they are. Customers who are not providing adequate returns and who have no strategic value or future profit potential should be divested. They not only contribute to loss, but also tie up resources that could be used to service better customers.

Firing a customer should generally be the last option, but it is nevertheless an alternative that needs to be exercised as needed. Not using this option will continue to drain the firm. Worse still, continuing to serve these unprofitable customers can rob the resources required to meet requests from profitable customers. This can lead to a defection of profitable customers to the competition, thus exacerbating the loss potential.

The important thing when involved in the firing of customers is to do it gracefully in order to avoid negative word-of-mouth publicity. In certain cases, businesses may have to contend with regulations before choosing the firing option. The best strategy is to encourage the customer to walk away voluntarily by directing it to self-service rather than full service, by making the process more complex, or by raising the price to match the additional demands on resources from this customer. Managers exercising the culling option should do the following:

1. Involve the senior management team and get its commitment to the strategy.
2. Evaluate the financial, nonfinancial, and strategic contributions of the customer.
3. Make sure new business is in hand to replace the customer to be dumped.
4. Evaluate the strategic and marketing implications of dumping the customer on other products as well as the impact on other customers.
5. Consider any regulatory implications of customer dumping.

Figure 9.2 illustrates the process firms should use in deciding their customer portfolio.

The following steps could be used in the process of getting rid of customers.

1. *Gathering data:* Managers resorting to the "culling" strategy should start by getting all the facts and figures and gathering empirical data. Detailed customer transaction information should be collected to identify various drivers of profitability. These data

Figure 9.2
Customer Profitability Analysis

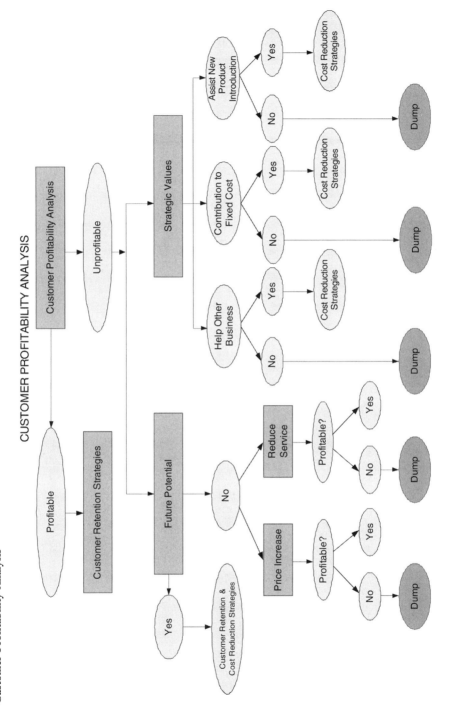

CUSTOMER PROFITABILITY ANALYSIS

include how recent the purchase was, past customer value, frequency of purchases, contribution margin, and so forth. Ideally, the data should be as detailed as possible to account for seasonality and should span several periods of time. Generally, firms are able to collect two to three years' worth of data. Some of the questions to consider include the following: When was the last time the customer bought something? How often and in what way did this customer buy? What was the average dollar amount per transaction for this customer? What was the total value of money this customer spent each year?

2. *Calculate the various cost components for supplying the product to the customer.*

3. *Estimate the profit for this customer,* in a manner similar to the calculation of customer lifetime value just described in the previous chapter.

4. If the customer is unprofitable, *examine the component of the costs to see how these can be managed or reduced to improve the margin.*

5. *Examine whether this customer has the potential to grow and contribute profit in the future.* It is possible that the customer may be unprofitable now, but has the potential to grow and contribute to profit later. For example, a small business may be unprofitable now as it is in the growth stage, but it has the potential to soon become a lucrative customer. In this case, the firm should not automatically fire the customer, but rather manage the costs to minimize the current loss potential.

6. *Examine whether the customer has a strategic value.* For example, during the introductory stage of the product life cycle, some products and services are naturally unprofitable. The customers who buy at that time help the firm introduce the product to the market by being innovators and profits come later from the early adoptors.

While some firms are open about culling, other firms do it quietly. Many firms regularly review their low-end customers' contributions and compare that to the cost of keeping them. They shed those that cost more than they generate in margin. On the other hand, banks and airlines are concerned about the negative image of firing customers and do it in an indirect way. For example, airlines charge fees to customers to stay in their frequent flyer program if they do not earn enough credits. Those who provide frequent business and miles are exempt from these fees.

Customer profitability analysis should be an ongoing exercise using financial and nonfinancial measures. Identification of the traits that are common to profitable customers should help managers focus effort on this segment to avoid defection as well as to explore cross-selling opportunities. Managers can do profit optimization by the following:

1. carefully recognizing and satisfying the needs of most of the more profitable group,

2. finding more profitable customers,

3. converting unprofitable customers into profitable customers, and

4. getting rid of customers who have no profit potential and drain company resources. The strategy of "fewer and deeper" customer relationships enables more profitable growth.

To be effective, managers must understand that having more customers is not necessarily a good thing. They have to understand that there are certain customers who can never create value for the organization in the present nor in the future. Firms are better off without these customers, and managers should stay away from them. Acquisition and retention of customers can help the company grow only if profitable customers are targeted.

NOTES

1. Larry Selden and Geoffrey Colvin, *Angel Customers and Demon Customers: Discover Which Is Which and Turbo-Charge Your Stock* (New York: Penguin Book, 2003).

2. Simon Lloyd, "The Culling Game," *BRW* 22, no. 13, April 6 (2000): 96–99.

3. Orla O'Sullivan, "Some of Your Customers Are Unprofitable. OK, Now What?" *ABA Banking On-Line Journal,* http://www.banking.com/aba/cover_1197.asp (accessed August 14, 2006).

4. Selden and Colvin, *Angel Customers and Demon Customers.*

5. Lynette Ryals, "Creating Profitable Customers through the Magic of Data Mining," *Journal of Targeting, Measurement and Analysis for Marketing* 11, no. 4, June (2003): 343–49.

6. "What to Do about Unprofitable Customers," FusionBrand, http://fusionbrand.blogs.com/fusionbrand/2004/07/what_to_do_abou.html (accessed on August 14, 2006).

7. O'Sullivan, "Some of Your Customers Are Unprofitable."

8. Larry Selden and Geoffrey Colvin, "Will This Customer Sink Your Stock?" *Fortune* 146, no. 5, September (2002): 127–32.

9. Ibid.

10. "What to Do about Unprofitable Customers."

11. Selden and Colvin, *Angel Customers and Demon Customers.*

12. Valerie Zeithaml, Roland T. Rust, and Katherine N. Lemon, "The Customer Pyramid: Creating and Serving Profitable Customers," *California Management Review* 43, no. 4, Summer (2001): 118–42.

13. Ibid.

14. Ibid.

Part II

SUCCESSFUL SELLING IN THE 21ST CENTURY

CHAPTER 10

SMALL BUSINESSES IN THE 21ST CENTURY: UTILIZING INTEGRATED MARKETING COMMUNICATIONS EFFORTS IN THE SALES PROCESS

Dan Rose

The 21st century is being shaped by many forces, namely, technology; changing human values, wants, and desires; the global economic, political, and physical environments; complexity; and demographics, in particular, the world population and wealth shifts away from North America and Europe. While no one can predict how these variables will influence the future of organizational size, the impact of small businesses will certainly change. On one hand, big businesses might become more important as large brands grow and mergers continue to take place. However, even as we start to see the influence of "megabrands," technological, demographic, and environmental changes are enabling small businesses to flourish as well. For example, technology enables a small start-up company in America to conduct business all over the world. Likewise, as the sales process becomes more automated and relies more heavily on databases, some of the traditionally high costs of selling are no longer necessary. Thus, the technology makes the sales process more efficient, while still strengthening the relationship bonds. Even though the future can obviously not be predicted, small businesses and all their diverse characteristics and needs will remain an important element of commerce in the 21st century.

IT IS BACK TO THE FUTURE FOR SMALL BUSINESS SALES

For small businesses, the science and art of selling in the 21st century will require adapting to and combining the traditional tried and true sales methods of centuries past along with the most current strategic marketing practices and technology available. The small businesses that succeed will be those that combine best practices of traditional and live sales efforts with the tremendous advantages of automated and online sales and customer relationship management practices. For many small businesses, the process will be like going back to the future.

For hundreds of years, sales efforts by successful merchants were anchored by their personal relationships with their customer base and the trust and attention they paid to those customers. This was true of the butcher, the baker, the innkeeper, the corner grocer, and nearly all other merchants. Small business owners knew, understood, and anticipated the needs of their customers. They greeted them warmly by name, knew their family, and made suggestions for new purchases based on the knowledge of that customer and their previous buying habits and needs.

In the 20th century, the use of mass media to market company products began to attract a wider client base for small business owners. In part, this helped these merchants to expand their sales base and introduce new customers to their companies. However, the personal and trusted relationship with the business owner or principal salesperson began to erode. This occurred in part because as the size of the client base grew so large, it became difficult, if not impossible, to maintain the type of personal relationships with all customers as had been done in the past. The 20th century also ushered in the concept of the sales force with multiple salespeople providing customer service and with it, the advent of sales turnover, lack of product or customer knowledge, and the related problems that occur with sales force management.

The past several decades have seen many small business owners further distanced from the frontline sales efforts and customer contact. This is due in part by the owners' time being drawn to increased legislative and compliance-related issues, more complicated operational issues, and vendor or supplier issues. Many small business owners today are too busy "just keeping up" with the daily responsibilities of operating their businesses to be able to provide the outstanding personal sales touch and service of yesteryear.

However, from approximately the early to mid 1990s through the present, some small business owners have successfully integrated the use of technology to help them provide the same type of personalized sales service to an even wider customer base as had their small business forefathers. Certainly the use of the affordable and personal business computer has helped small businesses with back office and operational tasks. Perhaps more importantly, technology has impacted the sales process as well. At the root of this effort is database marketing and the use of the Web to help facilitate small business sales.

THE CHANGING MARKETPLACE

The homogeneous mass market, which has dictated the offerings of U.S. producers since the dawn of the Industrial Revolution, is confronting its demise. If you do not believe it, look no further than assembly-line hamburger maker, Burger King, which was a forerunner in realizing that customers want it "their way" and their way is not necessarily everyone else's. As touted in its advertising, Burger King offered "customized" burgers based on a patron's preferences—down to the ketchup—a far cry from the typical one-way-suits-all quarter pounder. Markets are becoming niches and niches are growing smaller. As this market miniaturization occurs, customers gain more stature—and they know it. These customers are also becoming more technologically savvy and better educated about the products in the market. Reaching those customers through the sales force requires a new strategy. The scattershot approach, which was not necessarily all that effective in the past, will be even less so in the 21st century. The most obvious alternative, shifting to narrower and more specialized markets, is already being tried by many small firms with substantial success.

As described, these new strategies must be based in relationship marketing. The technology of today puts these relationships at risk, while at the same time making it possible to enhance them. Just as marketers can build large databases full of consumer information, customers can go online and create blogs or chat groups and instantly spread good or bad information about companies. This word-of-mouth information spreads so quickly that it is now termed "viral marketing." Much like the quick spread of bad viruses, word-of-mouth information spreads through the Internet faster than businesses had ever imagined before.

This scenario provides so many positive benefits for businesses. Personal selling has always been one of the most expensive, if not the most expensive, forms of marketing communications. With the growing importance of relationships as opposed to transactions, salespeople now need to spend more and more time with clients developing relationships. However, marketers can benefit from the changes of the 21st century by taking advantage of these new forms of communication and then integrating all these together into one, cohesive strategy. It is impossible for a firm in the 21st century to discuss sales, without discussing all other forms of marketing communications. Small businesses can reap large rewards by utilizing these new, nontraditional approaches to sales to increase efficiency. As shown in Chapters 8 and 9, managers can sometimes gain more beneficial knowledge by examining sales productivity instead of sales volume. The changes suggested in this chapter help to increase that productivity.

Virtually every marketplace has been or is being influenced and changed by the global impact of instant communication, affordable technology, and available resources to assist even the smallest businesses everywhere. In his groundbreaking book *The World Is Flat,* author Thomas L. Friedman explains the changing dynamics of the open market system and helps small businesses understand the need to alter their sales models and customer relationship management models. Friedman describes what he terms "Globalization 3.0" as follows:

> Globalization 3.0 is the newfound power for individuals (and businesses) to collaborate and compete globally....and the phenomenon that is enabling, empowering and enjoining individuals and small groups (read businesses) to go global so easily... is the flat-world platform. The flat-world platform is the product of the convergence of the personal computer (which allowed every individual to suddenly become the author of his or her own content in digital form) and fiber-optic cable (which suddenly allowed all those individuals to access more and more digital content around the world for next to nothing) with the rise of the work flow software (which enabled individuals (or small businesses) all over the world to collaborate on that same digital content from anywhere, regardless of the distance between them).[1]

The question every small business owner in the world who seeks to successfully sell products and services in the 21st century must ask himself or herself is this: "How can I leverage the power of Globalization 3.0 with modern sales and marketing techniques, while also providing the traditional and personal 'high touch' sales relationship with all of my customers and prospects?"

In this chapter, we seek to help answer the above question. We review a few traditional methods of small business sales techniques that remain valid today whether integrating technology or not. In addition, we look at the use of more recent sales and marketing approaches as well as technology for the purpose of sales efforts and supporting sales efforts. Specifically, we address the concept of niche marketing, direct marketing, the use of the Web and Web storefronts, and take an in-depth look at one of the most cost-effective methods of lead generation for small businesses in the early 21st century: search engine marketing.

So, why do we say we are going back to the future for small business selling in the 21st century? Because those small businesses that "get it" and succeed will be the ones that continue to integrate technology and deepen customer data into their sales process in order to provide their customers and prospects with highly relevant and personalized levels of sales communication. These small businesses will be going back to the same successful model the shopkeepers used hundreds of years before them, but they will conduct this approach on a much broader scale to much larger customer bases. And at the core of this effort will be the use of technology and database marketing.

PUTTING DATABASE MARKETING INTO CONTEXT

Before we explore the impact of database marketing on the sales process, we first need to put it into context against the backdrop of sales and marketing efforts in the last century. The last decades of the 20th century saw several changes and improvements in the small business sales and marketing approach. Marketing efforts designed to support the direct sales effort have been practiced by small businesses for hundreds of years. Chief among these efforts has been the use of mass marketing. However, among the most important changes in the past century was the shift in focus from mass-marketing efforts to more narrow, or direct marketing, efforts. This is true whether you are talking about the total marketing efforts or just sales.

Mass marketing, the principal means of promoting or marketing products and services in the 20th century, held great success for most businesses. The primary vehicles used for mass marketing were the daily newspapers, weekly or monthly magazines, radio, television, and outdoor billboards. The concept of delivering one overall branded message to thousands or millions of individuals at a time was deemed among the best ways to support direct sales efforts. In short, it was one message—the same message—delivered to all viewers, listeners, or readers.

In the second half of the 20th century, targeted marketing vehicles began to be used, and with good success. The same communications channels such as print, radio, and television began to evolve into more narrowly focused mediums. While television stations in every market across the United States began with just a few broadcast channels in the 1940s and the 1950s, the advent of cable television several decades later brought dozens and now hundreds of specialized programming channels designed to attract very specific types of audiences. The same narrowing of content, and subsequently the narrowing of audiences that content attracted, was realized in many print publications as well as radio stations. Instead of the *Saturday Evening Post, Life,* and the *Sporting News* magazines, all designed for mass appeal, publishers began to cater to much more narrowed markets such as *Rubber and Plastics News* or *Drycleaners Monthly*. Instead of just a few radio stations broadcasting music or information designed for mass appeal, dozens of narrowed radio formats began to be offered such as classical music, sports talk radio, or heavy metal stations. Again, these formats were designed to attract a more narrow and specific type of listener, thus allowing businesses the opportunity to more narrowly define their marketing message and reach an audience that would likely have a greater interest in that targeted communication. This was the early stage of matching relevant content or marketing messages to targeted audiences.

Marketing channels began to more narrowly define their audiences, in part, because marketers expressed the desire to sell or communicate to specific groups instead of the masses. These targeted marketing efforts became fundamental approaches for small business sales techniques in the last few decades of the 20th century. In the 1970s, a form of marketing began to gain significant momentum that is still evolving and being used heavily today. That is the use of database and direct marketing. Because of the much smaller level of resources that small businesses have at their disposal, database and direct marketing is critical to the success of a business and its selling efforts.

THE RELATIONSHIP OF DIRECT MARKETING AND
DATABASE MARKETING

According to Wikipedia, the online encyclopedia, direct marketing is defined as follows:

> Direct marketing is a form of marketing that attempts to send its messages directly to consumers, using "addressable" media such as mail and email...Direct marketing uses non-addressable media as well as addressable ones. The important thing is that it seeks a response and it is this which the recipient, usually a marketer, bases their future actions, or contact strategy on.[2]

For many small businesses, particularly manufacturers, the historical method of moving product to the end user might involve wholesalers, retailers, manufacturing representatives, inventory control issues, and related logistical challenges. Additionally, it is important to keep in mind that the cost of traditional face-to-face selling is extremely expensive. Thus, by employing direct marketing methods, small businesses gain greater control of the entire sales process while possibly eliminating unnecessary cost structures in the sales process. The generally accepted direct marketing channels, which can add to the sales efforts, include the following:

- *Direct mail* is the use of the postal service or other delivery providers to send printed materials such as letters, catalogs, flyers, or packages directly to a customer or prospect's home or business address. Emerging digital printing services are helping to facilitate unique individual messages to each recipient based on his or her profile.

- *Outbound Telemarketing* is the use of the phone to engage customers and prospects in sales-related activity.

- *E-mail* is the use of the Internet to send individually unique text- or html-based information to a customer's or prospect's home or business e-mail address.

- *Web Sites* are the use of the Internet to create a virtual presence representing your business, your products and services, and your ability to sell directly to customers on-line. The site content and design may change to match the profile of the individual user.

In addition, two emerging Direct Marketing channels follow:

- *Mobile Marketing* is the use of mobile communications to send individually unique text- or html-based commercial messages directly to cellular phones or personal digital assistants.

- *Digital Cable* is the use of digital compression technology to deliver individually unique commercial messages to each home or even each television set within a home or business to match the viewer profile.

This chapter is not intended to be an exhaustive examination of all direct marketing channels or even all sales approaches for small businesses in the 21st century. Instead, we are focusing on growing small business sales and marketing approaches that are readily available to marketers at affordable entry points. These approaches happen to employ technology-based direct marketing channels including the e-mail and Web site channels as well as the supporting technology of search engine marketing. Though not discussed in detail here, it is likely that both mobile marketing and digital cable will become viable channels for small business marketers to use in the support of sales.

DATABASE MARKETING

Without reliable customer data, any action taken to influence the customer is at best an educated guessing game.[3]

Sending the right message to the right audience at the right time is the ultimate goal of all marketing efforts. It is an evolving process that is being improved at a rapid pace. At the core of the effectiveness of marketing campaigns is the matching of the most relevant marketing message to the individual customer or prospect that is sent at the optimum time. Factors such as buying ability, demographic and previous behavioral profiles, recent purchases, implicit or explicit responses, and type of offer are among the elements considered when developing marketing campaigns. The art and science of doing this is well known at database marketing firms.

By using database marketing efforts to enhance marketing efforts, small businesses in the 21st century will have the ability to reconnect on a one-to-one basis with their customer base, just as the local shopkeeper has done the past several hundred years. The process will also help small businesses to communicate relevant, highly targeted messages to their prospects. The process can be largely automated, and the response rate and behavior of some of the messages (online) can be tracked and added to the customer and prospect database to better refine all future communications to the same individual.

BUILDING AND HOUSING THE DATA

For many small businesses, a modest customer and prospect database might be stored in a Microsoft Office Excel file and may include such basic information as name, address, e-mail address, and phone number. With just this basic information as a start, small businesses can employ the services of outside data companies such as Acxiom Corporation (http://www.acxiom.com), Equifax, Inc. (http://www.equifax.com), or InfoUSA (http://www.infousa.com) to purchase such supplemental data for their customers and prospects as household income level, a variety of demographic profile information including age, number and age of children, interest or involvement in specific activities, and even purchase date and price of current real estate owned. In addition, data can be continually added to such a small business database by directly asking or surveying customers, as well as noting their previous buying habits and specific purchases. These data become extremely valuable to a business and are the basis for successfully using direct marketing efforts as the cornerstone to the company's marketing campaigns moving forward.

For most small businesses, the reality of Globalization 3.0 as described in this chapter's introduction means that an affordable personal computer is now powerful enough to store, manage, and serve up very large files of business information records. Additionally, easy to use database software such as Microsoft Office Access is affordable and certainly powerful enough to manage the majority of all small business owners' database needs. An Access database can combine small business product specifications and pricing from Excel files (or paper) with invoices and client reports/call history from Microsoft Office Word documents with paper-based order forms and deposit them all in one location. This same Access database can store the type of customer and prospect behavioral and profile data described in the previous paragraphs, which will help the small business in matching appropriately targeted lists and specific content features or offers for future sales efforts.

There is no longer a financial or educational barrier to entry for small businesses to use this type of marketing technology. Small businesses that decide to invest in developing and improving a customer and prospect database and then using that information to personalize relevant communications to their customer and prospect base should realize a significant competitive sales advantage over those firms that do not.

Benefits of Personalization in electronic and paper direct marketing:

- 34 percent faster rate of response
- 48 percent increase in repeat orders
- 25 percent greater average value of each order
- 32 percent increase in overall revenue.[4]

SMALL BUSINESS SELLING THROUGH E-MAIL MARKETING

As referenced previously, this chapter includes a look at how small business marketers can apply database marketing techniques to two channels in particular: the e-mail and Web channels. These two channels are certainly closely aligned and complement one another, but they do remain separate; they must go hand in hand with the personal selling efforts. For maximum results, the goal of small business marketers in the use of e-mail marketing is to send personalized, targeted, and highly relevant messages in order to increase revenues, strengthen brands, and enhance customer relationships. In order to accomplish this, marketers need to apply database marketing techniques to the e-mail channel. According to Wikipedia, the online encyclopedia, e-mail marketing is defined as follows:

Email marketing is a form of direct marketing which uses electronic mail as a means of communicating commercial or fundraising messages to an audience. In its broadest sense, every email sent to a potential or current customer could be considered email marketing. However, the term is usually used to refer to:

- Sending emails with the purpose of enhancing the relationship of a merchant with its current or old customers and to encourage customer loyalty and repeat business.
- Sending emails with the purpose of acquiring new customers or convincing old customers to buy something immediately.
- Adding advertisements in emails sent by other companies to their customers.

Most companies can develop and manage campaigns internally by using relatively affordable e-mail deployment platforms available online. There are dozens of e-mail management and deployment platforms now available and their processes, best practices, and requirements will help all marketers maintain legal compliance. A few examples of these platforms appropriate for small business use include http://www.mailchimp.com/, http://www.constantcontact.com, and http://www.campaigner.com/.

From the start, it is important for small business operators and marketers to have a good understanding of the regulations and compliance issues surrounding the use of the e-mail channel as well as common best practices. While there is ample information and support available from platform partners such as those listed above to assist the small business marketer, let us further examine these compliance issues.

The passage of the federal CAN-SPAM (Controlling the Assault of Non-Solicited Pornography and Marketing) Act in December 2003, as well as several recently enacted state laws, prohibits the abuse of the e-mail channel; financial and other penalties are applicable for fraudulent use. As a general overview, you may communicate with existing clients or prospects as long as there is an existing relationship or a previous transaction. For contact with new prospects, marketers need to gain permission or "opt in" from the recipient after the first e-mail in order to continue communicating with that individual. Further, the bill permits e-mail marketers to send unsolicited commercial e-mail as long as it contains the following elements:

- an opt-out mechanism,
- a valid subject line and header (routing) information,
- the legitimate physical address of the mailer, and
- a label if the content is adult.

The law was intended to prevent or deter spammers, e-mail harvesters, those sending false or misleading headlines, and other unethical, and now illegal, practices.

APPLYING DATABASE MARKETING AND SALES EFFORTS TO E-MAIL CAMPAIGNS

By analyzing the customer or prospect database, we can begin to segment our audiences for the purpose of specifically sending different marketing messages to each customer or prospect segment based on what is believed to produce the highest level of response. A suggested approach to follow for small business marketers using the e-mail channel includes the following process:

1. Establish your overall campaign goal. This goal should maintain consistency with the overall customer contact and marketing strategy.
2. Pull the particular customer segment(s) with whom you want to communicate.
3. Match an appropriate and relevant marketing message to each particular customer segment with whom you are communicating.
4. Measure and analyze the response and conversion rates for each segmented campaign and notice differences based on testing of multiple approaches.
5. Adapt and refine the future communications based on those that have worked best in the previous campaigns.

This process will help small business marketers gain relevant and valuable information each time they use the e-mail channel to communicate with customers and prospects. This information can then be added to the customer database that the small business maintains for its clients and prospects. In time, the marketer will better understand the behaviors, needs, and profiles of his or her primary market. These valuable data will then be used to help small businesses plan future campaigns with specific content and offers that result in communicating unique messages to each individual, rather than sending the same message to everyone.

Establish a Goal

Each campaign goal should be consistent with the overarching marketing and communications objective for the small business. The goal will lead to strategic and tactical decisions for the call to action (Do you want the recipient to link to your Web site? Call you? Provide information?) and the intended outcome of the communication.

List Management

Each communication is an opportunity for marketers to add to their list of recipients for pass along or subsequent messaging. It is also an opportunity to further identify additional profile data, preferences, and behaviors of each e-mail recipient. Think through the process of adding additional recipients, such as forward to a friend elements in an e-mail campaign or the ability for someone to become a subscriber to a newsletter or product information directly from your Web site. The e-mail platforms previously discussed in this chapter have easy-to-use templates and processes to assist these efforts. In addition, small businesses should be aware of list hygiene, data append, and eCOA (electronic change of address) issues and incorporate appropriate updates to keep all contact lists current and accurate. E-mails that bounce back may be old or no longer valid. Marketers need to make an effort to contact these customers or prospects via phone or mail to confirm the validity of a current e-mail address.

Communicate

The communication message needs to align with the overall campaign strategy and business marketing goals. What is our value proposition in sending this e-mail and interrupting the recipient's valuable time? If you can provide a compelling, relevant, and valuable message each time you use the channel (instead of viewing it as an inexpensive alternative to other contact means), you will serve your customers' needs and strengthen the level of trust they have in your company. The message should be personalized, segmented, and relevant. What are your different content feeds or offers to your different audience segments, and how have you established the business rules to determine who will receive what type of message? This is the core of one-to-one marketing. It is a crawl, walk, and then run approach and will take most marketers time to truly engage in strong one-to-one marketing. However, most small businesses can begin with simple segmentations like zip code (providing content and offers specific to individuals from different communities) or prior purchases (providing content and offers to users of specific products or services).

Audience segmentation strategies may be very different for each small business. As one example, a public golf course operator might include audience segments based on gender or recipients with children in order to create content and offers for Ladies' day or Children's golf lessons. From these initially established profiles, small businesses will begin to segment the customers and prospects in the database records, as well as corresponding content feeds, and match them to the appropriate segmented lists.

Measure

Campaigns should be measured, compared, and analyzed in order to improve all future correspondence. Measurement goes beyond basic reporting structure such as bounce rates, delivery rates, and open rates. Small businesses should learn from click-through rates (when a reader clicks on a specific link within the e-mail) in order to track click stream data. This allows the marketer to learn where a specific customer (by name) has visited within the e-mail or Web landing page, what product information he or she may have reviewed, or what data he or she may exhibit an interest in. In addition, marketers should employ testing techniques to determine which particular version of a campaign message may yield stronger results. Based on those results, the balance of the campaign can be adjusted to maximize the effectiveness of a particular message or offer. The tracking and measurement of your campaigns can be viewed in real time from your personal computer. In addition, the data should be added to the existing customer or prospect database the small business currently maintains. This process can be automated and is offered by many of the e-mail platform tools previously discussed.

Adapt

The completion of each e-mail communication provides marketers with new information to learn from and to base their future communications upon. Which offers worked and which did not? Did customer segments react differently? Were the conversion or call to action response rates different? This information feeds into the existing collected knowledge and helps the marketer determine how best to use the process moving forward to maximize the potential of the selected e-mail platform tool.

SMALL BUSINESS SELLING THROUGH WEB SITES

> The marketplace is the place of exchange between buyer and seller. Once one rode a mule to get there; now one rides the Internet. An electronic marketplace can span two rooms in the same building or two continents. How individuals, firms and organizations will approach and define the electronic marketplace depends on people's ability to ask the right questions now and to take advantage of the opportunities that will arise over the next few years.[5]

Small businesses are well beyond the discussion point of questioning whether to have a business Web site. The answer is clearly yes. A Web site is as critical to the success of all companies as the phone is, and in many instances, the Web site can be more important than the phone. The composition of the small business Web site, as well as the functionality and user experience, is what helps to determine the success rate the site will have in terms of positively impacting sales.

When your prospects and customers are searching online, they are not looking for the traditional branding or sales information. Many times, they are looking for ideas to help them solve a problem. They want information they can use for their own benefit. Small businesses that apply the "think like a consultant" approach and offer something that helps visitors first, instead of trying only to sell them a product or service, will gain loyalty in the Web visitor.

Consider your small business Web site as the first and lasting impression new prospects will have of your company. How you communicate your story will directly impact your sales efforts. Many small businesses still have straightforward "brochureware" marketing sites. The objective of the site is to supplement traditional sales and marketing activities and generally promote the company. There is often a reluctance to give complete product details because the objective is to induce visitors to call or write to the company for more information and thus establish contact. This is an antiquated approach and results in the Web visitor simply clicking on a competitor's Web site for similar information. It is important to understand that the Web has given power to the consumer like no other media or technology. If you do not satisfy the needs of the customers or prospects online, they are just one click away from finding their solutions with someone else.

In a site that includes online sales, the objective is to close the sale electronically with payment (and sometimes delivery) made over the Internet. This type of site is designed to include comprehensive product information, as visitors will be expected to make a purchasing decision based on the information presented. These sites usually have three sections:

1. *Marketing and added-value information.* This information is intended to help inform, educate, and attract customers, giving them a feel for the contents and giving them confidence in the small business.
2. *The catalog.* Detailed information on product benefits, specifications, and pricing.
3. *Order processing.* This will include a secure method for specifying and paying for the order. More advanced systems may have a method for the customer to go back into the system to check progress and delivery of the order.

According to Wikipedia, the online encyclopedia, a Web site is described as follows:

A website is a collection of Web pages typically common to a particular domain name or subdomain on the World Wide Web on the Internet. The pages of a website will be accessed from a common root URL called the homepage, and usually reside on the same physical server. The URLs of the pages organize them into a hierarchy, although the hyperlinks between them control how the reader perceives the overall structure and how the traffic flows between the different parts of the sites.

From the last half-decade of the 20th century through the first few years of the 21st century, most small businesses have relied on outside consultants and service providers to develop their Web sites. These firms would host the sites on computers known as Web servers and develop the sites using a programming language known as HTML (HyperText Markup Language). The pages are then called up by using a software program known as a Web browser. While consultants and professional service providers remain experts in terms of providing strategy and do lend value to small business Web site management, the actual development and maintenance of many small business Web sites can be managed internally using packaged software that is readily available and affordable to small businesses. This is particularly true for static Web sites that do not change content as frequently. In those instances, Web site development tools such as Microsoft Office FrontPage or Adobe Dreamweaver can be used by small businesses to develop and maintain their sites themselves.

If the focus is on actually selling product online, there are three ways to build your online store:

1. Purchase packaged software that is "out of a box."
2. Use software offered by a hosting company.
3. Create your own system, writing the necessary code.

From the beginning, marketers need to decide what your online store is designed to achieve, realistically. Among the best advice is not to overengineer. Technology advances quickly and what you may be forced to code now, at a higher expense, may shortly be available in a more out-of-the-box form. For this primary reason, most small businesses should initiate their online store presence with a packaged solution.

Packaged software is available to help small businesses build e-commerce enabled sites (allowing the business to sell product online) and assist in the ongoing content changes that may be required to the site. Some of these packages include products like http://www.goemerchant.com/, http://www.store.yahoo.com, and http://www.wired-2-shop.com/. Small business owners and marketers will want a basic understanding of the Web storefront anatomy prior to development.

Web storefronts enable your customers and prospects to view your products, to add or delete items from their selection, and review their final selection prior to purchase. The payment process is easy to follow, fast, and secure. Shipping information, applicable tax, and any return policy are clearly presented, and customers are e-mailed with a confirmation of purchase and delivery date.

However, selling is only part of the equation here. Detailed records of all transactions are needed for accounting and tax purposes as well as for use in developing more effective marketing efforts in the future. If possible, small businesses will want this information to synchronize with their existing accounting and back-office software. However, it may also present an opportunity to review a new back-office system—but that is a separate consideration.

DATABASE MARKETING AND WEB SITES

Customization and relevancy are at the core of the 21st century marketing revolution. By creating a dialogue with customers electronically, their buying behavior can be analyzed and responses to their requests can be personalized. Customization provides value to customers by allowing them to find solutions that better fit their needs and saves them time in searching for their solutions, which cuts down on face-to-face personal selling costs. Instead of presenting a large amount of data to a given customer to sift through, custom catalogs can be presented, one customer at a time. Not only can a solution be uniquely targeted and developed for a customer, but also as the relationship grows, the more a small business will learn about the individual buying behavior, habits, and needs of their customers. As a natural result of this growing relationship, cross-selling opportunities will become apparent.

For small businesses selling and marketing in the 21st century, the mantra remains the same as in the past: it is all about the personal relationship between the buyer and the seller. Successful marketers will shift back their focus from products to the customer—the whole customer. The goal is to build an ever-deepening relationship with a customer to meet as wide a variety of the customer's needs as possible.

Small businesses that establish and improve the customer relationship are the small businesses that succeed in all types of selling. They will become the primary place consumers will go to meet their shopping needs. Companies that are able to capture substantial information about their customers' buying behavior can anticipate needs for products and services of all kinds—this is the heart of one-to-one marketing, where each customer is treated as a market segment of one. It is the same approach the storekeepers and small merchants have maintained for hundreds of years. Among the most cost-effective and successful methods of attracting qualified prospects to a small business Web site is Search Engine Marketing.

SEARCH ENGINE MARKETING

Oftentimes Search Engine Marketing (SEM) and Search Engine Optimization (SEO) are considered two different types of marketing. Actually, Search Engine Marketing deals with the actual techniques used to position a Web site within search engines to achieve maximum exposure of a Web site. There are several SEM methods, but the main two are search engine optimization and paid listings.

SEO, also referred to as Natural Search, is a separate set of methods that are targeted to improve the ranking of a Web site in search engine listings and could be considered a subset of SEM. The goal of an SEO effort is to increase the amount of visitors to a Web site by ranking high in the search results by creating site pages that are accessible to a search engine. The higher a Web site ranks in the results of a search, the greater the chance that that site will be visited by a user. Some techniques used in SEO include link building, keyword targeted content, designing an optimal page structure, and developing codes that include pertinent basic elements such as title tags, headers, and meta tags.

The majority of traffic from Web sites comes from search engines. Although the data vary depending on the sources you read, the bottom line is that search engines are used millions of times each day by consumers searching for a variety of products and services. The November 2005 Nielsen//NetRatings Report recorded that the activity of more than 60 search sites yielded a total search volume of approximately 5.1 billion searches for that month.[6] Having your business displayed at the top of search results is essential if you want to do any business from the major search engines. According to an April 2006 Search Engine User Behavior Study, iProspect reported that 62 percent of the current search engine user community click on a search result within the first page of results, and a full 90 percent of search engine users click on a result within the first three pages of search results.[7,8] This finding accentuates the need for small businesses to make certain that their Web sites are ranked within the first three pages of search results, mainly on the first page, for the keywords used by potential customers to find products, services, or information.

Obviously, small businesses can generate revenue from a Web site, but how the products and services available on the Web site are advertised has a large impact on the overall return on investment (ROI). If a small business purchases advertising through a program like Google AdWords or other services that charge per click, each click may cost only 10¢, but if it takes 200 clicks or $20 to make a $10 sale, then there is no profit being made. Pay-per-click (PPC) campaigns will also never stop costing money. In the long run, however, Search Engine Optimization can be very cost-effective.

The investment associated with some SEO programs depends on the company and the industry. A dog training school may be able to maintain a top 5 ranking with a monthly budget of $50, while a small Web site development company may be looking at several hundred a week, if not more, to maintain a top spot. While there are other ways to advertise a Web site, very few can compete with the vast targeted audience and affordability that search engines provide.

Search engines use automated software programs known as spiders or bots to survey the Web and build their databases. Web documents are retrieved by these programs and analyzed. Data collected from each Web page are then added to the search engine index. When a query is entered at a search engine site, your input is checked against the search engine's index of all the Web pages it has analyzed. The best URLs (Uniform Resource Locators) are then returned to you as hits, ranked in order with the best results at the top.

So how do you get your site indexed? Following are some critical elements adapted from the article series by Dave Davies,[9] owner of Beanstalk Search Engine Positioning, Inc., titled "Ten Steps To A Well Optimized Website." These are good guidelines to follow to have a higher ranking, naturally optimized Web site. Depending on the competition, some steps may take a few hours, some may take months, but in the end, if done correctly, you will have a well-optimized site that should place well and hold its positioning.

While there are several techniques associated with SEM, the two main methods are SEO and PPC. PPC has its advantages, especially if a small business can benefit from direct marketing to the most targeted customers. PPC programs are an online advertising model used by search engines, Web directories, and Web sites. The advertiser pays only when someone clicks on a sponsored link. Typically, in these scenarios, search engines allow advertisers to bid on a position and set a maximum spending amount either per day or per bid. For example, if a small business owner would like to purchase the keyword phrase "knitting needles," he or she could put a maximum bid of $1 for position one with a maximum daily budget of $30. If only ten impressions converted to clicks in a 24-hour period, the advertiser would have to pay only $10 for the day.

There are several benefits small businesses should consider when choosing PPC for direct marketing.

- PPC advertising is highly targeted and results are quantifiable.
- PPC keywords and phrases can be tested for very little money. Small businesses have the ability to set bid and daily spending limits based on their budgets.
- Feedback is *very* fast. Small business advertisers can measure results within 24 hours of the start of a campaign. Most of the search engines, including Google and Yahoo!, offer various performance reports that are available every 24 hours.
- ROI can be easily calculated using conversion tracking. Google and Yahoo! will track conversions even if your small business does not use a Web site analysis package.
- You pay only when somebody clicks on the ad. So if the first keyword tests are a disaster and nobody clicks, it does not cost anything.
- It is easy to get started. Once all the keyword research has been made and landing pages have been created, the next step is to submit the keyword, descriptions, and URLs to the engines.
- You can experiment with different keywords, titles, and descriptions.

In order to know what search terms to use, small business advertisers should first research search terms. To start, simply brainstorm terms that you think customers would use to search for your product or services. Also be sure to check if your competitors are ranking for those same words. If you need help deciding on more detailed search terms, there are several tools available to assist in your search, such as Wordtracker and Overture Bid Tool. The next step is determining which PPC product to use. Many search engines offer a variety of products to optimize your PPC efforts.

CONCLUSION

While no one can predict the future, noticeable changes have occurred in the 21st century that will change the way small business selling is conducted. All of the globalization, demographic shifts, and organizational structural changes coupled with the advent of great technology will help businesses with these changes. The thought of utilizing greater forms of technology may at first seem contradictory to the processes of building relationships. However, as this chapter has demonstrated, technology can actually strengthen relationships through the use of databases and direct marketing. These tools, along with other forms of communication, such as the use of e-mail, Web sites, and search engines, are key tools that small business marketers can use in an easy, cheap, and efficient manner. While the tools discussed in this chapter do not seem to fit the traditional view of selling, these tools can be used in conjunction to create an integrated marketing communications strategy, which can help the small business marketer compete with large marketers in the sales process.

NOTES

1. Thomas L. Friedman, *The World Is Flat: A Brief History of the Twenty-First Century,* New York: Farrar, Straus and Giroux, 2005.

2. "Direct Marketing," *Wilkipedia,* http://em.wilkipedia.org/wiki/Direct_Marketing (accessed on August 15, 2006).

3. Chris Helm and John Gaffney, "Less Talk, More Action," *1to1 Magazine* (October 14, 2004).

4. "Benefits of Personalization," *CRM Magazine,* October 2004.

5. Derek Leebaert (editor), 1998. *The Future of the Electronic Marketplace,* Cambridge, MA: MIT Press.

6. Nielsen//NetRatings, "Nielsen//NetRatings Reports the Fastest Growing Web Sites Year-over-Year among Top Internet Propeties: Apple, Google and Amazon Take the Lead," http://pic.photobucket.com/press/2005-12-netratings.pdf (last accessed April 20, 2007).

7. Dave Davies, "10 Steps to Higher Search Engine Positioning," http://www.beanstalk-inc.com/articles/search-engine-positioning/10-steps.htm (accessed August 16, 2006).

8. iProspect, "iProspect Search Engine User Behavior Study: April 2006," http://www.iprospect.com/about/whitepaper_seuserbehavior_apr06.htm.

9. Dave Davies, "Ten Steps To Higher Search Engine Positioning," http://www.beanstalk-inc.com/articles/seo/10-steps.htm.

CHAPTER 11

Understanding Diverse Purchasers in Business-to-Business Marketing and Industrial Selling

Michael F. d'Amico

Healtheon/WebMD.com is a Web site that provides health care and wellness information for consumers. However, Healtheon/WebMD.com also markets to hospitals, health maintenance organizations, insurance companies, and other business organizations. These business-to-business activities are a major part of its marketing efforts. Just as a consumer products marketer needs to know its customers' buying behavior, Healtheon/WebMD.com knows that it is important to understand the needs of its organizational customers and the nature of buyer-seller relationships in business markets. With regard to selling and relationship management, the business-to-business relationships are usually the biggest and the most important ones for most firms due to the quantity and volume of their purchases. This chapter investigates how organizational buying behavior differs from the buying behavior of ultimate consumers, which is a critical subject in order to develop a better understanding of company and customer relationships.

ORGANIZATIONAL BUYING BEHAVIOR

A business marketing transaction takes place whenever a good or service is sold for any use other than personal consumption. In other words, any sale to an industrial user, wholesaler, retailer, or organization other than the ultimate consumer is made within the business market. Such sales involve business-to-business marketing activities. What do organizations buy? Manufacturers require raw materials, component parts, equipment, supplies, and services. Construction companies and service providers require many of these same products. Wholesalers and retailers purchase products for resale, as well as equipment such as trucks, shelving, and computers.

Hospitals, zoos, and other nonprofit organizations use many goods and services to facilitate the performance of their business functions, as do federal, state, and local governments. In fact, the U.S. federal government is the largest single buyer of organizational products in the world. By participating in business-to-business exchanges, all these organizations display organizational buying behavior. Buying is a necessary activity for all business and not-for-profit organizations. In organizational buying situations, the purchase of goods and services (such as medical equipment and accounting services) often involves a complex process. Purchasing agents and other organizational members determine whether goods and services need to be purchased, gather information about the needed goods or services, evaluate alternative purchases, and negotiate the necessary arrangements with suppliers. Much organizational buying takes place over an extended period of time, involves communications among several organizational members, and entails financial relationships with suppliers. The federal government's purchase of solar panels for a space telescope would be a good example of such a long, involved process. However, there is considerable diversity in organizational buying. A restaurant's regular purchase of ketchup from a supplier would be a straightforward and simple process.

CHARACTERISTICS OF THE BUSINESS MARKET

The agricultural, financial, and manufacturing industries are quite different from one another, yet they share some basic characteristics that are typical of all business markets. First, particular business markets often contain relatively few customers in comparison to the consumer sector. As a consequence, each customer's purchases may represent a significant amount of revenue to marketers who seek their business, therefore increasing the importance of the relationship. Second, these customers are often geographically concentrated. For example, Silicon Valley, in the area surrounding San Jose, California, is the headquarters for hundreds of companies that make semiconductors, computer specialty products, and computer software. Of course, foreign competition exists, but business markets abroad also tend to be geographically concentrated.

A third characteristic of business markets is that buyers in such markets generally prefer to buy directly from the manufacturer or producer, although the 21st century has seen a growing trend toward outsourcing, which can mean that even the sales function has been outsourced at times. However, the preference to deal directly with the manufacturer may come from the desire to buy in large quantities or to avoid intermediaries in an effort to obtain a better price. It may also be a function of the technical complexity of the products that many of these buyers use and the fact that many such products are often made to order. (Consider how the U.S. government purchases weapon systems, for example.) For all of these reasons, the desire to deal directly with producers is understandable.

A fourth characteristic of business markets is that buyers usually have considerable expertise in buying. They buy, almost always, in a scientific way, basing decisions on close analyses of the product being offered and careful comparisons of competing products. Moreover, terms of sale, service, guarantees, and other such factors are likely to be carefully weighed by employees who specialize in purchasing. A purchasing manager is an employee who is responsible for the purchasing function within an organization. If the product is a highly technical one, properly trained engineers or scientists may also participate in the purchase decision. For a major purchase decision, a committee will likely be formed to evaluate factors such as the business-to-business marketer's product, technical abilities, and position relative to competitors. In such cases, strategic alliances may be formed to work out technological problems. For example, Fujitsu's engineers shared technologies and worked closely with product developers at Sun Microsystems, Inc., to jointly develop a new microchip for Sun's workstations.

A fifth characteristic of business markets is the importance of repeated market transactions. The focus of much business-to-business marketing has shifted from the single transaction to the overall buyer-seller relationship and makes use of relationship marketing. By establishing strong working relationships, suppliers and customers can improve distribution processes and other joint activities. In fact, many business-to-business marketers form strategic alliances, or at least informal partnerships, with their customers. For example, the Sherwin-Williams Company, the paint producer, let Sears, Roebuck and Company executives help select the salespeople who would service the Sears account. The company's logic was that the two companies had joint sales goals, so it made sense to jointly select the people responsible for achieving these goals.

All of these characteristics are just as important in the 21st century as they were in the 20th century. Indeed, some are now having an even greater impact on how business-to-business selling occurs. For example, while purchasing managers have always had a role in corporations, their role is even more pronounced today. As relationships grow and deepen, purchasing managers are gaining greater and greater power, and good salespeople must realize this. Likewise, strategic alliances are also having a more pronounced role on selling in the 21st century. In a time of increased accountability, strategic alliances that do not add value to the value chain will be dropped. Thus, it is becoming increasingly important for salespeople to demonstrate how they can add value to the relationship. Additionally, in the 21st century, the Internet is a very efficient medium for conducting repeat business. Because the Internet is having such a dramatic impact on business-to-business marketing, a separate section is devoted to this topic later in the chapter.

Although the sixth characteristic of the business market has been mentioned in earlier chapters, it is worth repeating here. Business-to-business marketing has become a global activity. Global competition can be intense, and taking a world perspective is essential. In many instances, a business-to-business marketer's main competition does not come from its home country. Indeed, a company may have no domestic competitors. Taking a global perspective is important for marketers selling in consumer markets, of course, but in business markets it is so crucial that it may determine whether a business survives. Managers in business-to-business marketing organizations often find that decisions about international strategy are the most vital decisions they make.

The characteristics of organizational markets mentioned here do not apply to every market. Furthermore, the list of characteristics is by no means a complete one. But it does give some indications of how industrial salespeople deal with these special buyers. The fact that there are often relatively few buyers, who may be geographically concentrated, and who prefer to deal directly with suppliers, encourages—indeed, often requires—the extensive use of personal selling and relationship marketing.

The technical nature of many of the products and the expertise of the people making the purchase decisions demand a well-trained sales force with extensive knowledge of the products they sell. Representing a maker of nuclear power plants is quite different from selling Legos or Hot Wheels play sets to Christmas-shopping grandparents. The various characteristics of business markets often combine to permit the marketer to identify almost all potential customers. This capability can make personal selling, which is usually expensive, a cost-efficient marketing tool within this sector.

THREE KINDS OF BUYING

The buyer of organizational goods and services, such as chemicals, machinery, or maintenance services, may go through a decision-making process that is similar to, but more complex than, the consumer decision-making process. Organizational buying behavior may be viewed as a multistage decision-making process. However, the amount of time and effort devoted to each of the stages, or buying phases, depends on a number of factors such as the nature of the product, the costs involved, and the experience of the organization in buying the needed goods or services, which all in turn affect the amount of personal selling required. Consider these three situations:

- An organization regularly buys goods and services from the same suppliers. Careful attention may have been given to selection of the suppliers at some earlier time, but the organization is well satisfied with them and with the products they offer. The organization buys from these suppliers virtually automatically. This is the straight rebuy situation. Everything from pencils to legal advice to equipment may be bought this way if the buyer is satisfied with the supplier's past performance and a search for alternative solutions is not initiated. Very little personal selling is involved in this type of purchase decision.

- An organization is discontent with current suppliers or suspects that "shopping around" may be in its best interest. It knows what products are needed and who the likely suppliers are. This is the modified rebuy situation. Here, too, any type of good or service may be involved. Personal selling plays some role in this type of buying decision, either to keep an account that is almost lost possibly by suggesting other products in your product line that the customer might not be aware of or selling can also play a role by converting a new user that is unsatisfied with the competition.

- An organization is facing a new problem or need and is not certain what products or what suppliers will fill the need. If the purchase is expected to be a very expensive one, the sense of concern and uncertainty is heightened. This is new task buying. Personal selling plays an absolutely pivotal role in this stage.

In each situation, the length of the decision-making process and the amount of time devoted to each buying phase may vary, depending on what is being purchased. These three separate kinds of buying have been associated both with specific types of organizational buyer behaviors and with specific business-to-business marketing activities. It is important to note that the key element that sets the categories apart from one another is the behavior of organizational buyers and their current needs and decision processes, not the complexity of the product involved nor the amount of money being spent.

Understanding the types of buying situations and behavior found in organizations is extremely important for organizational marketers, just as understanding consumer behavior patterns is important for marketers of consumer products. Each buying situation suggests a different sales strategy and an adjustment of its elements to fit particular circumstances.

A sales manager whose customer is facing a new task buying situation, for example, should understand that the target customer is uncertain about what steps should be taken to satisfy his or her organization's needs. Such a buyer probably will require a good deal of information about the supplier, its products, and its abilities to deliver and service the products. This suggests a sales strategy that stresses promotion, especially communication of information that will help the customer evaluate alternatives and understand why the company doing the marketing is the one to choose.

A buyer in a modified rebuy mode might require information of another type; this buyer knows something of what is needed and who likely suppliers are. In such a case, communications built around very specific problem areas might be appropriate. If the target buyer is searching for new suppliers, the marketer must find out why. Have deliveries been late? Have there been product failures? Are prices perceived as too high? The marketer must be aware of such problems and show the target buyer why dealing with this supplier can solve them.

In the case of the straight rebuy, the marketer who is in the strong position of being the supplier benefiting from the rebuy situation wants to make sure that the target customer does not become discontent and continues to make regular purchases. Maintaining the relationship through regular contact is the key marketing objective.

In many organizational buying situations, the buyer has either a mental or a formal list of likely suppliers. This list includes those suppliers known to be able to supply the product or service according to specification and to meet time, quality, or other requirements. Suppliers who are on the list obviously have a far greater chance of landing an order than those who are not. Those not on the list will have to exert some extra effort to get an order. Thus, the activities of vendors will reflect their status—either "in" or "out." At a minimum, a firm has to know about a job to bid on it. Firms not on the list might never receive an invitation to bid. That is why it is so important as a sales representative to keep all lines of communication open. Representatives need to make sure that their names are out there and that positive word-of-mouth promotion is "floating around" about them.

THE INTERNET AND E-COMMERCE

The Internet is dramatically changing business-to-business marketing and the way organizational buying occurs in the 21st century. Consider the General Electric Company (GE), a major corporation that markets power systems, aircraft engines, plastics, medical systems, and hundreds of other products in the business market. GE does $1 billion of business on its Trading Process Network Web site. A salesperson no longer needs to make a call to companies engaged in straight rebuys. Buyers just go to the company's Web site, find information about goods and services, select the products they need, and e-mail their orders. Many business-to-business marketers have found that providing extra customer value on the Internet both increases sales and reduces the cost of making a sales transaction.

An Internet Web site provides a number of advantages to organizational buyers. They appreciate having product and pricing information readily available through a company's Web site. Technical documents and marketing information no longer need to be mailed or faxed to organizational buyers, because they can be sent to customers and collaborators in the value chain over the marketing company's intranet, which is connected to the Web site. Sophisticated Web sites allow customers to select a particular product configuration and learn its exact cost.

Furthermore, with a good Web site, customer-service representatives may not have to spend as much time on the telephone answering questions about the status of orders in progress. Many Internet sites, such as the FedEx Corporation site, use a tracking number system that permits customers to learn the status of a shipment. Customers also like the idea of being able to get a price quote or product configuration information at their own pace, rather than using e-mail or voice mail to contact a sales representative or customer-service worker and then waiting for the company representative to get back to them later on. Simply by eliminating some telephone tag (leaving messages back and forth repeatedly before finally contacting each other), the Internet can save great amounts of time. FAQs (Frequently Asked Questions) lists on Web sites also provide added value to prospective customers.

In competitive bidding situations, the Internet can increase the number of bidders and include suppliers from around the world. GE has cut the length of the bidding process in its lighting division from 21 days to 10. Because requesting bids is so easy, purchasing managers contact more suppliers; the increased competition has lowered the cost of goods by 5–20 percent. Advanced software lets GE purchasing managers specify to whom they want their request for bids to go and describe the type of information, such as drawings, bidders should provide. The software then manages the bids as they come back, eliminating unacceptable bids and handling further rounds, finally notifying the bidders of the outcome. In sum, while some might feel that the Internet lowers the level of the relationship, in actuality, the 21st century has shown a trend toward technology enhancing the relationships. Future chapters of this book cover the use of technology in the 21st century in more detail.

THE CROSS-FUNCTIONAL BUYING CENTER

As mentioned earlier, many people may be involved in an organizational buying decision. How do salespeople manage to consider all these persons, their motives, and their special needs? It is a complicated and difficult task. However, the concept of the buying center helps sales managers to visualize the buying process and to organize their thinking as they develop the sales strategies. The buying center in any organization is an informal, cross-departmental decision unit whose primary objective is to acquire, distribute, and process relevant purchasing-related information. In somewhat simpler terms, the buying center includes all the people and groups that have roles in the decision-making processes of purchasing. Because all these people and groups take part, they are seen as having common goals and as sharing in the risks associated with the ultimate decision. Membership in the buying center and the size of the center vary from organization to organization and from case to case. In smaller organizations, almost everyone may have some input; in larger organizations, a more restricted group may be identifiable. The buying center may range in size from a few people to perhaps 20. Some international buying centers have been known to be as large as 50 people.

When thinking in terms of a buying center, keep in mind that the center is not identified on any organization chart. A committee officially created to decide on a purchase is likely to be only one part of the buying center. Other members have unofficial but important roles to play. Indeed, membership in the buying center may actually change as the decision-making process progresses. As the purchasing task moves from step to step, individuals with expertise in certain areas are likely to step out of the process as others are added. Again, membership in a buying center is informal, so no announcements are likely to be made of who has been dropped and who has been added.

Buying centers, then, include a wide variety of individuals who work in different functional areas of the organization. In other words, buying centers are cross-functional. One example comes from a study of the buying of air compressors for manufacturing plants. The following individuals and groups were all found to be involved in some part of the purchasing decision: president, vice president of engineering, vice president of manufacturing, plant facilities manager, maintenance supervisor, chief electrician, and purchasing department personnel. Each member of a buying center has an official place in the organizational structure as well as an unofficial one in the buying center. Official organizational roles may influence roles in the buying center. For example, the formal organization of a hospital might include a purchasing department that screens all marketers of hospital equipment, even though the physicians, surgeons, and hospital executives actually have more influence over the decision-making process. Furthermore, in general, roles vary with the complexity of the product under consideration. As complexity increases, engineers and technicians may have a greater say in purchasing decisions. If the product is not complex or if a regular purchasing pattern has been developed and agreed on, a purchasing agent or some other formally identified buyer is likely to have buying responsibility.

ROLES IN ORGANIZATIONAL BUYING

In a sense, in spite of its apparent complexity, buying behavior in buying centers is like buying behavior in households. There, different members of the household play certain roles in the purchase decision. We can identify five similar roles in organizational buying behavior: users, buyers, gatekeepers, deciders, and influencers.

Users are employees or managers who will actually use what is purchased. Although a retail sales clerk may be the user of a computerized cash register, he or she may have little influence on the decision to buy the product. The buyer has the formal authority to purchase the product and is often responsible for choosing a supplier and negotiating the terms of the purchase. A purchasing agent may fill the role of buyer. Alternatively, a purchasing agent may gather information, such as product specifications and prices, after which engineers or others within the organization make the buying decision. Collecting and passing on or withholding information is known as the gatekeeper function. In some cases, the "gate" may be opened or closed by someone who has very little to do with the process otherwise. For example, suppose a secretary requests new word-processing software. The office manager who supervises the secretary may act as gatekeeper by simply passing along (or failing to pass along) the request to higher management. Perhaps, though, the office manager has the ultimate responsibility to decide whether the secretary will get the new software. In that case, the office manager is also the decider—the person who makes the actual purchase decision. In any case, marketers must direct much of their effort toward gatekeepers because they control the flow of information related to the purchase.

The influencer affects the purchase decision by supplying advice or information. In a software purchase, a consultant may supply technical information and may thus act as an influencer. (Note that an outsider can play a role in the buying center.) A secretary in another department may act as an influencer by relating past experiences with a particular product. Influence can also take the form of information about what course of action those in high positions in the organization prefer; whoever provides such information is an influencer.

Remember that a person in a particular position may play several roles and that a particular role may be played by persons in several types of positions. Note also that the importance of a particular role varies from decision to decision. You can see that a buying center is often loosely constructed and somewhat difficult to identify clearly. Nevertheless, because of its potent influence, the marketer should devote time and effort to investigating the effects of the buying center on the marketing situation at hand.

DETERMINING EACH ROLE

While the above characterization is a helpful one, it does not provide any guidance to the salesperson who is trying to determine whom to talk to within a company. And, if you do not know the decision-making process within each company, you may not be selling to the decision maker. Selling to the wrong person presents an incredible waste of time and perhaps even creates a bad reputation. You also will not find out the right needs if you are not talking to the right individual. So how do you determine who that individual is to ensure that you are selling to the right person? In a recent article by Lain Chroust Ehmann, ten questions were outlined that you should ask the buyer.[1]

1. *Why are you investigating a new solution now?* Or in other words, what are the problems in your company? What is going wrong? Why do you need a new product? With this one question, you will begin to have an inkling of what the major issues are, what the customer's timing is, and what the decision criteria will be. You also may get a hint of where the contact fits in the overall scheme of things. You immediately know

what some of your challenges are going to be—and with whom you are going to need to speak.

2. *What is it about your current solution that is no longer working for you?* Like its sister above, this question is intended to open the doors for communication and help you to identify areas that will require additional investigation. It is just about continuing the questioning process to ensure that you have the right information and are working with the right person.

3. *How have you made decisions like this in the past?* Just for the same reason that we were always told that we had to take history in school, the past shows keys to the present. It shows what things were done, what went wrong, what went right, and may possibly gives clues into what may be done in the future. Sometimes prospects are reluctant to share information, seeing that sort of disclosure as akin to handing over their power. In these cases, salespeople have to find round-the-back means of getting to the same destination. Asking how previous decisions have been made not only can give you insight into what other parties may need to be involved in the process, but also what criteria were used to make the decision and who your competition may be.

4. *When do you hope to have the new product/service operational?* and

5. *Is there a compelling event that is driving this purchase?* Timing is everything. It is not just about what is happening, but when it will happen. Salespeople need to understand their buyer's sense of urgency and priorities. A deal that needs to be signed, sealed, and delivered before the end of the quarter will go to the top of your list, while one that is not going to be finalized until sometime in the next fiscal year does not command the same urgency. These questions will also let you know if you can realistically meet the customer's ideal time frame, alerting you to potential problems down the road, which will make sure that you can satisfy them and create a continued relationship.

6. *What objectives will this purchase assist you in reaching?* Okay, timing is everything, but so is strategy, right? If that is the case, you can better know what your prospect needs. To find out this information, revisit Chapter 4, but instead of researching your competition, think about your buyers. It is one thing to know where someone is presently, but it is much more beneficial to understand where they plan to go in the future. You will gain an added benefit from this question: buyers will think that you truly care about them, their needs, and their future.

7. *Is a particular department driving this decision?* This is a nice, indirect way of saying, "So, are you the decision maker here?" And you do not want to say the latter. That is offensive and will put people on the defensive. Would you want to answer that question? "No, I don't have any power" or "Of course I can make decisions" are likely to be the two answers you will get. And that does not find out any more information such as Is anyone else involved in the decision process? Just be careful with this question. This is a power and ego issue.

8. *What criteria will you be evaluating in order to make a decision?* This is further digging into the decision process. What step(s) are you involved with? What is it that you care about? What will your different needs be at different points in the process? If there is a

committee making the decisions, the chances are each member will have different needs at different points in the process.

9. *How will these different criteria be weighted?* Size matters. What if you are buying a car and you ask about all the various features; meanwhile, all the time you know that price is the only thing that matters. Then the salesperson spends an hour talking all about the features and performance of a car that is out of your budget when there is only one car on the whole lot that will fit that budget. You have to know which determining factors are the most important. You can do a bang-up job of meeting nine out of ten decision factors, but if you fail on the one that really counts, you can still lose the deal.

10. *If there was anything that would stop this project, what would it be?* Although salespeople never want to deal with the negative, would it not be helpful to get an immediate answer to this question? This question is an attempt to embrace the negative and get the customer to think outside the box. It will also help identify possible roadblocks and other parties you may need to co-opt or present to on your quest for the sale.

ORGANIZATIONAL BUYING PROCESSES: REMEMBERING THE IMPORTANCE OF EMOTION

Is organizational buying behavior based on rational buying criteria, or do emotional motives come into play? Consider the following example: A computer equipment firm had traditionally listed high prices for its products, but offered deep discounts from list prices. This practice was prevalent in the industry. The company decided to lower its list prices to capture the attention of purchasing agents. However, the company failed to take into account the professional needs of purchasing managers in large organizations, who proved their worth to their bosses by negotiating the deep discounts. These buyers ignored the lower list prices and purchased only from firms with which they could still negotiate deep discounts.

So what happened in the previous example? What was the key determining factor in each decision? Now that we understand the basics of organizational buying, it is time to review the psychological side of the processes to understand how decisions are made. There is an old sales adage that dates back to Aristotle: people buy emotionally and defend logically. You would think that this does not apply in the organizational buying context. With all the formal processes and procedures that occur, you would think it would be like following a list. However, because we are all human, we are all driven by the same basic underlying thoughts, emotions, and values. And they very much come into play even in the organizational buying context.

So, if industrial buyers go by feelings, not logic, what are salespeople doing wrong? Or, what could they be doing to get more sales? Because we are taught to treat the sales processes as a multistage process, with distinct stages, many salespeople do not stop and look for nonverbal cues that can provide insight into a prospect's feelings. Salespeople must dig deeper to understand a buyer's needs, not *also* in organizational buying, but *especially* in organizational buying where the relationship is key. If you can create a connection with customers, that builds the relationship, which in turn motivates customers to take action. That connection is based on many of the key emotions that are similar to forming a social relationship, such as, likability and compatibility.

Keep this thought in mind while you focus on how members of your sales force are trained to sell. Usually, training revolves around drilling in features and benefits, competitive analysis ("our ROI [return on investment] comes faster and is 12 percent higher"), and memorizing a long list of facts. This is all good; it means the reps will not be at a loss for words when they are in front of a prospect. But is it how purchases get decided? Increasingly, the evidence suggests this factual scaffolding is beside the point of how purchases get made. Few buyers will be primed to sign on the line when a rep shoots fact upon fact at them. Facts are fine—no one says they play no role at all. Sometimes they justify the decisions that are arrived at emotionally. But sales will get made when the salesperson masters the tougher objective of tapping into the customer's emotions.

Unfortunately, it is a lot easier to teach facts than to teach how to be emotional with people. And unfortunately, not everyone is that good at "reading" people to judge emotions. Sometimes it is about compassion and empathy and learning to listen to stories about a frustrating day at work. Sometimes it is about vulnerability. If you, as a salesperson can open up, then your buyers will be likely to open up. Sometimes it is about giving compliments and ego strokes, without sounding phony. One of the biggest emotions in organizational buying is ego. People want people at their work place to respect them and think they do a good job.

Then, to read the buyer's emotions, salespeople must exhibit similar skills. They must tune in instead to the emotional cues buyers give off and watch for body language, tone of voice, and any emotive words the buyers use. These cues will not give you a direct path into the buyer's decision. But practice reading them and they will become a road map into the buyer's mind and the forces that are helping to shape the decision. Salespeople must also realize that there is always an emotional component to every sale. Encourage the customer to express emotions and learn to listen for them. And on that same note, never argue with a customer's or prospect's feelings. It sometimes sounds almost like manipulation, but it is not. Instead, it is truly realizing that relationship marketing is not just a textbook term. It means that to you, the selling process must become an actual relationship. This concept is so easily ignored in organizational buying where it is so vitally important.

Now we discuss the flip side of the coin. Reasonable observers must acknowledge that good sales skills and effective advertisements often appeal to an organizational buyer's emotional need to buy "the best" or to take pride in the products purchased. However, one compelling argument explains why emotional buying motives are not likely to be the most important ones: No organizational buyer would put his or her job and reputation on the line by purchasing a product simply because a friendly salesperson satisfied some emotional need of that buyer. By entertaining a prospect, a sales representative may satisfy certain aspects of that prospect's needs for affiliation, but if the sale goes through, it is because the product meets all the rational criteria used by the purchaser to judge the product. That is, the emotional reasons are almost always supplemental buying criteria. There are many rational reasons *for* buying. The importance of each factor varies from situation to situation, and some factors may not come into play in a given purchase decision. This discussion focuses on a few of the most influential purchasing criteria.

PURCHASING CRITERIA

Product Quality

Product quality can be an extremely important purchasing criterion. Organizations may make certain purchases without carefully analyzing the products they are buying simply because the costs and risks involved in making a bad choice are not very great. Paper clips and thumbtacks are all pretty much alike, for example, and are often bought without close scrutiny. However, most goods and services bought by organizations are not like that, and organizational buyers are usually very careful. In fact, many products are made according to the buyer's own specifications, indicating that the buyer closely considers exactly what quality is required in a product purchased for a given task. In many industries, such as aerospace and defense, the reliability of the component part is the most important criterion.

Many organizations have adopted total quality management (TQM) programs that directly affect the organizational buying decision. A manufacturer that promises its customers defect-free products will not tolerate parts suppliers that do not adopt TQM programs of their own. Thus, not only must product quality conform to customer requirements, it may have to exceed the expectations of organizational buyers. High quality, as the customer defines it, is a major reason for buying.

ISO, the International Organization for Standardization, publishes international quality-control standards, which have rapidly taken hold in Europe and elsewhere around the globe. ISO 9000 is a standard of quality management, represented by a certificate awarded by one of many independent auditors, attesting that a company's factory, laboratory, or office has met quality management requirements determined by the International Organization for Standardization. The ISO 9000 standards do not tell a manufacturer how to design a more efficient earth mover or build a more reliable industrial robot, but they provide a framework for showing customers how a company tests products, trains employees, keeps records, and fixes defects. Think of ISO 9000 not as another variant of total quality management but as a set of generally accepted accounting principles for documenting quality procedures. With estimated tens of thousands of certificates issued worldwide, the standard is rapidly becoming an internationally recognized system, comprehensible to buyers and sellers. In addition, the International Organization for Standardization has published ISO 14000, which is a guide for environmental standards that relate to product design.

Related Services

Service is an important variable in organizational purchasing. Before a sale is completed, the marketer may have to demonstrate the ability to provide rapid delivery, repair service, or technical support. After the sale, the supplier had better be able to deliver the promised services, because "downtime" costs money and may be a great source of frustration for the buyer of, for example, an office photocopier, a computer, or an assembly-line conveyor system.

In business-to-business marketing, relationship marketing often means effectively being part of a collaborator's organization. Red Star Specialty Products, a Universal Foods Company, is the largest North American producer of yeast-based flavor enhancers. It offers clients applications support, technical seminars, prototype products, and a technically trained staff of field representatives. Maintaining and enhancing relationships with its customers by providing extra services is a vital aspect of Universal Foods' marketing efforts.

Price

Price can be the single most important determining factor in many organizational buying decisions. There is an old adage that says "Farmers are price takers, not price makers." It suggests that farmers (who are organizational marketers) face keen competition in a marketplace where the products sold are more or less the same. Not all organizational marketers are quite so much at the mercy of market forces as farmers, but many organizational goods and services face strong competition from products that are close substitutes. In such situations, an attractive price is likely to be the key to completing a sale. To heighten the effects of competition on price, organizational buyers often gather competitive bids from suppliers.

Organizational buyers can be expected to analyze price carefully, examining not just the list price but also any discounts, terms of sale, and credit opportunities that accompany a purchase agreement. Further, some buyers make a distinction between first cost (initial price) and operating cost (price over a specific time period). Such cost analysis, as well as their thorough knowledge of the product, allows organizational buyers to make detailed comparisons of value, increasing the importance of price as a buying criterion.

Value: The Perfect Combination of Price, Service, and Quality

Successful 21st century salespeople know the key to selling in many industries comes down to one word—value. Consultative salespeople are not just salespeople. They are exceptional salespeople who can ask all the right questions, get to know the buyer, and build a relationship with him or her, which provides many solutions to the buyer's needs. Salespeople of the 21st century must embrace the idea of both consultative and value selling.

There are three ways in which a salesperson can sell on value. First, salespeople must be value adders in dollar terms. In other words, they must sell profits rather than products and services. Next, salespeople need to be trained how to present profit improvement proposals that quantify dollars. And finally, salespeople must become problem solvers, comanaging with their customers as partners.

Consultative selling is true customer-driven sales strategy, instead of a product-driven process. A tricky part is when your product is a commodity, which forces prices to be low because of equalization by competition. Thus, salespeople must learn to understand and realize the value created in a customer's business by using your product. When you create that value you can cease being a commodity, which brings us to the next question. So, how does a salesperson establish value? The key goes back to knowledge. Salespeople must understand their customers' businesses and understand how their products will solve needs for their customers. Salespeople need to understand where the key areas and the cost centers are. Value comes not from the product, but from the ability to apply it to your customers' businesses so that costs are reduced or revenues are increased. Either approach creates value, which is something that almost all businesses are in search of in the 21st century.

Reliable Delivery and Inventory Management

For many organizations, the assurance of reliable delivery of purchases is essential. A related concern, inventory management, may also be an important buying criterion. Even a couple decades after the original push for just-in-time inventory management, the desire to reduce logistics and handling costs is still key in almost all companies. These issues are often addressed through the development of strategic alliances with collaborators.

Beneficial Organizational Collaboration

As business becomes more global and as information technology advances, organizational buyers are increasingly concerned with collaborative efforts and with building strategic alliances with other organizations. For example, strategic alliances related to inventory management may take the form of single sourcing.

Single sourcing occurs when an organization buys from a single vendor. Usually, in such situations, the organizational marketer works closely with the buyer to ensure that inventory items are delivered just as the buyer's inventory is being depleted. The seller may, for example, ship tires to an auto manufacturer so that they arrive exactly when needed in the production process and in the quantity needed. The degree of cooperation may be so great that buyer and seller share information technologies and a common database reflecting the customer's current inventory. Such single sourcing is likely to involve electronic data interchanges between companies.

A company enhances its effectiveness by concentrating its resources on a set of core competencies. Many organizations buy from collaborators who have competencies in tasks the organization chooses not to perform by itself. Hence, the potential for continuity in the relationship with the same seller because of common goals, mutual trust, and compatible business processes is an important reason for buying. This is particularly true for wholesalers and retailers who are members of a channel of distribution.

The Bottom Line

The relative importance of each of the major organizational buying criteria—product quality, service, price, value, and delivery—may vary with the buyer, the situation, or the product. For example, research showed that customers of Copperweld Robotics, a producer of industrial robots, wanted answers to three questions, in the following order: (1) Will the product do the job? (2) What service is available? (3) What is the price? Copperweld knows that, for buyers of industrial robots, service is a top priority. If one component of the robot does not work, the customer's whole production line shuts down. Providing service after a sale is crucial to Copperweld's efforts to create and maintain customer relationships.

In general, in any organizational buying decision, the buying criteria interact. Each contributes to the final decision, and each affects the importance of the others. Yet they often boil down to one overriding factor: the need to operate an organization at a profit. General Motors Corporation's (GM) truck and coach division emphasizes features like corrosion resistance and low fuel consumption in its advertising. The strategy is based on the belief that GM customers buy trucks not because they like them, but because they need them to earn a profit.

THE NATURE OF ORGANIZATIONAL DEMAND

The demand for goods and services in the multifaceted organizational marketplace differs greatly from the demand for most consumer goods. Some generalizations can be made about organizational demand and, in particular, about demand in the business segment of the organizational market. This demand is (1) derived, (2) inelastic, and (3) fluctuating.

Derived Demand

A reduction in consumer demand for housing has a tremendous and obvious impact on the building supply products industry. The demand for aluminum depends on the demand for products such as airplanes and trucks, as well as products packaged in aluminum. Downturns in the economy cause people to cut back on their use of airlines, which in turn reduces the need for airplane fuel and the parts and tools used in airplane maintenance. Ultimately, even the demand for such mundane items as the brooms used to sweep out airline hangars will decline as airline usage declines. All of these examples demonstrate a basic truth: All organizational demand depends ultimately on the related consumer demand. Organizational demand is derived demand—that is, it is derived from consumer demand. Derived demand ultimately depends on consumer demand even in purchasing situations quite removed from consumers.

No retailer would buy so much as a can of soup for resale unless management thought that the soup could be sold to a customer. Similarly, no manufacturer of cardboard box-making machines would buy even a pencil for use at the factory unless management believed that box makers would buy box-making machines, that packers would buy boxes, that wholesalers and retailers would buy boxed items, and that retailers would be able to sell those items to ultimate consumers.

Economists have coined the phrase *acceleration principle* to describe the dramatic effects of derived demand. According to this principle, demand for product B, which derives its demand from the demand for product A, may greatly accelerate if there is a small increase in the demand for product A. For example, consider the demand for Video Graphics Array (VGA) graphics cards, which derives from the demand for color monitors. Makers of color monitors may increase their purchases of VGA graphics cards by a percentage higher than the percentage increase in sales of color monitors, to protect against the possibility of running out as demand grows. Similarly, when demand for a consumer product declines, the demand for its component parts may decline even faster than the demand for the consumer product itself.

Understanding the effects of derived demand on marketing efforts is important for organizational marketers, and not just because those effects are potentially devastating. Derived demand also presents certain opportunities. Under some circumstances, the organizational marketer can stimulate demand for the consumer product on which demand for the organizational product depends. This approach involves drawing demand through the distribution channel until it reaches the seller. For example, advertisements suggesting that milk is better in unbreakable

plastic jugs may be sponsored by the producers of plastic jugs or the manufacturers of machines that make plastic jugs. Recognizing a trend of declining per-
capita beef consumption, the Beef Industry Council targeted advertisements to
consumers in an attempt to reverse the trend. Pork producers and lamb producers
have done much the same thing, even though all these organizations represent
farmers and ranchers who are several steps removed from the consumer in the
channels of distribution.

The Beef Industry Council's experience suggests another advantage of understanding derived demand. By keeping an eye on the ultimate demand on which
they depend, alert marketers can foresee developments that may soon affect their
businesses. In some cases, such marketers can take steps to influence these developments or to make adjustments that offset their effects. Responding to trends in
the marketplace is an important part of the job of all marketers, of course, but
organizational marketers must pay special attention. Unfortunately, their distance
from the consumer on whom they ultimately depend may make it more difficult
for organizational marketers to focus attention on developments that may affect
their sales.

Price Inelasticity

Compared with the demand for consumer goods, price has only a modest effect
on industry demand for an organizational good. Industry demand is relatively
price inelastic in the short run—demand for organizational goods and services is
not likely to change significantly as a result of price fluctuations. There are two
very good reasons for this price inelasticity. First, organizational buyers are in a
position to pass along price increases to their customers. If the price of the sheet
metal used to make Jeep fenders goes up, DaimlerChrysler, the maker of Jeep,
can raise the price of these products to cover the increased cost of the metal,
because the demand for Jeeps is strong. The second, and less obvious, reason for
price inelasticity is that the price of any one product is likely to be an almost insig-
nificant part of the total price of the final product of which it is a part. When the
price of sheet metal goes up, raising the cost of a fender by a few dollars, the
increase has little effect on the total price of a finished Jeep. Note, however, that
although organizational prices tend to be inelastic in general, buyers do pay attention to differences among prices among several competing sellers. Therefore, marketers must consider price in terms of each customer's special situation.

Fluctuating Demand

Most organizations prefer steady operating schedules. Thus, you might expect
organizational demand to be more or less constant. Actually, compared with the
demand for consumer goods, the industry demand for organizational goods is
characterized by wide fluctuations. There are three logical reasons for this.

First, organizational purchases can usually be closely linked to the state of the economy. As the economy moves through its up-and-down cycles, demand for many organizational products goes through cycles as well. During prosperous times, firms tend to maintain large inventories. When the economy slows or enters a downturn, retailers, wholesalers, manufacturers, and most other business customers tend to sell off or use up their existing inventories. They also tend to postpone purchases of new supplies, equipment, and other products. If the direction of the economy is uncertain, purchases are again postponed. This is especially true for machine tools, pumps, materials handling equipment, and other products that can be repaired and made to last until the economy improves. Hence, demand in this part of the organizational market, influenced by environmental dynamics, can fluctuate widely.

Second, many organizational purchasers have a tendency to stock up on the products they buy. They then do not need to make further purchases until their stock is somewhat depleted. Third, many organizational products have long lives, as in the case of buildings and major equipment.

CONCLUSION

This book has discussed numerous times the importance of relationship marketing in the 21st century. Business-to-business selling is one market segment where the value of relationships cannot be understated. With such high dollars and volume on the line, relationships are key factors in business-to-business selling. The 21st century has seen numerous changes that both enhance and hinder the formation and maintenance of business-to-business relationships. As was discussed in this chapter and in others through the book, this century has been one of increased technology, greater globalization, increased power of purchasing agents, greater and stronger strategic alliances, a growing emphasis on value-oriented selling, higher levels of accountability for managers and their corporations, a continued trend toward just-in-time inventory management, higher levels of fluctuating demand, and an overall push to improve the bottom line. All of these trends are having a dramatic effect on business-to-business selling in the 21st century. Good salespeople will learn to utilize these changes to their advantage in order to see an increase in relationship building and sales. This beats the alternative of getting lost in the waves of changes that this century has already brought.

NOTE

1. Lain Chroust Ehmann, "Exactly Who Decides?" *Selling Power* 26, no. 5, June (2006): 44–47.

CHAPTER 12

NEGOTIATING COMPANY AND CUSTOMER RELATIONSHIPS

Jon M. Hawes

As relationships become more and more complex during the 21st century, the use of negotiations within company and customer relationships has become even more prevalent. What is negotiation? "Negotiation is a decision-making process by which two or more parties agree how to allocate scarce resources."[1] Inherent in this definition are a number of important factors. First, two or more parties are involved. The company, of course, can be one party and the customer can be the second party. In some cases, there may be more parties involved. For example, governmental agencies impact the dealings between sellers and buyers of electricity. The media may also impact buyer-seller relationships in some settings. As a case in point, Wal-Mart currently receives so much scrutiny from the media that any negotiation in which the firm is involved will certainly be influenced by the potential public relations impact of any deal that might be reached.

Another important factor in the definition of negotiation is the allocation of scarce resources. Within a buying-selling situation, the allocation of scarce resources can simply be the products to be sold and the money needed to secure them. Obviously, the seller would like to get more money for fewer goods while the buyer would like to get more goods for less money. Often, however, more is involved. The utility or satisfaction to be obtained by participants of the exchange represents a broader and perhaps more meaningful conceptualization of this notion of scarce resources. Often, emotional considerations represent a significant consideration when determining the total satisfaction obtained by each party to an exchange.

Central to the notion of negotiation is the expectation of give-and-take. Rather than accepting an initial offer from the other side, we negotiate whenever we ask for an adaptation of what the other party initially offers to us. Negotiation involves offers, counter offers, adjustments, and revisions. We expect to make concessions, but we also expect the other side to do the same. As nice as it would be, give-and-take does not mean take and take and take and take. The norm of reciprocity creates an expectation of some degree of parity in terms of the pattern and amount of concessions across the parties.

Consequently, anytime that buyer and seller do not accept the initial offer of the other side and instead propose a modification of the terms to that agreement, negotiation has occurred. The decision-making procedure that occurs among the affected parties to achieve this is negotiation. This process can be tough on relationships, or the parties can work together for the common good. Hopefully, the latter approach is used.

What are the alternatives to negotiation? What could be done when confronted with a situation rather than negotiate a solution with the opponent? The first alternative that can be easily identified is to simply capitulate or give in to the other side. While we would not get what we want, we would avoid the effort needed to negotiate with the opponent. Rather than capitulate, we could instead just break off contact with the other side and hope we never see the opponent again. We might also take the dispute to a third party for potential resolution. Better Business Bureaus often get involved with commercial disputes. Some contracts also call for other forms of mediation or third-party resolution of disputes. Obviously, legal action in a court is a form of third-party resolution. Yet another option is just to hope that the other side will give in and change its practices in a way that suits our needs. Do not hold your breathe for this to occur! Finally, physically fighting with the other side is an alternative to negotiation. This does not represent a reasonable alternative within commerce, but this is what nations do when they go to war rather than negotiate a peaceful resolution to their differences.

With such a broad definition of negotiations, it is clear that many people engage in negotiations on a frequent and regular basis. In fact, we can argue that everyone does it, almost daily. Interestingly, while negotiating is so abundant within company and customer relationships, most of the participants have not received any training on the subject. Usually, people just "wing it" with their best seat-of-the-pants judgment on how to handle a negotiation. Unfortunately, the result is often poor tangible outcomes along with damaged relationships, even when both parties' intentions had been honorable.

The good news here is that there is clearly much room for improvement. While many firms have made considerable improvements in efficiency for a variety of other organizational functions, there is great potential for increased effectiveness both in terms of the tangible outcomes as well as in terms of improved relationships with others relative to the negotiation processes. With the stakes so high and with the historical level of training so low, even modest investments in a better understanding of the process of negotiation is likely to pay very high dividends. Considerable movement along the learning curve is likely and welcome for all concerned.

FUNDAMENTAL APPROACHES TO NEGOTIATION

There are two fundamental approaches to negotiation between a company and its customers. The first type of negotiation is distributive negotiation, sometimes called "bargaining" within the negotiation literature. In the popular press, this may also be called the "win-lose" approach. In this highly competitive situation, one or both parties view the allocation of scarce resources as a zero-sum gain where my loss is your gain (or my gain is your loss). In other words, I can get more only if you get less. The entire focus is upon claiming for your side all of the value that is possible while still convincing the other side to agree to the deal. Historically, this has been how many people approached negotiations. While it is sometimes the appropriate frame of reference, this style can be hard on relationships.

The second and perhaps more enlightened approach is known as integrative negotiation, or as a "win-win" agreement. Here, both sides recognize that the scarce resources can be expanded though cooperation or perhaps by creative thinking. This can result in a larger pool of resources that then will need to be claimed by each side. The fundamental difference between a distributive and an integrative agreement is whether or not the pool of resources or the "pie" gets enlarged. If it does, the agreement is said to be integrative. Figure 12.1 shows this distinction. Now, let us look more closely at each of these approaches.

DISTRIBUTIVE BARGAINING

Even in the 21st century, there are some times when distributive bargaining is the appropriate approach. This can be the case when there is no potential for relationship development, when the other side is focused only on price, or when time pressures prevent the development of trust or the sharing of interests. But when a negotiation participant seeks only to claim value by gaining through the other's loss as is the case in distributive bargaining, all sorts of aggressive tactics can be expected. Under this competitive context, the focus is on getting all you can get out of this deal without much consideration of the impact on any future interactions because there may not be any more deals. This is a very Adam Smith–type of view in which short-term profit maximization is the name of the game. Transaction-oriented rather than relationship-oriented selling would appear to be consistent with distributive bargaining.

Setting Distributive Goals

Preparation for a distributive negotiation should involve setting a target point, a reservation point, and an asking price (seller) or an initial offer (buyer). The target

Figure 12.1
Fundamental Approaches to Negotiation

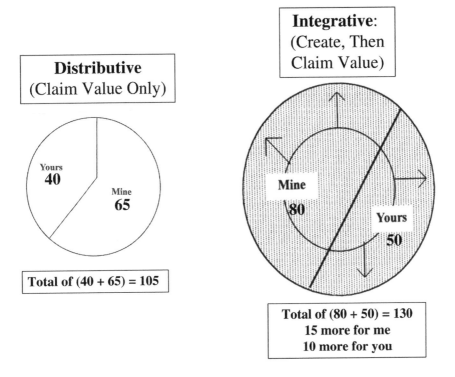

point is the best-case scenario on how the deal will end. For the seller, this would involve the most optimistic (high) price and quantity of goods that he or she could expect to sell. For the buyer, this would involve getting the best (lowest) price in the quantity needed.

Research has shown that ambitious targets are directly related to better outcomes. Negotiators who have high expectations often come closer to fulfilling them. Especially within the distributive context, target points should represent aggressive goals. They should be set high, but not so high that they are viewed as unrealistic and therefore not worthy of discussion by the other side. Targets should be ambitious but discussable.

While the target point is the ideal outcome hoped for, the reservation point is the worst deal that you would still accept. The reservation point provides guidance on the most that you would be willing to "give" and still do business with the other side rather than select your best alternative to a negotiated agreement (BATNA) with this party. BATNA is a very important concept within distributive negotiation. It suggests that there is more than one opponent with whom you could work. It implies competition within that market and multiple attractive sources. The most attractive of those available sources provides your best alternative to the negotiated agreement under consideration. Obviously, it would make no sense to accept an offer from the current opponent that is worse than what one of its competitors has already offered to you. In many cases, however, under the heat of battle in a highly competitive distributive situation, this unfortunately is sometimes done. The development of a reservation point prior to the interaction is an attempt to avoid this type of a mistake during the bargaining session. Thinking ahead is better than thinking behind and in hindsight wishing that you had made a different choice.

The third important element to effectively planning for a distributive negotiation is to determine what your first offer should be. Since the process of give-and-take is a central element in the negotiation process, the first offer is very much influenced by subsequent concessions; this is covered in the next section.

Making Concessions

The seller's asking price and the buyer's first offer impacts the settlement price. In many cases, these initial values become anchors that influence subsequent discussions about price. When the two parties ultimately agree to "split the difference," a very common method for finalizing the settlement, the first offers are directly related to the final outcome. In order to provide some room for give-and-take, the seller's first offer should be higher than the target point. This enables the seller to make concessions (decreases in price) yet still achieve the target price. For the buyer, the converse is true. The initial offer should be low enough to enable concessions (increases in price) but still achieve the buyer's target price.

Beyond the first offer, it is also important to more broadly consider the role of concessions within a negotiation. Remember that once the parties consider the interaction to be a negotiation, there is an expectation of give-and-take. This implies a belief as well about the pattern of concessions that are likely to occur. Without concessions on the part of either side, the negotiation is likely deadlocked. There is no positive movement and an agreement is not likely.

An extreme case of this has become known as "boulewarism," named after Lemuel Boulware who was the chief labor relations negotiator for the General Electric Company (GE) many years ago. He became famous for his "take it or leave it" approach to union contracts. Mr. Boulware's strategy was to offer the union leaders what he called GE's first, best, and only offer without an opportunity for give-and-take. Imagine the level of distress the union leaders would face if they informed their dues-paying membership that they had accepted the company's first offer. Union members would likely question the need for a union! Instead, the union leaders effectively argued that Boulware's strategy was unacceptable and filed an unfair labor charge against GE. This charge was upheld under the Wagner Act, forcing GE to bargain in good faith, meaning that it must engage in give-and-take.

Consequently, there is a very strong social norm for give-and-take during a negotiation. But beyond the avoidance of a take it or leave it offer, what else is involved in the process of give-and-take? Three very important elements of give-and-take are the magnitude, the pattern, and the timing of concessions. First of all, let us consider the magnitude of concession. This can be expressed as a dollar or a percentage amount, and it should be viewed by the other side as reasonable. This usually means that the magnitude of each side's concessions relative to the opponent is reasonably similar. The second aspect of concessions involves the pattern. Generally the recommendation here is for each subsequent concession to be of lesser value signaling to the other side that there is little to be gained by holding out for yet one more concession and that the negotiator has no more to give. Finally, the amount of time it takes to respond to the other side's most recent offer also sends a signal. The longer it takes to make the counteroffer, the less likely the opponent will try to hold out for yet one more concession. Figure 12.2 shows two alternative concession streams. Obviously, opponents would work much harder to try to obtain a concession in Round 5 in the hypothetical negotiation X rather than Y. Consequently, the signals sent in Negotiation Y are likely to better serve your needs.

As a practical example of this, I recently received a neighborhood newsletter from a realtor that included recent home sales along with various information relating to those transactions. One interesting statistic was the percentage of

Figure 12.2
Pattern of Concessions

Round	Negotiation X			Negotiation Y		
	Magnitude	% of Opponent's Concession	Time Elapsed	Magnitude	% of Opponent's Concession	Time Elapsed
1	$20	90	15 minutes	$20	105	5 minutes
2	$20	100	15 minutes	$15	95	10 minutes
3	$20	110	15 minutes	$10	90	20 minutes
4	$20	120	15 minutes	$5	85	40 minutes
5	?			?		

transaction value to asking price. Within this neighborhood, the recent statistic was 92 percent. In other words, homes sold on average for 92 percent of what the asking price had been. What a valuable statistic for a potential buyer trying to determine her first offer on a property within this neighborhood! Knowing that 8 percent was the average amount that recent sellers had been willing to discount home prices suggests that an aggressive but discussable first offer might be perhaps 15 percent under listing price. If this amount is not accepted (and in all likelihood it will not), the seller would likely make a counteroffer since the first offer had been "discussable." The potential buyer can then react to that new discounted price. If the seller offers a reduction off the list price of, for example, 3 percent, the potential buyer's next offer should be commensurate with the sacrifice that the seller offered from the listing price. In this case, the buyer should up her offer to about 3 percent more than her first offer. This would take the current bid to about 12 percent under the original list. If this is not accepted by the seller, another counteroffer is likely. If that comes in at about 2 percent under what had been proposed as the first counteroffer, the buyer knows that he is getting close to what the "average" home has been netting and may accept the offer. There could be, however, another round of concessions. Assume that the buyer counters this most recent offer by increasing her last offer by 1 percent. What would you expect to happen? My guess is that if the house had been on the market for more than the average number of days to sell (another statistic reported in the newsletter), the seller would accept the most recent offer and a deal would be made.

What can be learned from this real estate example? First, the amount of each concession was reasonably similar in magnitude, demonstrating to the other side that there was reciprocation for its sacrifices. Furthermore, the pattern of concessions signaled that the negotiation was nearing an end. The amount of each concession narrowed over time logically indicating to the other side that as these values approached 0, there simply was no more room for bargaining. Taking longer to make each concession can also signal that the making of concessions is almost over.

Dealing with Dirty Tricks

While the distributive negotiation approach is sometimes appropriate, when this win-lose approach to negotiation is used, relationships can suffer and some too-agreeable parties can be taken advantage of by tough opponents. If the other side uses a dirty trick, the best defense is early recognition of the tactic to enable an appropriate response. In the next section, we describe some of the most frequently used aggressive tactics in an attempt to help you identify them early. Before we cover that, let us discuss your options.

The best way to deal with the use of these dirty tricks is to minimize the chance for usage by creating a personal relationship with the opponent early in the interaction. An opponent is less likely to attempt the use of an aggressive tactic of questionable ethics on a person with whom he or she has a positive, personal relationship. Consequently, co-opting the tactic by befriending the other side before it is used is a good place to start.

If that does not work and you suspect that your opponent is using a dirty trick, most experts recommend that your first response should be to ignore it. There is a chance that you are mistaken in your identification of the tactic. In addition, it is possible that the tactic will not be repeated. As long as you do not give up pie because of the tactic, a strategy of simply ignoring it and continuing to bargain in good faith as you attempt to reach your negotiation goals makes sense.

What if the opponent then uses another highly aggressive tactic or a dirty trick? At this point, it makes sense to call him or her on it or to discuss the use of these tactics and suggest a return to more professional ways of interacting. Maybe the opponent can be persuaded in this manner to stop using these unpleasant approaches to negotiation.

But what if the opponent persists? The next suggestion is one of the following depending upon your BATNA. If your best alternative to this negotiated agreement is highly attractive, you should simply walk away from an opponent using the dirty tricks. You can do better and suffer less stress from dealing with one of the competitors. If the opponent is this unprofessional during the negotiation, imagine the difficulty that you may face in obtaining compliance to the terms of the agreement after the sale. Do not waste your time dealing with this unpleasantness.

On the other hand, what if your BATNA is lousy? In that case, you might (or might not depending upon the circumstances) want to respond in kind to the dirty trick. If the opponent is yelling at you, yell back at him. If this opponent plays chicken (see the next section) with you, you have the option of playing chicken with him. Sometimes, an opponent may just be trying to see how far you can be pushed. Once you fight back, it is possible that he will stop the aggressive use of dirty tricks for fear of your reciprocation. Be careful, however, because this response can put you in the same category as the nasty opponent. Do you really need this deal with this particular opponent enough to risk this type of behavior? Furthermore, what are the odds of full compliance to the terms of the agreement by the opponent after the transaction has been made? This might just be a deal you are better off not making.

Frequently Used Dirty Tricks

So what kinds of dirty tricks do some of these opponents use? Remember, the objective of this listing is not to encourage you to use the tactics. Instead, the goal is to enable the reader to recognize these techniques early in an interaction so you will not fall prey to the opponent. By no means is this list complete. There are hundreds of gambits for aggressively persuading others to accept your offers.[2] And there are a hundred variations for how each tactic can be used. Be careful!

When there are multiple people on an opposing negotiating team, the *good cop/ bad cop* is often used. This dirty trick is very simple and straightforward, yet highly effective. One person takes a highly aggressive, unyielding approach to the negotiations. This is the bad cop. He becomes unpleasant and highly annoying during the interaction. Another member on the team takes a much softer approach during the interaction. This good cop smiles occasionally and is reasonably pleasant during the negotiation. Due to the psychological impact of the so-called contrast effect, she seems REALLY nice in comparison to the bad cop.

At some point during the interaction the bad cop excuses himself, perhaps to retrieve something from his car or to use the restroom. When he is gone, the good cop sympathizes with you about the difficulty of dealing with the bad cop. She then offers to work out a deal while he is gone, saving you from the unpleasantness of dealing with him. While the deal she offers you would normally not be viewed all that favorably, it sounds great in comparison to the alternative of dealing with the bad cop upon his return. Their hope is that you will readily agree to the good cop's terms prior to the return of the bad cop.

Another frequently used dirty trick is the *highball/lowball tactic*.[3] This takes on two basic forms. The first application of the highball/lowball also has its power based on the contrast effect. With apologies to my friends in the used car business, please consider the following example of a highball/lowball application.

You are shopping for a used car: let us say a 2001 Chevy Cavalier. You have a fairly good knowledge of the market after having visited several other dealerships. You arrive at the next dealership, notice a nice-looking green 2001 Chevy Cavalier (the color you prefer) on the lot and begin inspecting it. Soon a salesperson approaches you and asks what you think of the car. In response, you ask what the price is. He promptly responds that the price is $9,600. You realize that this is way too much money for the car and exclaim, "You have got to be kidding me!" The salesperson says, "Well, let me go inside and check my numbers. Would you please wait here while I check?" When he returns in a few minutes, he offers you what appears to be a sincere apology and says that the price is only $6,900 and that he could not be sorrier for transposing the numbers.

What is your reaction to this? Most of us would feel vindicated for our good understanding of the market. Due to the contrast effect, we also feel that we have just received a discount of $2,700. For many shoppers, this car really begins to look attractive at this point. And, we feel a strong obligation to continue in the "negotiation" because we have already extracted such a major "concession" from the salesperson. In this situation, many buyers do not bargain hard for significant additional concessions and the negotiation very likely concludes with a purchase of the car at nearly $6,900. Had the salesperson started by saying that the car is

$6,900, most buyers would work much harder at attaining major concessions from that value.

The other application of this basic tactic really could be better described as the lowball/highball trick. There are a thousand variations of this scam, but it works something like this. A customer buys a new car and gets what she believes to be an exceptionally good price. She finances it at the dealership and drives it home that day. She pays $1,000 down and is told (in writing) that her payments will be $237 per month for 48 months. Of course, she parks it in the driveway and all of her neighbors, family, and friends come over to see it. What a beautiful car!

Early on the third day, she gets a call from the salesperson who tells her that there was an error in the financing and that they have to come to her house to pick up the car. She fears the embarrassment of people finding out that she no longer has the new car and is afraid that they will think the car was repossessed or at least that her credit was not approved. Due to this social risk as well as the concept of cognitive commitment, many people in this situation will respond to the return request by saying something like, "Isn't there any other way to resolve this? I really like the car." Often, the salesperson will reply "the number of payments was incorrectly listed—you would need to make 60 payments of $237, not 48" or "the numbers were transposed on the paperwork and your payments would need to be $273 per month." Often, the customer agrees to the new terms without bargaining or even making a counteroffer.

Chicken

"The game of chicken (also referred to as playing chicken) is a 'game' in which two players engage in an activity that will result in serious harm unless one of them backs down."[4] Remember the movie *Rebel without a Cause*? In that movie, two characters drive cars at top speed toward a cliff. To the idiots involved in the madness, the one who swerves first loses and is identified within that peer group as the "chicken."

The same type of game also happens during a negotiation. "If you don't drop your price by 10 percent we will pull you from the approved vendor list!" "If you don't deliver to us in three days we will bad-mouth you to the point where you will never sell another product in this city!" These and similar outrageous threats are made by customers all too frequently in commerce. Failure to comply with such a serious threat from the opponent carries considerable risk. The best defense to this type of extreme demand is to have really attractive alternatives to this deal with other clients.

The Nibble

Speaking of chicken, how about the nibble? This is a much less intense form of dirty trick. The nibble is done almost at the point of deal completion, usually by the buyer, but the seller could also get involved. This tactic is executed just prior to signing on the dotted line by making one more request for a small concession. When done by the customer, the request could be for a cash discount, a "baker's dozen," a free gift with the purchase, or a free tank of gas when buying a car. If the seller is the initiator, the request could be for a small unexpected prepayment prior to delivery, for a special rush-order fee, for an "order processing fee," or some other form of deal sweetener to improve the seller's margin on the deal.

The reason the nibble is so often used is because it so often works, even though it can be hard on relationships. At this point in the process, the opponent usually feels like the negotiation is over and may conceptually breathe a sigh of relief. In addition, many of us are reluctant to risk losing the deal by refusing to make such a small concession now given how far we have come in the process. The best defense against the nibble is a comment like, "I am sorry, but we just can't do that." If that does not work, consider making a counter "nibble" of slightly higher magnitude. Fortunately, not all distributive negotiations involve dirty tricks. In fact, some interactions lead to an integrative outcome and a discussion of this follows.

INTEGRATIVE NEGOTIATIONS

The fundamental difference between a distributive and an integrative negotiation is whether the pool of exchanged resources (the pie) gets expanded. Pie expansion is a thing of beauty. When both sides get all that they want instead of only part (maybe only half in a classic compromise), there is just cause for celebration. Participants to such a negotiation are often quite satisfied with the deal, and the relationship between the parties often flourishes as a result.

The classic example of an integrative negotiation involves two sisters. There is only one orange in the house. Both girls simultaneously decide that they want the orange. Both run to the kitchen to claim the last remaining orange. Consider how this dilemma would be resolved in a distributive negotiation. Under the classic compromise situation, one girl would cut the orange in half and the other would get to select her half of the orange while the other gets the remaining half. To be sure, each girl would get about half of what she wanted. Now, consider an integrative resolution. Here, each sister would discuss the situation. Interests would be shared. Questions about why the orange was wanted would be asked. Time would be taken to consider a variety of potential resolutions to the issue.

In this classic example of sisters each wanting the last remaining orange in the house, it becomes apparent that an integrative solution is possible in which both girls can get all that is wanted. When asked *why* she wants the orange, the first sister says that she wants to eat the pulp. No big surprise here. But when the second sister is asked *why* she wants the orange, she responds that she needs the peel as an ingredient for a recipe she is preparing. So, the first sister takes all of the pulp as she wanted, and the second takes all of the peel as she wanted. By asking questions, sharing information, taking some time to think, and by creatively resolving the problem, each girl has all of her interests fulfilled.

With such an ideal outcome, why are not all negotiations resolved integratively? Unfortunately, it is not always possible. But it is possible far more often that most negotiators believe to be the case. As a matter of fact, most negotiations have the potential for at least some pie expansion even though participants believe that most negotiations are a zero-sum game.

It should also be mentioned that integrative outcomes are harder to achieve. Integrative negotiation takes longer, involves creative thinking, and requires a higher level of trust among the participants so that they become willing to share interests rather than just positions. Interests are the fundamental, underlying, and often hidden needs that a party is trying to achieve from a deal. Positions are what a party says it wants and are exemplified by the terms of sale that are quoted to the other side.

Even with a solid recognition of the benefits of integrative negotiation, that outcome is often hard to achieve. An important factor here is the fact that conflict tends to prevail over cooperation in many negotiating settings. Furthermore, often parties come to a negotiation with a past history that makes trust building and information sharing difficult to achieve. Consider, for example, the next negotiation between the National Hockey League Players' Association and owners of those teams. Given the history of lockouts and strikes in the past, there is not much love in the room when these parties get together.

So how can negotiators experience the benefits of an integrative outcome? How can each side get more pie than would be obtained under a distributive outcome? The next section describes five methods for expanding the pie.

Pie Expansion Tactics

There are at least five tactics that can be used to expand the pie and create an integrative solution within a negotiation.[5] These can best be explained by way of the following example. Consider the negotiation between a happily married husband and wife concerning their next vacation. Here are the facts. They want to go together. Each works outside the home and gets two weeks of vacation time. If requested soon enough, each can pick almost any two weeks in the year. The husband says that he would like to go to the mountains, and the wife says that she would like to go to the ocean. The classic distributive solution would be to spend perhaps one week at the ocean, then travel to the mountains for the second week. While they would be together, each party gets only one week at the first choice location. Another popular distributive choice would a form of turn-taking. The wife could get her ocean vacation this year, but plan on a trip to the mountains next year. Integratively negotiated outcomes are better.

The first type of an integratively negotiated outcome is very straightforward, but often overlooked: *expand the pie*. Each party could ask the respective boss for more vacation time. Occasionally, the supervisor will approve this request. If not asked, there is no likelihood of the boss voluntarily offering the extra time. Why not ask?

Another way to create an integrative outcome in which there is more pie to share across the participants in through the use of *nonspecific compensation*. In this tactic, one side gets her way and the other side is "paid back" for compliance in an unrelated way. In the current example, the couple could go to the ocean for their vacation, but the husband could receive nonspecific compensation. For example, suppose that the husband had been asking for his wife's permission to allow him to start a part-time career in NASCAR but that she had so far refused to comply. She might get her preference on the ocean vacation, but then relent and grant permission for the husband's NASCAR ambitions. A key issue here is that the payback be unrelated to the vacation. The pie would be expanded because the wife gets all she wants (100 percent) relative to the ocean vacation and the husband gets something that until now was unattainable creating additional satisfaction or utility for him as well.

Another related tactic is called *cost cutting*. In this situation, one side gets its way. The cost for the other side's compliance with this outcome is also considered, however, and reductions are sought enabling a more positive outcome than would otherwise have been the case. In our vacation example, let us assume once more that the wife gets her way. The couple plans an ocean vacation. But the wife, in the spirit of true cooperation, asks the husband what it is about ocean vacations that he does not like. If what he does not like includes noise and crowds, the wife could select a relatively quiet and sparsely populated spot for their ocean vacation that would cut the husband's cost for complying with the decision. She gets her first wish fulfilled, but his utility is improved by the removal of what he disliked about vacationing near the ocean.

A fourth method for securing an integrative negotiation is through the use of *logrolling*. This tactic requires that at least two issues be under consideration in the negotiation. Let us reframe the current vacation example as a two-issue problem. We already have the issue of location: mountains or ocean. A second issue might involve hotel quality: high or low.

We already know about each party's preferences about location. How about hotel quality? Perhaps the wife has a preference for high-quality hotels while the husband prefers a low-quality hotel due to the cheaper price. In addition, perhaps each party also has a different valuation relative to the importance for the two issues of location and hotel quality. Maybe the wife is more concerned about hotel quality than location and the husband is more concerned about location than hotel quality. This is an ideal setting for logrolling. If each party gets to its first choice on the most important issue, the vacation will take place at a high-quality hotel (wife) in the mountains (husband). Since the decision is based on what is most important to each party, each gets more than half of what was wanted, enabling pie expansion.

Finally, we come to the most difficult opportunity to achieve an integrative outcome. This method is called *bridging* and involves a radical conceptualizing of the problem in a new way. Suppose that instead of selecting one of the stated positions (mountains or ocean) that is already on the table, the husband and wife search for a solution that fulfills their more fundamental interests. The husband can ask the wife, "*Why* do you like vacations at the ocean?" or similar questions. The wife should also ask the husband, "*What* is it that attracts you to vacationing at a mountain location?" By exploring their reasons behind their originally stated positions, they may be able to find a solution to the problem that they both like.

For example, let us suppose that the wife likes the ocean for vacations because when she goes there she enjoys sunbathing and swimming at the pool. Perhaps the husband likes the mountains because when he is there he finds many opportunities for hunting and fishing due to the remoteness of the site. If they give this some further thought and freely share with each other what they fundamentally enjoy about the vacation experience, the couple may determine, for example, that a two-week vacation together in a hotel near a highly remote Canadian lake in July enables both to get all of what they want. This is an optimal solution that was possible only because both sides worked together to explore creative solutions that were not initially considered.

CONCLUSION

Negotiation is hard work, but the payback can be very attractive. Now more than ever, the opportunity to work with others to explore modification and improvement of offerings enables greater productivity, higher customer satisfaction, and often more profitable deals for both parties involved. When buyers and sellers negotiate issues of concern rather than simply seeking out alternative partners, working relationships often improve and long-term strategic alliances become more likely.

Here is some good advice on negotiations. Prepare well, set ambitious but discussable goals, seek and develop more attractive BATNA, be honest, and treat opponents with respect. When the time is right, share your interests, not just your positions with the other side. Furthermore, learn from your previous negotiation encounters. Identify where you have done well and in what areas you should work for improvement. If you do these things, you will be well positioned for negotiation success.

NOTES

1. Leigh Thompson, *The Mind and Heart of the Negotiator* (Upper Saddle River, NJ: Prentice Hall, 1998): 2.

2. For many examples of gambits, see Roger Dawson, *Secrets of Power Negotiating* (New York: Career Press, 2000).

3. "The #1 Sales Scam," *Reader's Digest* 164, February, no. 982 (2004): 138–141.

4. "Game of Chicken," *Answers.com,* http:www.answers.com/topic/game-of-chicken (accessed August 22, 2006).

5. Roy J. Lewicki, David M. Saunders, and Bruce Barry, *Negotiation,* 5th ed. (Boston: McGraw-Hill/Irwin, 2006): 84–86.

CHAPTER **13**

Understanding Emerging Sales Technology

Richard A. Rocco and Alan J. Bush

> The introduction of sales technologies into my sales territory has been both a great opportunity and a big headache.
>
> —Sales manager for a health care company

Whether you are managing a small business or global organization, today's highly competitive business environment requires that companies constantly seek an edge to gain new customers, manage existing customers, as well as increase productivity and performance across the organization. The salesperson is the organization's "face" to the customer and the foundation of the company's relationship, so a firm's customer relationship building strategy is highly dependent on the behavior and capabilities of its salespeople. The concept of merging relationship marketing with personal selling is labeled relationship selling, and some of the most promising tools to enhance customer relationships and productivity in the sales discipline have evolved from applications of information technology. These tools are commonly defined as sales technologies, and the emergence of these technologies marks a new era in professional selling.

Consider the case of a 55-year-old traditional salesperson who manages a customer contact list in a "black book," maintains monthly sales reports in a spreadsheet on a home computer, and retains customer orders on paper forms in a file cabinet. You may know someone just like this sales rep: someone set in his ways and too busy to deal with anything new because his current process works fine for him. The obvious problem with this scenario is that the salesperson's information is stand-alone, provides limited accessibility while traveling, and is at risk for loss. Although it is common for this person to call his spouse or office manager when he needs to retrieve information, there is nothing in place to provide the salesperson with a timely, automated perspective on what is happening with his customers or business.

Instead of discovering at the end of the month or quarter that regular orders are trending down 15 percent, there are various sales technologies available that can provide, for example, the salesperson with daily updates on unusual order variances or provide an alert when there are overdue orders. This provides more time to understand the situation with the customer and determine if the change is simply due to fluctuating customer volume, or something more serious like a dissatisfied customer or competitive activity. Without this timely knowledge, it may be too late for the rep to remedy the situation and save the business.

A sales rep's ability to be effective and "look good" to his or her customers by meeting or exceeding customer demands requires timely and accessible information. The emergence of sales technologies provides companies and their sales organizations with an opportunity to develop a competitive edge by leveraging information technology and customer data with sales specific applications and electronic devices in order to enhance traditional sales tasks and better manage customer relationships. However, when you ask a salesperson about his or her experience with a sales technology, the response usually contains some frustration with a dose of optimism.

A Vice-President of Sales for a large health care organization observed that sales force automation (SFA) technologies will succeed only if the company and the salesperson have a shared perspective on servicing the customer, a mutual agreement on desired results, and recognize the effort will be a learning process. In this regard, the sales team will be open to embracing any legitimate technology that will help them meet their goals and less resistant when things go wrong. Otherwise, it becomes a long, challenging process that will test everyone's patience and budget. In this context, the utilization of sales technologies, in particular, SFA, does not need to be frustrating if you enter into the process with an informed perspective on the opportunities and issues associated with these tools.

The perspective that this chapter advocates is derived from the Japanese saying "failure is a gem," where success with any sales force automation technology can be attained not only by learning the success stories, but through an understanding of the failures. By leveraging this perspective and focusing primarily on sales force automation, the content of this chapter will be beneficial for those simply trying to understand the area as well as those trying to avoid or minimize a "challenging process" when introducing sales technologies into an organization.

AN INITIAL PERSPECTIVE ON SALES TECHNOLOGY: WHAT IS IT?

An accurate perspective on the term "sales technology" is that it represents any information technology applied to a sales situation that facilitates, enhances, or enables a sales task.[1] This broad definition captures various technologies like pagers, cell phones, PDAs (personal digital assistants), personal computers, word processors, spreadsheets, databases, as well as planning and contact management software. Simply, these are all examples of technology that has been extensively applied to the sales function to facilitate, enhance, or enable some aspect of the selling tasks. For instance, the introduction of ACT! contact management software and Lotus 1-2-3 spreadsheet software provided salespeople with powerful stand-alone tools to better manage their customer information and call planning as well as organize and report sales data. The challenge today is that the scope of these applied information technologies and their subsequent impact on business performance encompasses a significant body of literature that could occupy its own book. However, research shows when approaching the topic of emerging sales technologies with companies operating in both business-to-business and business-to-consumer markets, many consider SFA as one of the most promising technology tools to support an organization's relationship marketing strategy, increase field productivity, and improve sales performance.

The SFA concept initially received attention in the early 1990s and significantly evolved into the 21st century as better applications, improved technology, and a greater understanding about SFA implementation issues fostered greater interest within sales organizations. In part, this is the same period where technology acceptance in the greater population improved as personal computers and other electronic devices became more common in people's lives. As SFA technologies evolved into the sales landscape of many leading companies, hundreds of vendors entered this multi-billion-dollar market in the course of the past two decades in an effort to provide innovative, integrative, and user-friendly SFA solutions that propose favorable outcomes for those companies willing to make the required investment. Despite a history of mixed outcomes, many sales professionals now consider SFA to be an emerging application of sales technology that is the most likely tool to foster significant improvements in sales productivity and customer relationships into the early 21st century.

As sales executives increasingly recognize the importance of technology to the success of the sales organization, the scope of sales force automation solutions continues to grow beyond just software or stand-alone devices. In order to help organizations capture the significant potential benefits of SFA in their organizations, vendors increasingly must provide a wide range of products and services to manage the complex information technology environment as well as seamlessly integrate their products with enterprise-wide information systems in an effort to link sales to corporate information systems. This requires that vendors provide expertise in one or multiple areas inclusive of SFA software, wireless devices, communication systems, systems integration, and consulting services. Although there are hundreds of companies that provide some type of SFA product or service, some of the best-known companies in the SFA and customer relationship management (CRM) markets include Oracle-Siebel, SAP, salesforce.com, inc., and Research In Motion.

EMERGING SALES TECHNOLOGIES—LEADING BY EXAMPLE

A great example of a company providing emerging sales technology solutions in the area of sales force automation is Research In Motion. This firm is the designer, manufacturer, and marketer of innovative wireless solutions like BlackBerry wireless handheld devices. Leading companies across all business sectors increasingly rely on user-friendly, integrative wireless mobile devices like BlackBerry to provide their management and sales organizations with 24/7 wireless access to the information and communication necessary to be more responsive to customers and more decisive in executing their daily business activities. BlackBerry can provide the sales professional with wireless access to e-mail, phone, Internet browsing, and corporate data applications along with key contacts and calendar information.

One of the most important emerging capabilities for sales technologies like SFA is the ability to tap into an organization's enterprise system that manages valuable corporate information. BlackBerry is an example of a wireless mobile that can provide this important capability because BlackBerry devices are based on a wireless platform solution that provides salespeople with secure data from their organization's enterprise system to ensure access to both relevant and current information when needing to react to competitive situations or respond to customer needs. Therefore, an organization can utilize BlackBerry to extend its specific SFA software to the device in order to provide account information, sales opportunity alerts, or any of the multitudes of capabilities inherent in the SFA software. The benefit is that the company now can extend any relevant internal data to field sales reps in order to enhance their ability to service the customer needs in a more responsive and productive manner.

THE SALES FORCE AUTOMATION TECHNOLOGY CONTINUUM

Although BlackBerry provides a leading example of advanced sales technologies, the reality is that firms have different sales needs, goals, and budgets. The range of what one considers sales force automation technology can vary from stand-alone, personal sales productivity tools to fully integrative, two-way wireless devices that are linked to a company's enterprise system (see Figure 13.1).

Figure 13.1
The SFA Technology Continuum

As businesses look to select the best solution for their sales organization, the complexity and cost of the sales technology initiative increases significantly as you move along this continuum. A common sales technology in use today in the middle to upper range of the continuum (depending on features) is Internet access from the field through a personal computer that allows the sales rep to check e-mail and, in many cases, access specific resources on the company's intranet through a customized sales portal. The advantage with this technology is accessibility to the company's information from any Internet access point without requiring a dedicated wireless platform device. Although these devices provide enhanced functionality, customization, and convenience for sales reps, the advantages must be weighed with the cost of providing the devices as well as support services when a rep encounters a device failure or software issue.

Since many businesses do not have the sales technology expertise or staff to support complex sales force automation projects, leading sales technology vendors like BlackBerry increasingly provide a range of support programs and services to assist companies with the various components of the system deployment inclusive of the SFA device, enterprise server, and wireless network. Although the success or failure of sales force technologies depends on many factors that are discussed in the remaining sections of the chapter, BlackBerry provides a leading example of emerging sales force technology solutions that have the potential to enhance the responsiveness, productivity, and performance of a sales organization in the 21st century.

THE BUSINESS CHALLENGE: WHY INVEST IN SALES TECHNOLOGY?

Organizations invest millions of dollars into CRM and SFA technologies with an expectation that these tools will provide an advantage over their competitors or enhance sales force effectiveness. Vendors market CRM and SFA systems as well as the latest wireless devices to these companies by setting expectations that these solutions will provide a desirable return on investment. Although it seems intuitive to assume that the application of technology, specially the implementation of sales force automation, will lead to increases in salesperson effectiveness and efficiency, SFA initiatives regularly fall short of expectations despite continual advancements in technology. The failure rates of SFA implementations have been reported as high as 55–85 percent.[2] Despite the historically low odds for SFA success and the risk of placing executives in the awkward position of explaining their poor investment, organizations are surprisingly resilient in investing in sales technologies. Why?

Reflect on the earlier illustration of the traditional sales representative utilizing a "paper and file" customer information management approach. Although the individual rep may be considered successful from a sales value standpoint and well liked by his customers, this type of salesperson poses a risk to the company. In today's competitive marketplace where hard-fought market share gain is both time and resource intensive, the regrettable loss of a customer is a critical failure for both a salesperson and the company. A statement like "I did not see it coming" should no longer be accepted as an excuse. The simple truth is that a postmortem analysis on lost business often demonstrates that early signals were present that, if detected in a timely manner, could have allowed the salesperson or company to remedy the situation and retain the customer. Since the sales team often represents the closest point of contact in an organization's customer relationship strategy and a primary goal of the sales process is to provide value to the customer, organizations should seek out the best available tools to leverage these relationships and enhance value. This is why organizations remain resilient in their sales technology investment despite known past failures.

Beginning in the 1970s, the increasing cost of sales in organizations relative to other organizational costs finally forced companies to commit resources in order to enhance their understanding of the professional selling process and seek ways to better manage their selling costs. Technology offers one possible solution because any automation of the various sales administration functions would relieve an organization of the significant time and costs associated with the fundamental tasks of documenting sales calls, capturing sales-related data, and generating period sales reports. The sales administration function in most organizations at the time was ripe for improvements due to the volumes of paperwork, manual handling, and potential for data errors.

A second target area for companies in the 1980s was trying to enhance sales productivity in the same spirit that the total quality management movement delivered improvements to manufacturing and other areas of the corporation. The initial technologies utilized in sales organizations like the fax machine, pager, cell phone, personal computer, and scanner provided improvements in productivity through better communications and automation of traditional office tasks. Although cell phones are a common technology today, consider its impact from a historical sales perspective. Prior to the introduction of this technology, the salesperson was relegated to conducting business on land lines, limited accessibility while traveling, and receiving messages through the office secretary or answering service when there was time to "check in." The introduction of cell phones, voice mail, and pagers ushered in the notion of 24/7 access for customers and increased productivity gains for the company due to the ability to facilitate business during the traditional sales downtimes (for example, car, train, and plane travel).

Individuals working in the field have noted that the major challenge in harnessing technology for sales applications beginning in the 1980s to the early 1990s was the limited capabilities inherent in early generation computing technology. The early stuff was unstable, which required a mix of vendor and IT (information technology) department resources, as well as the fortitude to make things work. The corporate initiative to lower costs and increase productivity forced firms to find creative solutions because there was not much readily available in the early days. As an IT function companies were great at managing data on the corporate mainframe, but struggled with finding efficient, timely solutions to get information both in from the field and out to the field.

While these early technologies evoke a list of traditional communication tools like fax machines, pagers, and cell phones, current sales technologies have evolved into advanced integrative software and hardware solutions that can provide real-time, two-way data interchange that takes advantage of the rapidly evolving mobile wireless device market. Although some specific examples of the various sales technologies and SFA applications have already been discussed, the reasons why an organization would want to invest in technologies has moved beyond basic cost and productivity improvement needs. The rationale for investing in sales technologies into the 21st century now includes enhancing relationships with customers, identifying sales opportunities, and creating a competitive advantage with information.

Consider the example of a productive senior sales representative for a leading transportation/distribution company that has been assigned 50 accounts and typically visits less than 20 on a regular basis. Although it is not atypical for a sales representative to dedicate the most time to the top accounts in the territory (highest sales or most profitable), neglected accounts often mean that new business opportunities may be overlooked or competitors have an open door to convert the business. By implementing an SFA system, this transportation/distribution company established a sales call system that tracked customer visits during the month and established recommended sales call frequency based on account potential and sales goals. Fundamentally, the deployment of this SFA system (laptop computer based) encouraged this salesperson to review a sales call dashboard on a regular basis and break the habit of calling on only certain customers. The benefit to the rep by keeping in touch with accounts on a more regular basis was a $1-million increase in sales during the first year of the SFA implementation. The reasons included an ability to strengthen relationships with the neglected accounts as well as capturing additional sales opportunities through these smaller and seemingly "lower-potential" customers. Other similar sales success stories across this organization justified the investment required to implement the system.

THE UPSIDE OF SALES TECHNOLOGY: REASONS TO ENCOURAGE THE USE OF SFA

At a sales and marketing conference focusing on CRM and SFA topics, sales executives representing over 30 different companies across multiple industry sectors were asked to name their primary reasons for investing in SFA technologies. In other words, the group was interested in knowing the primary issues or needs that a sales technology like SFA could positively address in the drive for a best-in-class sales organization. The top responses were the need to maximize the amount of customer-facing time for their reps, enhance individual rep productivity, and strengthen a rep's relationships with key customers.

These responses did not surprise the executives at the meeting because the issues are dominant sales management challenges across a broad range of industries and sales roles. The responses signal that executives consider that tools like SFA can potentially play a supporting role in enhancing a sales organization by supporting sales needs in areas like strategic customer management, sales process design, and sales productivity. For instance, in the area of strategic customer management, SFA technology can signal a salesperson through his or her wireless device, either through e-mail or the alert feature, that one of his or her customers has an issue, allowing a faster response. While this is valuable, SFA can further enhance the customer-salesperson relationship by enriching sales with customer relevant information delivered at the time of consumption. In other words, instead of responding to the customer right away, but having to say, "I'll get back to you on the issue," SFA has the capability to provide powerful analytical tools that can help bring information together from various company data silos and enrich the salesperson's ability to "solve" the customer problem at the point of need.

A recurring complaint of professional sales representatives is that they get bogged down with the administrative and routine service aspects of the job. Consider that the daily responsibilities of average sales reps are often dominated by inventory management, reporting tasks, e-mails, phone calls, supporting existing key customer needs, and travel. This erodes their capability to pursue new business prospects and actively identify cross-selling opportunities as often as they would like. Reduced "sell" time has the consequence of less income potential. As noted earlier, SFA can improve the time component in selling as measured by "responsiveness." However, it provides an even more compelling value by impacting the time component through the measure of "amount of selling time."

Consider the case of a medical sales representative who was spending a few hours every day managing inventory issues across a large sales territory in order to ensure that the right products were available at the right time to each hospital and new or replacement orders were processed in a timely manner to cover future needs. This was often time-consuming because the sales rep had to coordinate information, either in person or on the phone, among the hospital, the field office, and the corporate headquarters. This sales rep indicated that the process of managing orders and inventory was a daily frustration in their effort to provide the highest level of service to their accounts. In short, they had better things to do with their time. Fortunately, this particular organization initiated an SFA project utilizing a PDA with sales force automation software and wireless connectivity (through a cell phone interface) in order to allow the sales force to directly manage inventory, customer orders, and e-mail communications in the field. Although there were significant challenges with both the technology and sales force acceptance (discussed in a later section), the result of this SFA project provided benefits for both the company and the sales representative. On the corporate side, millions of dollars were saved through electronic order processing and better visibility of inventory. On the sales side, less time was spent placing orders and tracking inventory. The impact was less frustration across the organization and more hours each week available to focus on selling.

SFA can also offer companies an effective tool to support and enhance relationship selling by improving the quality and speed of information flow among the sales force, customer, and organization.[3] A strong example is Yellow Transportation, Inc. This company was confronted with poor distribution of sales-related information, inconsistent sales practices, and poor communication between customers and internal marketing groups as well as sales managers who often had to rely on the sales force to get information due to a lack of division-wide information sharing.[4] Yellow Transportation looked to sales force automation as a potential tool to address these issues. Ultimately, the implementation of a SFA program allowed it to track shipping information, increase information flow, and assist the entire sales organization with field access to critical customer information. Yellow Transportation ultimately experienced greater efficiency/effectiveness via SFA as its sales force was able to spend 30 percent more time with customers.[5]

The potential benefits of sales force automation are extensive. Numerous publications and case studies have discussed the benefits of SFA, and the following points represent a summary of the most commonly noted benefits for the use of sales force automation.

1. Provides access to timely account and customer information.
2. Provides access to timely product, inventory, and market intelligence information.
3. Provides potential for customer segmentation and needs assessment.
4. Allows customization to customer and account preferences.

5. Identifies potential cross-selling opportunities.

6. Improves communications with other sales reps, managers, customers, and the company.

7. Provides insights on customers based on value or other key organizational measures.

The emerging use of technology by salespeople is clearly evident through the growing use of sales force automation products and cutting-edge communication technology deployed in the field. When executed correctly, SFA can provide the aforementioned key benefits to a sales organization. However, the unfortunate news is that many companies have failed to realize significant value from their SFA investments, and many implementations generally fall short of expected results.

THE DOWNSIDE OF SALES TECHNOLOGY: SALES FORCE AUTOMATION FAILURES

As noted earlier in the chapter, SFA failure rates are notoriously high across various implementations and industries. This begs the question of how advanced sales technologies like SFA, which have the potential to provide substantial benefits to the sales organization, can have high failure rates? The answer to the question often lies beyond the technology itself.

A fundamental truth in any SFA program is that burden for the implementation of sales technology rests primarily on the shoulders of the salesperson. This point was supported when a group of senior sales and marketing executives were asked if their initial SFA implementation was successful. Less than 35 percent of the respondents felt that their first SFA implementation met the established objectives. When probed to understand the causes for the corresponding 65-percent failure rate, the executives noted the most significant issue impeding their initial effort as well as subsequent SFA implementations was the sales force itself. Many of the sales managers felt that the potential technical difficulties with SFA rank far below the issues associated with sales force resistance. However, this understanding was not realized for many of them until well into an initial implementation. The reasons for the resistance to utilizing SFA include the sales representatives' view that SFA is a "big brother" tool designed to oversee their activities more closely, hesitance to devote extra time to managing or collecting information that primarily benefits the company, and general apprehension about learning a new technology (inclusive of the device and/or software application). The apprehension about using new technology is a specific area that warrants further attention.

THE "SALESPERSON TECHNOLOGY DIVIDE"

There is a generation of sales professionals that simply resists the use of new technology in their lives and who represent a significant impediment to organizations that fail to recognize the unique needs of this sales rep segment when implementing sales force automation technologies. The division between those sales reps willing to embrace the latest technologies and those who actively resist technology defines the salesperson technology divide. This pervasive phenomenon in sales organizations impacts a company's ability to enhance sales performance through new technology. Unfortunately, this particular segment of the sales force is not often formally recognized by the organization during an SFA implementation until it is well into the implementation phase and difficult choices have to be made to resolve the resistance issues.

Consider the example where an expanding sales territory for a communications company is divided between an existing 50-something established sales rep and a new 20-something sales representative. In order to enhance sales opportunities and capture timely customer input, the sales manager informs them of a new sales force automation product that the company is introducing across the organization. While the younger sales rep is eager to embrace the use of a tablet-style PC containing the new sales automation software, the older sales rep is not comfortable learning the new system. Eventually, the older rep informs his sales manager that "he will not use it" and wishes to conduct business as usual. Not wanting to risk losing the older, higher-performing sales rep, the sales manager with this communications company hired a back-office employee to help the sales rep administer the use of the system.

Although the phenomenon is representative of the classic "old school" versus "new school" debate, failure to recognize the problem can have significant ramifications for corporations in the form of increased sales force turnover, increased technology implementation costs, and reduced sales productivity. In the case of this communications company, the hire of an additional office employee to help run the older sales rep's SFA application was not a planned expense and required replication into other regions of the country to address the same issue with other older sales rep's resistance to the new sales technology tools. The key point is that organizations must recognize that the people issues, specifically sales rep issues, are an important contributor to the success or failure of an SFA implementation and issues like the technology divide can confound an organization's effort to deploy an SFA initiative.

UNDERSTANDING SFA FAILURES: CASE ANALYSES APPROACH

Although this chapter has initially provided a general perspective on sales technology, specifically sales force automation technologies, there are still many implementation issues concerning SFA failures that extend beyond the individual salesperson and require further discussion. With this in mind, we extend the perspective of learning through SFA failures by leveraging our recent research on understanding sales force automation outcomes that was first published in *Indus-trial Marketing Management* in 2005 and now incorporated into the next eight sections via a case analyses approach. This research consisted of field interviews with executives from three global business-to-business organizations for case analyses representing a diverse set of industries (communications, health care, and transportation/distribution) that have experienced SFA failures and imple-mentation challenges.[6]

Embodying the Japanese saying "failure is a gem," the one important common characteristic across all three companies was their ongoing work attempting to improve their SFA despite their challenges and failures. Based on their SFA expe-riences across a combined sales force of over 4,000 reps, significant insights emerged that both enhance one's understanding of SFA outcomes and provide valuable lessons for increasing a firm's chance for a successful SFA initiative. A number of common themes emerged during the executive interviews, which are reflected in the following five sections. These common themes from our research provide important insights into the implementation factors that contribute to SFA outcomes, help identify potential barriers or "best practices" for managers in developing and implementing SFA systems, as well as yield a model of SFA outcomes.

Organizational Goals for SFA Differ

The SFA implementation goals and objectives for the three companies varied significantly, in part due to differing industries, business strategies, and sales struc-tures. The goals of the communications, health care, and transportation/distribu-tion organizations, respectfully, include enhanced information exchange through the SFA (driver: sales management), using the SFA to provide logistics improve-ments vis-à-vis better management and tracking of inventory (driver: logistics/IT), and leveraging sales force automation to consolidate information as well as increase efficiency (driver: corporate).[7] In understanding these differences, it was evident that the means to achieve their goals and objectives with SFA were similar.

Reflective of a traditional push strategy, their SFA system implementation strat-egies seemed to focus on communicating to the sales forces that it is in their best interests to buy in to the technology. Given this type of implementation strategy, it was curious that each company noted major organizational changes that involve a more relationship marketing, cross-functional organizational process wherein their SFA system was being employed to help enable the new strategic process.[8] The differing goals and objectives aside, the disconnect between their organiza-tional process changes and SFA implementation strategy was a significant point during the interviews. The three organizations seemed to focus on a push strategy that emphasized a technology buy-in rather than a pull strategy that asks their sales forces to take part in the changes in the organizational processes. Regardless of the differing goals and objectives, our case analyses reflect that lack of sales-person involvement in the process change is a key factor related to possible SFA failure.

Assigned Responsibilities for SFA Vary

The successful voyage of any ship is due in part to the captain, so another aspect of the executive interviews focused on the person or functional area responsible for implementing the SFA system. Again, we found three different "captains of SFA technology." The roles included the VP for logistics, a corporate level SFA manager, and field sales management. Although it may seem odd at first, the responsibility of the SFA initial implementation by the VP for logistics was driven by the logistics and inventory goals of the organization. Frankly, this role had the largest stake in the outcome and consequently assumed the SFA captain role.

Our findings reflect a failed assumption that the sales force would have significant input into the SFA development and implementation process. As noted in the previous section, if there is a change in an organizational process, all functional areas as well as the salespeople should be pulled into the process to mutually agree on the changes before implementation of the new SFA. It may represent an even greater issue when departments like logistics and IT facilitate the implementation because those functional areas do not have the same perspective as more customer-facing roles, such as sales and marketing, in the organization. Therefore, our case analyses reflect another key factor related to possible SFA failures, which is the organizational role responsible for the SFA development and implementation may impact SFA outcomes. An apparent disconnect between the SFA implementation role and the sales force increases the likelihood of a challenged or failed implementation.

The Importance of Communicating the Value of SFA to Sales

A prevalent frustration with each of our executives during the case analyses process was their inability to determine the value of the SFA system to the end user—the salesperson. As noted in the first of these five themed sections, the corporate goals and objectives for the SFA were clear for each of the three companies. However, since they had difficulty clearly stating the value of the technology to the user, the salesperson, it makes sense that the implementations had difficulty gaining salesperson buy-in. One does not have to ponder the reasons for SFA resistance when the salespeople in the field are still wondering "what is in it for them." The SFA manager noted to us that "the SFA technology does add more work and more cost to the process. Early into the system, there is little return. The key issue with SFA is to show the value to the sales organization. The company should try to achieve early sales rep buy-in to the process if you expect to be successful."[9] This point was not fully appreciated in these organizations during their initial implementations. Therefore, the case analyses suggest that not effectively communicating value of the SFA system to the sales force is another factor related to possible SFA failure.

SFA Effectiveness Can Be Hampered by Technology Itself

Advances in technology do not necessarily correlate with ease of use or improved reliability. In fact, it seems that many new technologies initially create more or different issues for the organization than the technology being replaced. In fact, the interviews confirmed that the organization not only has to prepare for the costs and issues directly associated with the implementation of its SFA technology, but also must be prepared for other "uncontrollable" factors that are associated with operating the technology. One particular example was the challenge in getting the salesperson's PDA to connect with the many different cell phone models/brands being used in his organization. Since the communication of the information from the PDA to the corporate server was dependent on the cell phone, it significantly added to the implementation challenge as well as the sales rep's frustration level. One executive noted that "the SFA technology is what enables the organizational processes to take place. If the salespeople are unaware or resistant to the process changes, technology that does not help enable this change is doomed for failure."[10] Therefore, the case analyses suggest that the SFA technology itself can be another factor related to possible SFA failure.

SFA TRAINING

A comment from one of the executives during the case analyses process confirmed the value of training as a key component in the SFA implementation process. The executive stated that "early into the system deployment we realized little return from our SFA initiatives. Much of this is due to lack of [sales force] training."[11] One company suggested the reasons why training was not emphasized during the implementation was the lack of sales involvement (corporate driven) and extended implementation time (too busy fighting fires). As one might expect, the lack of input and lack of experience with SFA technology can leave the sales organization frustrated and resistant to "buying in" to the technology as a part of their sales process. This is even more of an issue when an organization has independent sales reps. Many of these issues and the lack of trust among salespeople could have been alleviated with more training on relationship selling and the importance of sharing information as it relates to customer retention.[12] Our case analyses for this fifth area suggest the lack of SFA training with the sales team can be a factor related to possible SFA failure.

INSIGHTS AND IMPLICATIONS FROM THE SFA CASE ANALYSES: A MODEL OF SFA OUTCOMES

The concept and understanding of technology acceptance is well known in the IT field, but is only now being researched extensively in marketing and selling applications like sales technology. In considering the specific area of sales force automation technology, many adoption studies commonly tap the information technology literature to apply Technology Acceptance Model (TAM) and the Theory of Reasoned Action model in an effort to explain sales force usage and acceptance of the SFA. The two important components of TAM are perceived usefulness and ease of use, which simply try to understand whether the sales reps consider that the sales technology will be useful to them and whether it is easy to use. Respective of usefulness, the TAM model provides an understanding that the belief in the consequences of the benefits in using the technology is an antecedent of an individual's perceived usefulness.[13] Therefore, our initial research paper reflected two important perceived consequences the salespeople had toward the SFA as follows:

1. The process itself.
2. Technology as an enabler of the process.

The case analyses of the three organizations provide support for two key points that SFA outcomes are dependent on whether or not the sales force agrees with the process change and outcomes are also dependent on the technology itself. For instance, these companies initially did not consider the salesperson as a key component of the organization's process change. The implication of this was the creation of a disruptive situation for the sales organization that contributed to the SFA failure. When implementing an SFA program one should understand whether the organizational or structural process change is disruptive or incremental to the sales force. Further, one should understand whether the salespeople perceive that the technology will help them do their jobs better under the new process change. If the technology enables the process, the SFA program will have a greater chance for a successful outcome.

A third insight from our case analysis relates to the importance of salesperson acceptance or "buy-in" with the SFA system. Many of the executives' statements during our interviews support the importance of factors like properly communicating the value of the SFA and sufficient training as means to impact salesperson buy-in to the SFA system. However, organizational processes and individual salesperson factors can also play a contributing role in SFA buy-in as well. An important insight is that an organization needs to consider the likelihood that not every salesperson will "buy in" to the SFA. This was the case with all three organizations. Each company had the foresight to set a target sales force buy-in percentage threshold that ranged from 50 to 70 percent. Anything at or above that percentage range considered for successful sales force buy-in ("yes") and anything below that percentage was considered an unsuccessful buy-in ("no"). Based on the insights from our case analyses, a model for SFA outcomes was developed (Figure 13.2).[14]

SFA Nonimplementation Issues: Understanding the Impact on SFA Outcomes

Nonimplementation aspects of sales force automation initiatives refer to organizational processes that influence SFA outcomes. An important finding from the case analyses was the significance of SFA nonimplementation issues to success or failure of the SFA project. As noted earlier, all three organizations noted a change in their strategic focus or organizational processes that incorporated a more relationship selling, cross-functional perspective. This change occurs prior to the SFA implementation since the entire organization, inclusive of the sales force, should accept and buy in to the changes in organizational processes (for example, shift from transactional to relational selling). If the sales force fails to understand the fundamental changes in the firm's strategic orientation, SFA failure is a likely outcome.

As represented in the model, the executive interviews support a position that incremental change in organizational processes is going to be easier for the sales

Figure 13.2
SFA Outcomes

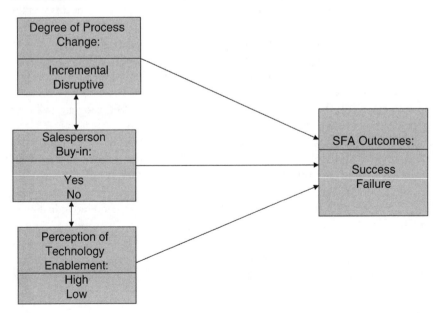

force to accept and buy in to than one that entails deep structural or disruptive changes. In the face of disruptive changes, the SFA technology implementation challenges increase significantly. The key implication from the case analyses is that senior management must realize the importance of process change and how it might be perceived by the sales force in order to positively influence an SFA initiative's chance for a positive outcome.

However, even with sales force buy-in with the process change, another facilitating nonimplementation issue for SFA outcomes is the salesperson perception of how well the SFA technology will enable the organization process change. Two of the organizations in our case analyses encountered early problems with their SFA implementation because the technology itself was not well accepted. The message to management is that while incorporating the sales force into the organizational process change is important, salesperson perception of the technology as an enabler of that process change is a contributing factor for continued SFA technology utilization in the field and successful SFA outcomes.

SFA Implementation Issues: Understanding the Impact on SFA Outcomes

SFA implementation issues are the areas related to the SFA initiative itself that directly or indirectly influence outcomes. Many SFA studies note that acceptance of the SFA by the sales force is an important implementation issue of SFA outcomes and the insights of the case analyses support this point. Regardless of the sales technology, without the buy-in of the majority of the sales organization it will be an uphill battle for any company to realize its expected goals.

From the company side, SFA managers should first clearly identify the SFA nonimplementation issues and then carefully focus on the salesperson buy-in. It is unrealistic to assume that the entire sales force will buy in to the SFA initially. For instance, the three organizations in the case analyses reasonably set buy-in goals from 50 to 70 percent. Given this potential acceptance gap, companies should be prepared to budget for expenses resulting from the previously discussed salesperson technology divide or training initiatives that utilize education and sales mentorship programs to foster SFA adoption.

From a salesperson's perspective, issues with the SFA technology implementation occur when there are changes in the core selling process for the sales force (for example, add more time) and when the changes do not fully satisfy the salesperson's individual needs. In other words, salespeople are most likely to resist the SFA technology when it is disruptive to their existing sales process and/or they fail to understand the benefits of SFA as it relates to their sales performance.[15] Most salespeople just want to feel that they had some input in the process and, if they commit the time to adopting the technology, that it will truly enable or enhance their capabilities instead of disabling them. Hence, successful implementation requires salesperson buy-in to organizational processes and new technology. Otherwise salespeople can easily become distrustful when asked to share their black book information via the SFA system. For organizations considering an SFA implementation, this requires an overall change in management philosophy that recognizes sales buy-in to the corporate process change, salesperson representation in the SFA development phase, extensive sales force training, sufficient technical support systems, as well as clearly communicated benefits, goals, and incentives for all involved parties.

EMERGING SALES TECHNOLOGIES IN THE 21ST CENTURY: LOOKING FORWARD

The term "emerging" sales technologies reinforces that this is an area still early in its development in many ways. In considering the continuum of sales force automation technologies, selection of the appropriate "tool" is important relative to the organization's goals and budget. However, any tool cannot be very effective unless you know "how" to use it. The important message in this chapter is that a true understanding of sales technology extends beyond the technology itself. The lessons from the three companies and contributing sections reveal that implementation and nonimplementation issues are more likely to be linked to SFA failures than problems with the technology itself. One of the most critical factors for determining the success or failure of an SFA program is the buy-in of the salesperson.

While there is a large body of evidence that reflects both significant business successes as well as abject failures in utilizing sales force automation technologies, the best organizations recognize that the successful implementation of any sales technology as a supporting tool for their customer relationship strategy requires endurance. Although it may sound intuitive, many organizations fail to include the end user (salesperson) in the SFA process. Early representation of the sales force and the sales process is an effective way to increase acceptance and encourage usage of SFA with the sales force. Ideally the sales force needs should be represented during the initial stages of organizational process and SFA implementation changes.

Although there are often distinct perspectives and needs when considering the acceptance of SFA (organizational, SFA technology, and sales force), these three must be considered together when developing and implementing the SFA process. For instance, one of the noted organizations in our case analyses took several years and several SFA iterations to realize the importance of focusing on all of these entities together to avoid SFA failures and increase the chance for successful outcomes. While the 21st century promises continued technology advances that can be applied to the selling process, enlightened managers and organizations will understand that increasing one's chance for successful SFA outcomes requires focus on the process and people ahead of the product.

NOTES

1. Gary K. Hunter and William D. Perrault, Jr., "Sales Technology Orientation, Information Effectiveness, and Sales Performance," *Journal of Personal Selling and Sales Management* 26, no. 2, Spring (2006): 5–113.

2. J. Galvin, "Increase SFA Adoption with Sales Process Mapping," Gartner Group Research Report SPA-18-2377, Gartner Group (2002).

3. Cheri Speier and Viswanath Venkatesh, "The Hidden Minefields in the Adoption of Sales Force Automation Technologies," *Journal of Marketing* 66, no. 3, July (2002): 98–111.

4. Alan J. Bush, Jarvis B. Moore, and Rich Rocco, "Understanding Sales Force Automation Outcomes: A Managerial Perspective," *Industrial Marketing Management* 34, no. 5, May (2005): 369–377.

5. Mike Fillon, "Keep on Trucking," *Sales and Marketing Management* 147, no. 6, June (1995): 17–19.

6. Bush, Moore, and Rocco, "Understanding Sales Force Automation Outcomes."

7. Ibid.

8. Ibid.

9. Ibid.

10. Ibid.

11. Ibid.

12. Ibid.

13. Ibid.

14. Ibid.

15. Ibid.

CHAPTER 14

THE ETHICS OF MANAGING CUSTOMER INFORMATION: CAN CUSTOMER RELATIONSHIP MANAGEMENT BACKFIRE?

Linda M. Orr and Victoria D. Bush

> The Industrial Age has given way to the Information Age. The development [of information technology] has been so rapid that society as a whole has *not* had the time to digest its ethical implications.
>
> —Richard T. DeGeorge
> author, *The Ethics of Information Technology and Business*

The Information Age has given us the power to access information about anything from the comfort of our own homes on our computers. While this provides many advantages, it can sometimes be a cause for concern. For example, at a recent presentation in Japan, a Dell laptop computer caught on fire. Pictures were instantly transmitted around the globe, causing a public relations nightmare for Dell Inc. From the consumer side, privacy continues to be a major concern. During this past year, various surveys put the number of identity theft victims in the United States alone at somewhere between 700,000 and 9 million people, depending on how broadly the crime is defined and how recently the survey was taken. These examples reveal that the sheer volume of information available to customers and organizations is overwhelming.

This information explosion raises several key questions for marketers to consider: (1) how do you convince customers to share information, (2) how do you assure them that their information will be safeguarded, and (3) how can you ethically manage this information within your organization? This chapter focuses on these issues that have arisen during the Information Age and offers several solutions for organizations to consider.

CONVINCING CUSTOMERS TO SHARE INFORMATION

Successfully handling the correct type and amount of information and communications both to and from customers is not only a necessity for 21st century marketers, but can also be a competitive advantage when done correctly. Customer relationship management (CRM), both as a strategy and as a more specific computer technology, is here to stay and will certainly continue to grow. The development of technology and advancements in software systems enable businesses to maintain larger and more accurate amounts of information. Thus, organizations must now better understand the potential pitfalls of misusing these communication flows and information about customers.

It is well known that customers fear an Orwellian loss of privacy, but marketers fear the opposite. Marketing managers fear that their customers may opt out of their organization's efforts to build and maintain databases. This is true now more than ever as industries, such as the direct marketing industry, are beginning to develop "do not call lists." Thus, safeguarding personal data is a corporate responsibility. If the information is valuable enough to be collected and warehoused, then it is valuable enough to be carefully managed and protected, just as much as any other corporate asset. However, marketers have to convince consumers that they believe this and that there is integrity within the firm's operations.

The first hurdle that businesses must overcome is to convince customers to become shoppers. Before an organization has an opportunity to discuss privacy issues once it has customer data, it must first get the customers to know who it is and what the organization has to offer. This hurdle is getting higher and higher every day and harder and harder to overcome. The 21st century is truly a century of information. Information is available from every direction at every point throughout the day. Consumers are now multitaskers, capable of receiving and processing large amounts of information at all times. Just take the younger generations. They spend over three hours a day on average on the Internet. Usually, the television, radio, and/or i-pod is running at the same time. Adults cannot escape this abundance of information either. We now have BlackBerries and/or cell phones with us at all times. Even on a plane ride, when we would once be out of touch, we can now get Internet access. If we do not take advantage of Internet access on a plane, we can still distract our minds with newspapers, magazines, books, videos, or music.

Thus, marketers have many avenues to get their messages out there, but how can marketers get customers to pay attention? Furthermore, how can marketers get customers to process and believe your messages? The gaining attention part is a little bit more straightforward and easily understood. To accomplish this objective, most marketers use a variety of attention-getting techniques, such as popular music, celebrities, sex, humor, rapid scene changes, bright colors, or anything else that is novel or exciting. However, the use of some of these devices is sometimes counterproductive to achieving the next objective of the consumer actually processing and remembering the advertisements. Sometimes, marketers go too far with things like sex or humor and the message is lost or the audience is actually offended. How many times have you heard, "that was a great Super Bowl ad, but I have no idea what product was being advertised"? Likewise, many of us recall ads from Calvin Klein and Abercrombie & Fitch Co. or even the Benetton Group back in the 1980s because their ads were so offensive to some groups.

Consumers pay attention only to what agrees with their preexisting sets of attitudes, beliefs, perceptions, experiences, and preferences. Technical terms exist for the processes that are occurring in the consumers' minds, such as selective attention or cognitive consistency. The facts are simple: not only will consumers not pay attention to something that does not grab their attention, but also, consumers will not pay attention to something that is sharply opposed to their current belief system. We all interpret things the way that we want to interpret them.

Another concept that affects how consumers process advertisements is called "schemer schema."[1] This theory states that as consumers become aware of marketer activities, they attempt to determine the marketer's objectives and then think strategically about this to the point that they may then modify their behavior—meaning if they think the marketer is trying to get them to do "A," then they will purposely do "B." While this theory was proposed in 1986, it is even truer today in the 21st century. Consumers are even more educated and better able to discern a marketer's objectives. Thus, marketers need to understand not only what their customers want, but also what "turns them off."

With all the proliferation of information and messages that bombard them, consumers are becoming, in essence, "desensitized" to advertising messages. Thus an alternative approach is for marketers to focus their efforts on personal selling and direct marketing—both of which rely heavily on customer databases, that is, information. As marketers get more information, they can collect and analyze data and better understand their consumers and, therefore, know exactly how to reach their customers. Marketers can design better strategies if they know who their potential customers are, where they are, what they are doing, and what types of media to which they pay attention.

In summary, the negative side of the Information Age is that, yes, customers are harder to reach through the clutter. They are desensitized and more skeptical. However, the positive side is that as a marketer, the explosion of information can be used to better understand potential customers. Then, once marketers get customers to buy their products and collect information about them, consumer privacy issues must be considered.

ENSURING CONSUMER TRUST IN INFORMATION

As companies continue to collect, use, and even disclose personal information, they must do so in a manner that does not invade the privacy of their customers. As human brings, we are very sensitive to our "privacy" or even our own "personal space." We do not want someone standing too close to us in the checkout line at the store, much less at the ATM. We do not want the world to know our personal information, from the mundane details like address and phone number to more important things like medical and financial histories. If a business respects a customer's privacy, it can potentially earn trust and loyalty, which are two critical elements for success. If trust and loyalty are violated, it is almost impossible to get them back.

There are several key elements discussed in the following sections in which managers must follow in order to maintain the customer's innate right to privacy. These points apply no matter which channel a consumer interacts with your business. This means that businesses have the opportunity to collect information at many interaction points—stores, call centers, Web sites, direct mail, e-mail, professional salespeople, and so forth—and information collected at any of these touch points needs to be respected.

Additionally, two kinds of customer trust must be considered when gaining consumer trust: fiduciary and personal. As businesses, it is sometimes easier to earn fiduciary trust than personal trust—meaning consumers may feel safer giving organizations their credit card information, but may be less willing to let organizations store their personal information. The irony is that the more personal information marketers have, the better marketers can be prepared to meet their customers' needs. Thus, more information then allows better communication with customers directly and in a customized manner, which eliminates some unnecessary clutter, and it also allows for the opportunity to build the relationship and, ultimately, increase trust. Thus, the information explosion of the 21st century has caused marketers to play a delicate game of gathering and protecting consumer information and building, maintaining, and growing trust to create longlasting relationships. What follows are several strategic paths to consider that will help ensure customer trust in sharing information.

ACCOUNTABILITY

Above all else, businesses must completely own all accountability. As part of accepting accountability, you need to designate an individual or group of individuals to govern the information and ensure that consumer's privacy is being protected. That individual may be a chief privacy officer in a large company or a high-level manager in a smaller company. In the words of Harriet Pearson, Chief Privacy Officer for IBM, "I'm an example of what has become basically a new profession."[2] A position that was once unheard of now exists in most *Fortune* 500 companies.

This seems like a fairly simple concept, but it is based on the fact that when something is everyone's job, it is very easy for it to be no one's job. There has to be at least one person who is ultimately accountable for privacy. In addition to appointing a person responsible for privacy management, a company must implement proper procedures to protect personal information and also make sure that these procedures contain guidelines for handling complaints. All relevant employees should then be trained in these policies and procedures.

Privacy must also be respected when information is transferred to another company or outside the firm to a subcontractor for processing. These days, it is very common for CRM systems to be run by third-party firms, such as one of the largest Internet CRM programs, salesforce.com. Even though someone else is handling the data, if it is your company's data about your customers, you must make sure that they are being handled carefully. Thus, just as you choose employees and customers carefully, you must choose your suppliers carefully. If you feel that a supplier or business partner is not operating at the highest ethical standards, you should not do business with it.

As a business owner, you simply cannot count on other companies to be ethical with their data. The vice president of a large mortgage lending company recently remarked about how its customers always complain because they think the company is selling their data. For example, even if you have recently applied for a mortgage, other, unsolicited credit offers may start appearing in your mailbox. However, it is not the mortgage company that sold your data. When you allow any company to pull your credit report, the credit bureaus then sell your credit score to other firms. This type of behavior can impact the credibility of the original loan company, which subsequently can impact potential for gained or lost trust from a customer. In this particular situation, if you are the loan company, there is not a lot you can do until the laws change. However, no matter what kind of business you are in, you can be aware of how information is being managed and/or sold. In the end, your company is accountable in the customers' eyes. If you simply and honestly tell them that no matter where they go and no matter who pulls their credit, their information will then be sold, they may then appreciate your honesty. Thus, disclosure becomes another topic of importance.

IDENTIFYING AND DISCLOSING PURPOSES

Not legally speaking, only ethically speaking, a company should tell its customers why their data are being collected and what it plans to do with them. If they know that a third party will at some point have access to the information, as in the previous example, or anything else that may jeopardize consumer privacy and trust, the customer should be informed. The law does not state this. This is one situation where best marketing practices are way ahead of the law. It is always better to inform your customers ahead of time than to have them come back to you after something bad has happened.

On this same note, how much is too much to share? Obviously, you do not need to tell your customers that George Smith will log on to his computer at 11:30 and check your data for accuracy and then close the file. This sounds like an obvious point, but consider this. Most companies collect basic information and sometimes even demographic information with every purchase. If the consumer is informed at the time of purchase that his or her information is being collected for future advertisements and mailings, and this is correct, most feel that this is an ethically correct use of information. However, what if at a future date, the marketer decides to perform some data analysis and determine if perhaps there is a certain demographic segment that prefers the marketer's product? What if it was something as simple as watching product sales for swimsuits increase in the southern United States exactly two months before a similar increase in the northern United States? That example is so obvious that most of us already know that, but the point is the same. Is it okay for a business owner to go on "fishing expeditions" with data if the customer was not informed about the purpose previously? Many researchers say this just makes good business sense, but many consumer watch groups feel this is unethical behavior. The answer lies somewhere in between and combines the principles of accountability and disclosure.

PRIVACY STATEMENTS

A number of organizations have actually published privacy statements and then violated them. For example, the New York Attorney General's office recently filed suit against an organization called Gratis Internet. The suit alleged that Gratis Internet sold personal information gathered from millions of consumers that it had promised confidentiality to in its privacy statement. This organization literally used statements such as "we will never give out, sell or lend your name or information to anyone."[3]

Regardless of actual decisions as to what your business's data policies and procedures will be, you must formulate a privacy statement communicating these policies and then be responsible for upholding them. Additionally, these statements must be published in readily available and easy to find locations. This act will not only protect you legally, but will help the process of trust building. There are a few simple steps to consider when developing and writing privacy statements. According to Kirk J. Nahra, partner with Wiley Rein & Fielding LLP in Washington, D.C., when considering customer data submitted via Web sites, privacy is of utmost concern. He states, "any corporation that collects information on its Web site should review (1) whether there is a privacy policy for the site, (2) whether the company is in an industry or market where there are specific required components for such a Web site policy, and perhaps most important, (3) whether the policy accurately states the privacy practices of the company."[4] In other words, statements about consumer privacy via the Web are just as important as any other privacy statements. You want to use your privacy statement as a sales tool to build trust, not to further confuse and insult your customers.

CONSENT: OPT IN AND OPT OUT

As a part of the disclosure process, businesses should obtain consent from individuals before data are collected and must give individuals the right to opt out at any future time. This process can be done in a simple manner and be written in conjunction with the privacy statement. If companies are collecting highly sensitive data, such as medical or financial information, consumers must be advised in very specific terms of their rights to "opt in." For example, a doctor should always ask permission before obtaining records of a patient from another doctor. Likewise, consumers should be informed of how to opt out and be able to do it at any time.

According to Richard T. De George, author of *The Ethics of Information Technology and Business,* consumers should be informed so they can assess their own risk of disclosing information. He suggests that four conditions should be considered. A consumer should "1) be informed or aware of the risk, 2) know the source of the risk and how great the danger is, 3) know how to protect against the risk to the extent possible, and 4) know the alternatives."[5]

ACCURACY

More than 90 percent of American and Canadian companies have some form of CRM software or technology. However, in 2002, the Canadian Marketing Association found that only 42 percent of these companies update their databases. First, this is just plain not smart from a business standpoint. Why spend the money to collect and store information if it is not accurate? Organizations risk insulting and loosing customers when the information they gather is inaccurate or outdated. For example, direct mail lists should be up-to-date and accurate. Many times they are not. If you are a business sending out mail to the wrong address or person, you are wasting money. Even something as simple as a misspelled name could offend someone. Thus, if you are taking the time to collect and store data, you should also take the time to maintain their accuracy. This principle is not only ethically correct, it just makes good business sense.

ADMITTING MISTAKES

Finally, if you do make a mistake, if you lose customer information, if you offend someone with an ad campaign, or if you do anything else that causes a loss of trust or causes a problem, you must admit fault. As was discussed in Chapter 3, admitting mistakes is an integral part of a business's reputation, and once reputation is destroyed, it is very hard to regain. This is a common sense statement that is so readily not followed in the business world.

Mistakes will happen. Oftentimes, these mistakes are the result of simple human error. For example, in October 2005, an employee of Montclair State University accidentally stored the social security numbers and majors of students on the University's Web server...a server available to anybody in the public realm. Earlier this year, discarded back and credit card information for 240,000 subscribers to the *Boston Globe* was accidentally recycled into paper used to print routing slips. Thus, regardless of who is at fault, you must admit fault and try to diagnose and correct the problem in a timely and effective manner.

MANAGING THE ETHICS OF INFORMATION

Privacy concerns and information overload present two issues that go far beyond business ethics lectures. They affect all areas of a business, from the legal and public relations departments to marketing and its focus on CRM to even human resources and its concern for employee retention. A well-designed, well-implemented policy can help a company in all of these areas, on both the tactical and the strategic levels. In the wake of the many recent corporate scandals, headline-grabbing hacker attacks, and other invitations to cynicism, businesses need to go out of their way to establish trusted relationships with consumers. A strong, clearly communicated information management policy is an effective way to win that trust...and maintaining that policy over time allows companies to build trust into long-term relationships.

Policies must be developed that build, establish, and maintain fair data handling and storage guidelines. Likewise, businesses must be ethical when communicating with their customers and be willing to be open and transparent with them. Ensuring secure data is good for CRM, which can help companies gain competitive advantages by building strong customers relationships that are built on a strong foundation of trust. Several issues should be considered by organizations to make secure data handling is an everyday reality within those organizations. These are discussed further in the following sections.

SAFEGUARDS

In May 2006, the United States Department of Veterans Affairs (VA) learned that an employee, a data analyst, took home electronic data from the VA that was stored in his home on a laptop computer and external hard drive. Subsequently, the employee's home was burglarized and the computer equipment, along with various other items, was stolen. The electronic data stored on this computer included identifying information for roughly 2.2 million veterans. Before that, in May 2005, in what could be the largest data security breach in the world to date, information on 40 million credit card accounts might have been stolen. The breach occurred at CardSystems Solutions, Inc., in Tucson, Arizona, a third-party processor of payment data. Out of the 40 million accounts that were stolen, roughly 20 million were VISA-brand cards, 13.9 million were MasterCard-brand cards, and the remaining cards were for American Express, Discover, and other various retail-owned cards.[6]

These breaches follow several high-profile data loss incidents that potentially exposed American consumers to identity theft. In 2005, CitiFinancial said tapes containing unencrypted information on 3.9 million customers were lost by United Parcel Service while in transit to a credit bureau. Additionally, data leaks have been reported by Bank of America Corporation and Wachovia Corporation, data brokers ChoicePoint Corporation and LexisNexis, and the University of California at Berkeley and Stanford University.[7]

This is unfortunately the world in which we live. As smart as the companies are that design software, thieves will always be just as smart, if not smarter. The business owner's choice is quite simple. You have to spend the necessary time and money necessary to safeguard information. These decisions are mostly based on technological knowledge that is outside the realm of this book. But, steps must be taken to ensure that databases are password protected and that access to them is limited to only those people who are properly qualified. Paper records and computer hardware need basic protection like padlocks or safes.

Privacy-enhancing technologies exist and should be used, such as data encryption. Likewise, when records are destroyed, it must be done properly and completely. It is merely unfortunate that these steps must be taken to ensure consumer protection and privacy to avoid identity theft or any other form of financial loss. Companies can enhance their relationship with customers if they make the information about what they are doing to protect consumers available to them. As a consumer, would you stop doing business with a company if you hear it misused your information? Would you be more willing to remain loyal to a company that was very cautious with your information? For most people, the answer to both of those questions is probably a resounding yes.

COMPANY DATA CHECKPOINTS

Once again, should you gather more data than you need and save them for future fishing expeditions? This is an ethical question that must be answered by your business and your personal ethical stance. But, once you decide what types of data to collect, there are much broader issues at stake about how you will store that information and who within your company will be allowed access. Should all employees have access to all data? Should this be monitored? How can this be monitored? What are the potential ramifications for employee morale? What are the implications for productivity?

Very few businesses have so little data that it is safe to allow everyone in the company to have complete access to everything. The common manner in which to resolve this dilemma is to separate employees by their level in the corporate hierarchy or job function and then make this separation a means by which to distribute data. Many times, frontline salespeople will have less information at their disposal than high-level managers. However, this method, although probably necessary, does create some problems. For example, if you have ever bought a car, it is likely that you have dealt with certain other individuals besides your salesperson. Typically, at every negotiation, the salesperson has to keep going back to the finance department to find out if the next jump down in price can be arranged. This is, of course, not done for ethical reasons, but instead as a negotiation tactic.

When firms use the previously mentioned corporate hierarchy method for data distribution, salespeople do not have access, so they may need to contact their managers to request customer data that are useful in resolving a problem. This slows response time and can then frequently cause the customer to be annoyed, but is a useful tactic when delicate customer information is being analyzed. However, employees can then also become disgruntled because by limiting access to data, they feel less important.

However, whatever the ramifications, data must be secured and only the people who need the data should have access to them. Likewise, when breaches do occur, policies must be very clear in terms of consequences for employees committing unethical and/or potentially illegal acts. Additionally, once a customer is no longer a customer, should you get rid of everything, or save it to analyze defection rates? Again, at this point, it becomes an ethical issue in which some people are opposed to fishing expeditions. However, no matter what the decision, once a customer is no longer a customer, if information is retained, his or her data probably should then be moved to another location, in which salespeople do not have access to it on a continual basis.

CONSUMER DATA CHECKPOINTS

On the other side of the equation is individual access from the consumer's viewpoint. Should your customers have access to their own personal information? However, some industries make their money off not doing so. For example, many years ago, individual consumers were not allowed to know their own credit scores. Even now, with the rapidly changing laws, we are allowed one free credit report a year, and we can get our credit scores, but we have to pay for them. If you finance your home through a mortgage broker, it is not really supposed to tell you which bank it is using until the end. Why, as a company, would any kind of personal information not be available? Ethically, individuals should be given access to their own personal data within an appropriate time frame and for a minimal cost.

Likewise, customers should know what data are stored so that they should be able to challenge the accuracy of them. For example, one company called a consumer almost 20 times due to nonpayment of an outstanding bill. The problem was that the consumer never even had an account with the company trying to collect an obviously erroneous invoice.

This is the kind of unbelievable bureaucracy that must be avoided. There is a very delicate balance between safeguarding data and making them accessible. The answer to most dilemmas of this type is to try to do what is ethically correct as a business and use some common sense! Along this same line of thinking, a company must put procedures in place for accepting and responding to complaints that consumers may have about the firm's data handling practices. Data at some point will become outdated and no longer be accurate; thus, procedures must be developed so that accuracy is maintained.

In sum, organizations must realize that the power of information can be used as an incredible asset, but can also be misused rather easily. Companies need to consider how to manage the customers' perceptions of information privacy and accuracy as well as how the information is used internally. Breaches of security are rampant, which damages any potential of long-term relationships with customers. As mentioned in earlier discussions, Kirk J. Nahra, a partner with Wiley Rein & Fielding LLP, specializes in privacy and information security litigation. He suggests a checklist of questions[8] for organizations to consider in this new age of information technology:

1. Do I have an effective information security program?
2. Do I have a security breach notification policy?
3. Do I have an appropriate privacy policy?
4. Do I know the privacy policies of my business partners?
5. Do I know the privacy policies of my vendors?
6. How am I handling my mistakes and the mistakes of others?
7. Do I have a policy for employee privacy?
8. Have I audited my information security activities?

Each of these questions is helpful for organizations to consider when designing and strategizing about what kind of information they gather from customers. Periodically auditing how information is collected, stored, and destroyed on an ongoing basis will help organizations avoid costly data mismanagement mistakes.

SUMMARY

The 21st century is a century of information. This information "overloads" us as consumers and as business owners. However, this vast supply of information also creates a potential gold mine of ways to gain and maintain customer relationships. Proper information analysis and understanding can help marketers understand how to break through the clutter and gain the attention of their potential customers. Information can help businesses better understand how their customers will process the marketing messages used to communicate the firm's offering. Then, the information that has been collected can be utilized to maintain the relationship with the customer and make that relationship grow. However, accountability comes with the collection of that information. Businesses must be responsible to consumers for safeguarding and protecting their information. They must develop policies about how this information will be used and then communicate these policies to their customers and to all their employees and suppliers. If these steps are done and done correctly, information and proper respect for consumer privacy can be a key enabler to building and maintaining trust and customer relationships in the 21st century. If not, huge problems will arise.

NOTES

1. Wright, Peter, "Schemer Schema: Consumers' Intuitive Theories about Marketers' Influence Tactics," in *Advances in Consumer Research,* Vol. 13, Richard Lutz, editor (Provo, UT: Association for Consumer Research, 1986), 1–3.

2. "Privacy Is Good for Business," http://www-03.ibm.com/innovation/us/customer-loyalty/harriet_pearson_interview.shtml (last accessed April 11, 2007).

3. Evers, Joris, "Credit Card Breach Exposes 40 Million Accounts," *c/net News.com,* June 17, (2005), http://news.com.com/Credit+card+breach+exposes+40+million+accounts/2100-1029_3-5751886.html?tag=st.rn (accessed August 5, 2006).

4. Nahra, Kirk J., "A Privacy and Security Compliance Checklist for the Internet Era," *Journal of Internet Law* 9, no. 12, June (2006): 6.

5. De George, Richard T., *The Ethics of Information Technology and Business* (Malden, MA: Blackwell Publishing, 2003), 172.

6. Evers, "Credit Card Breach Exposes 40 Million Accounts."

7. Ibid.

8. Nahra, "A Privacy and Security Compliance Checklist for the Internet Era."

INDEX

About the Editors and Contributors

GENERAL EDITOR

BRUCE D. KEILLOR is coordinator of the American Marketing Association's Office for Applied Research-Direct Marketing and Professor of Marketing and International Business at The University of Akron. He is also a research fellow at Michigan State University. Dr. Keillor specializes in international marketing strategy and direct multi-channel marketing and has authored more than 60 articles published in journals worldwide. He has also contributed to numerous books. In addition to his academic credentials, Dr. Keillor has also been an active entrepreneur as co-owner of a direct-marketing software company he helped found in 1994. Dr. Keillor also has extensive executive education and consulting experience as a copartner in BBA Associates, a global marketing consulting firm.

EDITORS

LINDA M. ORR is Assistant Professor of Marketing at The University of Akron. She is a co-editor of *Direct Marketing in Action: Cutting-Edge Strategies for Finding and Keeping the Best Customers* (Praeger, 2006). Her research areas are strategy, with a specific focus on learning, innovation, and marketing capabilities. She has also conducted academic research and business consulting in selling and sales management, sports marketing, and political marketing, and she has consulted to a variety of businesses, including both *Fortune* 500 companies and nonprofits. Additionally, she served as Assistant Marketing Director for Warner Bros.

Records Inc. in Nashville, and in a variety of managerial capacities in the finance and restaurant industries.

JON M. HAWES is Distinguished Professor of Marketing and Director of the Fisher Institute for Professional Selling at The University of Akron, where he teaches Business Negotiation, Sales Management, and Professional Selling. He has been an active contributor to the trust literature for many years and the article he co-authored, titled "Trust Earning Perceptions of Buyers and Sellers," is the most cited article in the history of the *Journal of Personal Selling and Sales Management.*

CONTRIBUTORS

ALAN J. BUSH is Professor of Marketing at the University of Memphis. Dr. Bush has also taught at Louisiana State University, Texas A&M University, and the University of South Florida. Over the past 20 years, he has published over 70 articles in the top marketing and sales journals such as *Journal of Marketing Research, Journal of the Academy of Marketing Science, Journal of Business Research, Journal of Retailing, Journal of Advertising, Journal of Advertising Research, Journal of Personal Selling & Sales Management,* and *Industrial Marketing Management.* Dr. Bush has also written two textbooks: *Professional Sales Management* and *Integrated Marketing Communications.* His current research interests are primarily sales force research, sales force automation systems, and sports marketing.

VICTORIA D. BUSH is an Associate Professor of Marketing at the University of Mississippi. Her research interests include cultural diversity in buyer-seller relationships, advertising ethics, and Internet marketing. Her research has been published in *Journal of the Academy of Marketing Science, Journal of Advertising Research, Journal of Advertising, Journal of Public Policy and Marketing,* and *Industrial Marketing Management,* as well as other journals and proceedings.

MICHAEL F. D'AMICO is Professor of Marketing at The University of Akron. Previously he taught at Texas Tech University and Michigan Technological University. His co-authored principles of marketing text went through 14 editions; he has authored or co-authored approximately 150 journal and proceedings articles and other publications. He is past president of the Marketing Management Association, Pi Sigma Epsilon, and Mu Kappa Tau.

JASON DILAURO is a Vice President and Senior Financial Advisor for Merrill Lynch in the Bath, Ohio, office. He focuses on assisting clients in making the transition from working years to retirement. By building income streams from well-designed portfolios, clients find the peace of mind in knowing they will be able to live the rest of their lives without financial concerns.

INGRID J. FIELDS has an extensive background and wealth of sales and sales management experience from telecommunication and technology companies such as AT&T, Lucent Technologies, and Technology Builders. Recently, Ingrid and her husband, Bob, co-founded and operated their own family business, called Fieldstone Villages, LLC, developing land and building residential homes. Ingrid has been involved in several Leadership Continuity Programs, is an active University of Akron Executive Advisory Board Member for the Fisher Institute for Professional Selling, and has been a radio show guest host for "Solutions Selling and Marketing for Business Owners" and a Panelist for USC's Digital Storage Forum. She has been a volunteer in the UC Irvine's MBA student mentor program and has joined in MS fund-raising events.

DANIEL J. LESLIE is a Financial Advisor with the Northwestern Mutual Financial Network. Dan is a Chartered Life Underwriter and Certified Financial Planner, and a certified coach and trainer in the financial services industry. He holds various investment licenses and specializes in working with high-income professionals and business people. Dan began his management career with Northwestern Mutual as a College Unit Director in 1998; he went on to become a Field Director with Northwestern Mutual and takes over as Managing Director in Akron, Ohio, in January 2007. He and his wife, Heidi, work on the fund-raising committee for Akron General Medical Center and the McDowell Cancer Treatment Center. Dan is also on the Executive Advisory Board for The University of Akron's Fisher Institute for Professional Selling and is the Vice President of the Akron-Canton Association of Insurance and Financial Advisors.

ANGELA MCMILLEN is a political consultant in Ohio and holds a Masters of Applied Politics from The University of Akron. She has consulted on political, judicial, and legislative races as well as governmental issues. In addition to her political work, Ms. McMillen has raised over $1 million for nonprofit organizations through grant writing, event planning, and direct mail fund raising. Prior to consulting, Ms. McMillen was a Deputy Treasurer in Medina County, Ohio, and a public accountant with Ernst & Young.

JAY PRAKASH MULKI is Assistant Professor of Marketing at Northeastern University. He has B2B selling experience in the energy sector in domestic and international markets and held senior management positions in *Fortune* 500 companies before entering the doctoral program. His primary research interests are in the areas of personal selling and sales management. His research has been published in *Journal of Business Research, Journal of Personal Selling and*

Sales Management, and International Journal of Bank Marketing. He has also published in the conference proceedings of the *Association for Historical Research in Marketing, Southwest Academy of Management Conference, National Conference in Sales Management,* and the *International Research Seminar in Service Management.*

RICHARD A. ROCCO has been a marketing professional in the health care industry for the past 17 years and has held a wide range of senior positions in the areas of CRM, global product management, and pricing and reimbursement strategy. He has been a thought leader at sales and marketing conferences to share his insights on topics including customer centricity, managing customer data as a corporate asset, SFA, and CRM. Mr. Rocco is presently a Doctoral Candidate at the University of Memphis. His research interests include sales force research, CRM, and sales force automation systems. Mr. Rocco recently co-authored an article on SFA outcomes that was published in *Industrial Marketing Management.*

DAN ROSE has 20 years of experience in sales, marketing, and communications. In the early 1990s, he capitalized on the Internet's growing commercial applications by launching an award-winning technology firm, later recognized as one of the fastest-growing companies in the Midwest by the Case Western Weatherhead School of Management. Rose has successfully built and sold three separate companies in the technology and communications space. He has been recognized as "Entrepreneur of the Year" by *USA Today*/NASDQ/Ernst & Young and as "Small Business Advocate of the Year" by the U.S. Small Business Administration. He is currently the CEO of Precision Dialogue, an online direct marketing firm, and co-owner of THMG, a data analytics marketing firm, both located in Ohio.

DAVE STEIN earned a living as a professional trumpet player and musical arranger before embarking on a high-tech career. Dave learned to leverage the discipline and logical thinking of a musician first into a career as a programmer, executive, then into success as a coach, consultant, and sales strategist, and now as the CEO and founder of an exciting new company. From 1980 until he founded The Stein Advantage, Dave was employed by several leading-edge technology companies in a number of roles: programmer, systems engineer, sales representative, sales manager, Director of Worldwide Sales Development, VP of Sales, VP of Marketing, VP of International Operations, VP of Client Services, and VP of Strategic Alliances. Until 2005, Dave focused on training, speaking to, and coaching experienced sales teams and their executives, which took him to 48 states and 23 countries. He is the author of *How Winners Sell: 21 Strategies to Outsell Your Competition and Win the Big Sale, Second Edition* and regularly contributes to leading sales journals, business magazines, and business sections of newspapers. He is also the featured monthly columnist for *Sales and Marketing Management* magazine and sits on the Executive Advisory Board of the Fisher Institute for Professional Selling. He is a professional member of the National Speakers Association, as well as a member of the Society of Sales and Marketing Training (SMT), the American Society for Training and Development (ASTD), the Strategic Account Management Association (SAMA), and the Aircraft Owners and Pilots Association. In early 2005, Dave founded ES Research Group, which provides independent, authoritative advice to corporations about sales performance.